Bushopedia

A Comprehensive Alphabetical Guide to George W.
Bush, the Bush Administration, Other Aspects of the
Far Right, and Related Topics

Bill Potts

Potts Publishing Edition

Published in the United States by Potts Publishing, PO Box 746, Roseville, CA 95661-0746.

Printed by DeHart's Media Services, Inc., 3333 Bowers Avenue, Suite 130, Santa Clara, CA 95054-2928.

ISBN 0-9785704-0-5

Book and cover design by Bill Potts.

Introduction

"Our lexicon is finished now,"
Said Dr. Johnson, "and, I vow,
This entry 'wool' is not our best.
'The hair of sheep,' how ill expressed!
For wool's the magic stuff of life.
It warms our bed; it decks our wife.
So enter this, and under-rule,
<u>'There is no substitute for wool.'"</u>

Thus reads an ad placed in London area buses and underground trains[1] by the British Wool Council in the 1950s.[2] It appears that Dr. Johnson's lexicon was not, in fact, finished. Lexicons and encyclopedias never are. It's the same with Bushopedia.

The American political scene is changing very rapidly, with new scandals, new revelations, new indictments, new convictions, and new (and lower) poll ratings for those in power. I've had to bite the bullet (and my tongue) and get this book to the printer with so many things unsaid and so many villains unmentioned. The temptation, to which I've succumbed time and again, is to keep adding—inserting a new entry, or amplifying or modifying an existing one. Some of the characters leave the scene, exiting stage right,[3] so to speak, and present tense suddenly becomes past tense. Bush nominates someone: Create an entry. He or she is approved by the relevant Senate committee: Add the date and the vote count. He or she is approved (or, very rarely, rejected) by the Senate: Note that, along with the

---

[1] In Britain, the word subway is used for an underground pedestrian crossing.
[2] As the ad first appeared in about 1955, its copyright, if any, has almost certainly expired. In any case, the British Wool Council appears to no longer exist.
[3] A small handful may have exited stage left.

date and the vote count. Congressman Cribble is indicted: Create a new entry (or, if he was already included, modify the existing entry). Now he's convicted: Add that to the entry.

With a sufficient number of co-authors, this book might have been close to a thousand pages, looking for all the world like an ex-president's memoirs. It isn't, though. It's a little under 350 pages, with a correspondingly reasonable price.

Time constraints mean that some had to be left out. I'm sorry, Congressman Bob Ney (R-OH), that I didn't include you. You surely have as much right as Tom DeLay to an entry. I'm also sorry, Congressman John Doolittle (R-CA). I'd love to discuss the reports that have appeared in the press and on the Internet, regarding the creativity involved in having your wife, Julie, be your fundraiser, with a nice 15% commission on contributions. That activity has apparently increased your family's value by $180,000 since 2001.[4] Maybe it's legal; maybe it's illegal. That's something that would be up to the courts to decide. It does seem to be somewhat malodorous though.

It would be nice to include all of Jack Abramoff's little playmates, but I wanted to get the book out in time for people to have a chance to learn something, so they can make an informed choice in the mid-term elections, rather than learning everything after it's too late.

You might have noticed that this book has a footnote or two. Actually, it has a little over 760 of them. Note that they are footnotes and not endnotes. You have to be especially dedicated to read endnotes. You may, in fact, have a sneaking suspicion that endnotes are put there to make you think that a certain degree of scholarship went into the work. The author hopes that you won't check them. Not all authors, of course, but at least one. I won't reveal her name though.

---

[4] *Congressman Doolittle, wife profited from Cunningham-linked contractor, Commissions taken on campaign cash, Dean Calbreath, The San Diego Union-Tribune, March 19, 2006, http://beyonddelay.org/news/pressclip.php?view=2052.*

Every footnote in this book is either a comment (sometimes pithy, sometimes humorous, sometimes not), a clarification, some extra information, or a reference. Those that are references are in italics. Some of the web references may not pan out, as the larger newspapers, for example, move stories to their archives after a certain time. Some of the TV network websites are particularly good as long-term references. CNN, for example, seems to leave every story on its website, on the original page, forever. Where a website such as truthout.org or commondreams.org has a copy of a newspaper article, it's usually available indefinitely, so I've tried to use such references, where possible, in preference to the original site. I've checked multiple websites for anything I present as being factual, although I've usually cited only one.

The entries (or, if you prefer, articles) contain many references to other entries. The first occurrence, within an entry, of the name of another entry is in *bold italic*. Subsequent references in the same entry are in normal type. The one exception is George Bush. You know there's a George Bush (or rather Bush, George Walker) entry, so it would be redundant and annoying to keep using bold italic to remind you.

While we're on the subject of George Bush, his entry is not one of the really long ones. On the other hand, he appears in many entries (e.g., Goat story), so a list of them is provided at the end of his entry.

There are over 240 entries in this book, some consisting of a single paragraph, some running to many pages. Read and enjoy.

A

Abraham, Spencer: Secretary of Energy until his resignation on November 15, 2004, which took effect upon the confirmation of his successor, *Samuel Bodman*. Ironically, he headed an agency whose elimination he proposed on no fewer than three occasions, having said that it had *"no core mission."* Prior to his appointment by George Bush, he was a one-term Republican Senator from Michigan, defeated in the 2000 election by Democrat Debbie Stabenow, who was running for the first time.

He spent much of his time in the Senate trying to limit both fuel efficiency standards for SUVs and research into renewable energy, to abolish the federal gasoline tax and to open the Arctic National Wildlife Refuge (ANWR) to drilling. Not surprisingly, the League of Conservation voters gave him a zero rating. In his failed bid for reelection, he received a record $700,000 from the automotive industry, and almost $450,000 from energy and natural resources companies, including Enron.[1]

During the George H.W. Bush administration, he was a staff aide to Vice President Dan Quayle. He is also a founder and member of the *Federalist Society*. In an April 17, 2002 article, in Counterpunch,[2] on Abraham's transition from senator to Energy Czar, Jeffrey St. Clair referred to him as "Senator Lunkhead."

---

[1] *The Three Horsemen, David Helvarg, The Nation, January 29, 2001,* *http://www.thenation.com/doc/20010129/helvarg (requires subscription).*

[2] Counterpunch (*http://counterpunch.org*) is edited by Alexander Cockburn (who is a Nation magazine columnist) and Jeffrey St. Clair.

Abramoff, Jack: A now-indicted lobbyist, once referred to by *Tom Delay*, as "one of my closest and dearest friends."

Abramoff is on trial and facing a probable ten-year jail sentence. His initial indictment alleged that, in September 2000, he and a partner, Adam Kidan, faked a $23 million wire transfer to defraud two lenders out of about $60 million to finance the purchase of SunCruz Casinos (a fleet of Florida gambling boats). The deal eventually fell through and the owner of SunCruz Casinos, Konstantinos "Gus" Boulis, was later killed in what appears to have been a gangland hit.

The Abramoff/Kidan investigation is only one of many involving Abramoff. Others involve both Abramoff and his entrepreneur friend, Michael Scanlon. At issue are very large payments from, in addition to others, Indian tribes who operate casinos.[3] Most importantly, an FBI task force is also looking into Abramoff's and Scanlon's relationship with quite a few Republican members of Congress. One of those members of Congress appears be the person who regards (or used to regard) Abramoff as one of his closest and dearest friends, Tom DeLay (*see last paragraph of* **DeLay, Tom**).

Abramoff and his lawyers negotiated a plea bargain on five casino-related criminal charges, in return for which he has been providing information on his financial dealings with those congressional Republicans and with others in the political arena. In addition to actual money, those dealings involve providing Republicans with fully paid trips to expensive resorts.

Republicans have tried to paint the Abramoff scandal as one that also involves Democrats. The fact is that no evidence indicating that Abramoff contributed any money to Democrats has emerged. Given his status as a **Bush Pioneer**, this is hardly surprising. His Casino clients have, however, made

---

[3] *Ex-Lobbyist is Focus of Widening Investigations, Susan Schmidt, Washington Post, July 16, 2004, http://www.washingtonpost.com/wp-dyn/articles/A53609-2004Jul15.html.*

contributions to both Republican and Democratic campaigns. The interesting thing, though, is that all but one of them increased their contributions to Republicans and, correspondingly, reduced their contributions to Democrats after establishing their business relationship with Abramoff.

Because of the number of members of Congress involved, the Abramoff scandal promises to be one of the biggest in United States history. Along with George Bush's plummeting approval ratings, it provides the Democrats with a marvelous opportunity to retake control of the House of Representatives in the November 2006 mid-term elections. It's less likely, but the Republicans might also lose control of the Senate.

On March 29, 2006, Abramoff and his partner, Adam Kidan, were both sentenced to five years and ten months for conspiracy and wire fraud. Interestingly, they were to start their sentences after 90 days, allowing time for them to co-operate in "a Washington corruption investigation" (presumably the one involving such GOP stalwarts as Tom DeLay) and a probe, in Florida, of the murder of Konstantinos Bulis (*see second paragraph of this entry*).[4]

In May 2006, the Secret Service released logs of visits to the White House. It turns out that Abramoff visited the White House about 200 times in Bush's first ten months in office. This is interesting, in view of the fact that Bush claims to be unfamiliar with him.[5]

Abrams, Elliott: Senior Director for Democracy, Human Rights and International Relations, and former Assistant Secretary of State in the Reagan administration. This is a staff position on the National Security Council and is one of

---

[4] *Ex-lobbyist Abramoff gets prison sentence: Fraud in Florida casino deal fetches 6 years in federal prison, CNN, March 29, 2006,* http://www.cnn.com/2006/LAW/03/29/abramoff.sentence.ap/index.html.

[5] This is basically the same claim Bush made regarding Enron's Ken Lay.

the Bush administration's truly appalling appointments.[6] As Abrams' position is not cabinet or immediate sub-cabinet level, there was no requirement for confirmation by the Senate. Abrams is one of a number of *neocons* in the Bush administration.

The appalling nature of Abrams' appointment becomes immediately apparent when we consider his involvement in the Reagan-era Iran-Contra affair, which led to his conviction for unlawfully withholding material information from Congress. Faced with a multi-count felony indictment, Abrams had agreed to plead guilty to two misdemeanors. George H.W. Bush eventually pardoned him (along with other Iran-Contra figures).

In a 2001 article,[7] David Corn says that Abrams *"billed himself as a 'gladiator' for the Reagan Doctrine in Central America — which entailed assisting thuggish regimes and militaries in order to thwart leftist movements and dismissing the human rights violations of Washington's cold war partners."* One of Abrams' more egregious offenses was his cover up of an incident in El Mozote, El Salvador, in which a U.S.-trained military unit had massacred hundreds of civilians. Even though the occurrence of the massacre was subsequently confirmed, along with many other atrocities, 85% of which were attributed, by a U.N. commission to the Reagan-assisted right-wing military and its death-squad allies, Abrams declared, *"The Administration's record on El Salvador is one of fabulous achievement."*[8].

Abu Ghraib (pronounced Abu Gu·rayb'): The prison in Baghdad, where Saddam Hussein incarcerated and tortured those who opposed him or appeared to oppose him (or possibly looked at one or more of his thugs the wrong way).

---

[6] In his announcement of the appointment to the press, former White House press secretary Ari Fleischer referred to Abrams as an "outstanding diplomat."

[7] *"Elliott Abrams: It's Back," The Nation, June 14, 2001, http://thenation.com/doc.mhtml?i=20010702&s=corn.*

[8] Ibid.

More recently, it has been the scene of flagrant violations of the *Geneva Conventions* by U.S. military and civilian personnel. The abuse and possible torture are particularly troubling for two reasons: first, it has been reported that most of the occupants of Abu Ghraib were simply rounded up on the street in an indiscriminate dragnet; second, approval of the methods used seems to have come from the highest levels in the Bush administration, with former White House Counsel, now Attorney General, *Alberto Gonzalez* advising George Bush on the possible legal loopholes and former Attorney General *John Ashcroft* providing Bush with at least one memo in a similar vein, which, in apparent contempt of Congress, he refused to hand over to the Senate Judiciary Committee. In a strictly partisan vote (10-9), on June 21, 2004, the Committee elected not to press the matter.

It's interesting to note that, although the issue of Abu Ghraib was (and still is) a very important one, with the possibility of severe consequences for him, George Bush did not make any effort to pronounce it correctly. His own personal variants included "Abuga Rayp," "Abu Garon," "Abu Garah" and "Abu Garef." More recently, his mispronunciation has become moot, as he has ceased to deal with the subject.

It has been reported that Abu Ghraib is just one prison in a *Gulag* (along with *Camp Delta* at Guantánamo Bay) of similar prisons being run by the U.S. military. Although the implied comparison with the Soviet-era Gulag relates more to secrecy than to harshness of treatment, neither attribute is considered acceptable in our allegedly more enlightened times.

On March 9, 2006, the U.S. military announced that it would be closing Abu Ghraib and moving 4,500 detainees to an expanded Camp Cropper, which is at Baghdad International Airport. Expansion of Camp Cropper to handle the influx was expected to take about three months.[9]

See, also, **Taguba report.**

ACLJ: American Center for Law and Justice. *See* **Robertson, Pat.**

Adelman, Kenneth: Prominent *neocon* and member of the Defense Policy Board. Before Operation Iraqi Freedom, Adelman was one of a number of neoconservatives sounding the drumbeat in favor of the attack and invasion, which he forecast, in a Washington Post article,[10] would be a "cakewalk." In the same article, he said:

> *"Hussein constitutes the number one threat against American security and civilization. Unlike Osama bin Laden, he has billions of dollars in government funds, scores of government research labs working feverishly on weapons of mass destruction—and just as deep a hatred of America and civilized free societies."*

Although it was obvious that Iraq was no match for U.S. military power, Operation Iraqi Freedom turned out to be somewhat more difficult than a mere cakewalk, with terrible loss of life on the Iraqi side (including tens of thousands of civilians[11]) and a disturbing number of deaths and severe casualties among the U.S. and British forces especially, both during and after the "combat phase" of operations.[12] Also, the *"scores of government research labs"* seem to have disappeared into thin air and the idea of *"working feverishly"* seems to be right out of a 1930s B movie script. As for Sad-

---

[9] *U.S. to move 4,500 detainees from Abu Ghraib, CNN, March 9, 2006, http://www.cnn.com/2006/WORLD/meast/03/09/iraq.main/index.html.*

[10] *Cakewalk In Iraq, Washington Post, February 13, 2002, http://www.Washington post.com/ac2/wp-dyn/A1996-2002Feb12.*

[11] Possibly over 100,000, according to a reliably researched report produced by Johns Hopkins University and published by *The Lancet,* Britain's leading medical journal.

[12] In March 2006, the U.S. troop death toll passed 2300. That total represents only those who died immediately. It does not include those who died, subsequently, from their wounds, nor does it provide any idea of how many have been wounded or of the grotesque injuries sustained (missing limbs, lost eyesight, permanent paralysis, face missing, etc.).

dam Hussein's *"hatred of America and civilized free societies,"* that was mere speculation. The evidence was and is that he was an opportunistic thug and brutal dictator. Greed and a desire for power and self-glorification seem to be much more likely attributes than hatred.

In any case, Adelman appears to have been somewhat unfazed by the outcome and unprepared to admit unambiguously that he might have been wrong.

ADF: *See **Alliance Defense Fund**.*

Administration: *See **Cabinet** and the entries referenced, in bold italic, within the Cabinet entry.*

affirmative access: George Bush's variant of affirmative action. In the 2000 presidential campaign, when asked if he supported affirmative action, he replied that he supported affirmative access. When pressed by his opponent, Al Gore, for a definition, he was evasive. The FindLaw website has an interesting November 1, 2000 article on the subject, written by Michael Dore.[13]

affirmative action: Public policies and initiatives designed to help eliminate past and present discrimination based on race, color, religion, sex, or national origin. Opponents of affirmative action (including George Bush) refer to it as a quota system. Their tactics typically play upon (or create) the fear, among many Caucasian men, that they will be arbitrarily denied employment in favor of a less-qualified member of a minority (so-called reverse discrimination and unwarranted preferences). Some reverse discrimination does indeed exist—but only in about 2% of cases pending before the EEOC (Equal Opportunities Employment Commission) in the mid-1990s.[14]

al Muhajir, Abdullah: Name adopted by José Padilla. *See **enemy combatant**.*

---

[13] *http://writ.news.findlaw.com/dorf/20001101.html.*

[14] *The Origins of Affirmative Action, by Marquita Sykes, http://www.now.org/ nnt/08-95/affirmhs.html.*

Al Qaeda: Also al-Qaeda, al-Qaida, and other variants. *See Bin Laden, Osama.*

al-Zarqawi, Abu Musab: Terrorist leader, killed in Iraq on June 8, 2006 in a "safe house," as a result of a U.S. air strike. After the onset of the Iraq war, he was associated with Al Qaeda. He could have been eliminated, along with his associates, in 2002, if not for indecision and apparently skewed priorities in the National Security Council. *See Rice, Condoleezza.*

Alito, Samuel: Bush's third nominee, announced on October 31, 2005, to replace Associate Justice Sandra Day O'Connor on the U.S. Supreme Court, who announced she would retire as soon as a replacement was confirmed.

Bush first nominated *John G. Roberts,* but elevated his nomination to that of Chief Justice, following the death of William H. Rehnquist. The Senate confirmed Roberts' appointment on September 29, 2005 and he thus became Chief Justice Rehnquist's replacement. Bush then nominated his White House counsel, old friend and ardent admirer, *Harriet Miers,* who eventually withdrew her own name from consideration.

Alito, whose nomination was praised by most Republicans and by the right wing in general, was appointed to the Third Circuit Court of Appeals in 1990 by George H.W. Bush. His decisions (and dissents) on that court have led to comparisons with Supreme Court Justice Antonin Scalia and to a nickname, "Scalito," meaning "little Scalia," that makes him almost sound like a Mafioso. This is consistent with Bush's determination to appoint justices in the Thomas and Scalia mold.

Alito will almost certainly move the Supreme Court further to the right, with probable negative consequences for gun control, church/state separation, *reproductive rights* (e.g., *Roe v. Wade*), and other rights. From the point of view of those who identify themselves as progressives, he has been consistently on the wrong side of such issues.

> *"Judge Alito is an ultraconservative outside the judicial mainstream. He has a long record of hostility toward reproductive rights, privacy rights and civil rights."*[15]
>
> *—Karen Pearl, interim president,*
> *Planned Parenthood Federation of America*

On the positive side, Alito appears, like **John Roberts**, to be squeaky clean, apart from his role in a case involving a company in which he had a large investment. In 2002, he was accused of conflict of interest in upholding a lower court's dismissal of a lawsuit against the Vanguard Group, a mutual fund company in which he had invested several hundred thousand dollars. Even though he denied having done anything improper, he did the right thing by recusing himself from further involvement.[16] There remains of course the question of why he did not recuse himself from the start.

The Senate Judiciary Committee scheduled Alito's hearings to start in early January 2006, much later than George Bush would have liked. On January 19, a party-line vote of 10 to 8 moved his confirmation to the full Senate, with a recommendation that he be confirmed. After a failed *filibuster* attempt by the Democrats, he was confirmed on January 31 by a mostly party-line vote of 58 to 42.[17] If all those who voted against him had supported the filibuster (i.e., had voted against cloture[18]), it might have been possible to block his confirmation. As it was, the filibuster was ended by a 72 to 25 vote for cloture.

---

[15] *Alito's dissents key for debate, Bart Jansen, Portland (Maine) Press Herald, http://pressherald.mainetoday.com/news/state/051107alito.shtml.*

[16] *Possible Supreme Court Nominees, Christopher Lee, Washington Post, October 28, 2005, http://www.washingtonpost.com/wp-dyn/content/article/2005/10/27/AR2005102700813.html.*

[17] Four socially conservative Democrats voted to confirm Alito. They were Robert Byrd (WV), Kent Conrad (ND), Ben Nelson (NE) and Tim Johnson (SD). One Republican, Lincoln Chafee (RI), voted against him.

[18] Cloture is the termination of debate. *See **filibuster**.*

Allawi, Iyad: Leader of the Iraqi National Accord party and Iraq's former interim Prime Minister, appointed to that position in June 2004 by the outgoing administrator of the Coalition Provisional Authority, Paul Bremer III,[19] and replaced in April 2005 by Ibrahim Al-Jaafari. At the time of his appointment, rumors were circulating that Allawi had personally executed six Iraqi prisoners[20] at the Baghdad police station a few days earlier. Those rumors were apparently confirmed in the January 24/31, 2005 issue of the New Yorker,[21] with further confirmation by Paul McGeough of the Sydney Morning Herald.[22]

Seymour Hersh refers to Allawi as "Saddam-lite,"[23] which is fair comment, given that Allawi was once one of Saddam Hussein's thugs.

Contrary to the Bush administration's ambitions and expectations, and in spite of election fraud favoring him, Allawi's party got insufficient votes in the January 30, 2005 election for him to remain as Prime Minister.[24] In the subsequent December 2005 election, Allawi's party lost ground, in spite of U.S. support for their campaign, and won only 25 seats.

Allbaugh, Joseph: Former Director of the Federal Emergency Management Agency (*FEMA*) and former Chief of Staff to George Bush when he was Governor of Texas. He was also

---

[19] On December 14, 2004, George Bush awarded Bremer the Presidential Medal of Freedom.

[20] The report was that he shot seven, all in the head. However, one was subsequently said to have survived.

[21] *A Man of the Shadows, John Lee Anderson, posted 2005-01-17 at http://newyorker.com/fact/content/?050124fa_fact1.*

[22] *US official confirms Allawi shot six dead, Paul McGeough, Sydney Morning Herald, January 19, 2005, http://www.smh.com.au/news/After-Saddam/US-official-confirms-Allawi-shot-six-dead/2005/01/18/1105810916006.html.*

[23] *Seymour Hersh: "We've Been Taken Over by a Cult", Democracy Now, January 26, 2005, http://www.democracynow.org/article.pl?sid=05/01/26/1450204&mode=thread&tid=25.*

[24] *Get Out the Vote: Did Washington try to manipulate Iraq's Election? Seymour M. Hersh, New Yorker, July 25, 2005, http://www.newyorker.com/fact/content/articles/050725fa_fact.*

National Campaign Manager for the Bush/Cheney 2000 election campaign.

Although he's no longer part of the Bush administration, he exemplifies the kind of people Bush has appointed to positions of considerable responsibility. He appears to have been deeply involved in the very underreported Funeralgate scandal[25] and, according to Lieutenant Colonel Bill Burkett, (Texas Air National Guard, ret.), he was involved in the scrubbing of Bush's National Guard records (*see James, Daniel*).

> *"Less than two weeks after Katrina devastated New Orleans and the Gulf Coast, the former FEMA head was on the scene to drum up business for his clients."*
>
> —*Subheading of Bill Berkowitz article, September 12, 2005*[26]

Since leaving FEMA, Allbaugh has been a lobbyist, doing business as The Allbaugh Group. He has several clients who have obtained or are likely to obtain contracts for salvage operations or reconstruction in the aftermath of Hurricane Katrina.[27] Among them are KBR (formerly Kellogg Brown and Root, a Halliburton subsidiary), the Shaw Group and UltraStrip.

Until his resignation (under a very heavy cloud) on September 12, 2005, **Michael D. Brown** occupied Allbaugh's former position at FEMA, now part of the **Department of Homeland Security (DHS)**.

Alliance Defense Fund (ADF): A legal firm, founded in 1994 and based in Scottsdale, AZ, whose primary purpose is to defend "family values," and to work against the American

---

[25] The history of Funeralgate can be found at *http://prisonplanet.com/analysis_louise_122302_allbaugh.html*.

[26] *Joe Allbaugh's Moneymaking Mission to the Gulf Coast, Bill Berkowitz, Media Transparency, September 12, 2005, http://mediatransparency.com/story.php?storyID=84.*

[27] Ibid.

Civil Liberties Union (ACLU). It was established by over 30 fundamentalist Christian ministries.

The names of its most prominent founders read like a who's who of leading fundamentalists. They include Bill Bright, who founded the multi-million dollar Campus Crusade for Christ, *James Dobson*, founder of the *Family Research Council* and Focus on the Family, Rev. D. James Kennedy, of Coral Ridge Ministries, Don Wildmon, founder of the American Family Association, and around 30 others.

According to People For the American Way (PFAW), ADF defends the right of Christians to *"share the gospel"* in workplaces and public schools. They claim that efforts to curb proselytizing in those places are anti-Christian.[28]

In August 2005, ADF announced that it would *"provide training on America's federal and state judicial systems to high school age students from all across the U.S. as part of the Teen-Pact Judicial Program (West), co-sponsored by the Georgia-based TeenPact Leadership School."*[29] Regarding potential students, TeenPact itself says, *"They will come away from TeenPact with a realization of their spiritual capacity as young people and a desire to change America for Christ."*[30] It seems probable that, in addition to litigating in favor of regressive policies, graduates of the school may very well move on to appointments as circuit court judges and, for some, Supreme Court justices—depending, of course, on future presidents having a world view similar to that of George Bush (along with a sustained Republican lock on all three branches of government).

ADF is not an organization to be taken lightly, having for example had success in anti-gay cases all over the U.S. Their 2001 budget was over $15 million.

---

[28] *People For the American Way, Right Wing Watch, Right Wing Organizations, Alliance Defense Fund, http://www.pfaw.org/pfaw/general/default.aspx?oid=4457.*

[29] *Moving the ball forward: ADF to train high school students on America's judicial system, ADF, http://www.alliancedefensefund.org/news/story.aspx?cid=3495.*

[30] Ibid.

American Center for Law and Justice (ACLJ): *See Robertson, Pat.*

American Enterprise Institute (AEI): A think tank for conservatives, neoconservatives, and conservative libertarians. Established in 1943, it has about fifty resident scholars and fellows. AEI scholars have argued in favor of prayer in schools[31] and of censorship of the arts.

Board members are typically CEOs of large corporations. Benefactors include the Scaife Foundation (*see Scaife, Richard Mellon*). Former trustees include *Dick Cheney,* and Ken Lay, who was the CEO of Enron and George Bush's friend and contributor.

Prominent fellows and scholars include *Lynne Cheney* (senior fellow in education and culture), former House Speaker, *Newt Gingrich,* former chairman and former member of the Defense Policy Board, *Richard Perle,* unsuccessful Supreme Court nominee Judge Robert Bork, and former Bush speechwriter, David Frum.[32]

appointments, judicial: *See judicial appointments.*

Arkansas Project: A $2.3 million project of the *American Spectator magazine,* in the 1990s, funded by *Richard Mellon Scaife* and aimed at discrediting President Clinton. According to *David Brock* and others, *Theodore Olson,* who was the U.S. Solicitor General from mid-2001 until his summer 2004 resignation, was deeply involved in the project—something Olson denied at his confirmation hearings in May 2001.

Ashcroft, John D.: Attorney General of the United States,[33] until his resignation on November 9, 2004. Paul Krugman[34]

---

[31] Contrary to the impression created by organizations like AEI, voluntary prayer is already permitted, as it should be, as long as it isn't disruptive (e.g., spoken loudly during class). Organized or coercive staff-led prayer is not.

[32] Source: *People for the American Way (PFAW), Right Wing Watch, http://www.pfaw.org/pfaw/general/default.aspx?oid=4456.*

[33] The Attorney General is not a general and should not be addressed as "General Ashcroft" (or "General Gonzalez") or as "General." The correct

has labeled him the worst Attorney General ever, which is a conclusion shared by a very large number of people.

> *"[I]t is impossible not to cheer the exit of the most destructive attorney general of the past 100 years, who responded to a great national crisis by steering the Justice Department on a narrow, stony path between the unconstitutional and the incompetent.*
>
> —*Editorial, The Nation, November 29, 2004*

John Ashcroft's career has included two terms as Attorney General of Missouri, Governor of Missouri from 1984 to 1993, and U.S. Senator from 1995 to 2000, when he was defeated by his then recently deceased Democratic opponent Mel Carnahan.

Carnahan, who had succeeded John Ashcroft as Governor of Missouri, was killed in plane crash only weeks before the 2000 elections. His wife, Jean, took his Senate seat, which she lost in the 2002 mid-term elections. Possibly to his credit (it may, in fact, have been nothing more than a bad tactical decision), Ashcroft suspended active campaigning after Carnahan's death.

While in the Senate, Ashcroft was one of the four "Singing Senators," along with Trent Lott (R-MS), Larry Craig (R-ID) and Jim Jeffords[35] (R-VT). Unfortunately, his solo efforts, while he was Attorney General, were met with a certain amount of both disbelief and derision.[36]

---

form of address is "Mr. Attorney General" (in the first instance), then simply "Sir." Many people get this one wrong, including talk-show host Larry King and numerous members of Congress (who should know better). Even Ashcroft's successor, in accepting Bush's nomination, referred to "General Ashcroft." The plural is, of course, "Attorneys General" (rather like "mothers in law") and not "Attorney Generals." Source: *Letters and Forms of Address, New York Public Library Desk Reference, Third Edition, 1998, McMillan USA, ISBN 0-02-862169-7.*

[34] Paul Krugman is an economist and a columnist for the New York Times. After George W. Bush's first inauguration, in January 2001, his column moved to a political, rather than purely economic, emphasis.

[35] Jeffords is now an independent.

[36] In February 2002, Ashcroft surprised an audience at a North Carolina seminary with his rendition, accompanied by taped music, of his own composition, "Let the Eagle Soar." His staff subsequently complained

> *"Attorney General Ashcroft is committed to confronting injustice by leading a professional Justice Department free from politics, defined by integrity and dedicated to upholding the rule of law."*
>
> *White House website (whitehouse.gov)*

Of all of Bush's cabinet nominations, Ashcroft's was, by far, the most contentious. He squeaked through his Senate Judiciary Committee hearing on a 10-8 vote, with Russ Feingold breaking ranks with his fellow Democrats[37] and avoiding a 9-9 tie. In the full Senate, eight Democrats,[38] including Robert Byrd, broke ranks,[39] resulting in a 58-42 confirmation. Even if no Democrats had broken ranks, he would still have made it, given that James Jeffords had not yet switched from Republican to Independent and changed the balance of power.[40]

Robert Byrd's willingness to trust Ashcroft was summed up in his January 21, 2001 statement on the Senate floor:

> *"Although I do not agree with all of his views, as I've already indicated, I have no cause to doubt that* (sic) *Senator Ashcroft's word or his concern regarding his fealty to an oath that he took before God and man. And as far as I'm personally concerned, it would be an act of supreme arrogance on my part to doubt his intentions to honor that oath. Given Senator Ashcroft's background and positions of which* (sic) *he has been nominated, and his assurances to the Senate that he will faithfully uphold the law of the United States, I shall vote to confirm him."*

---

that he was handing out copies at meetings and asking them to join in. A Justice Department lawyer was asked why she opposed the sing along. Her answer was brief and to the point: "Have you heard the song? It really sucks." Source: *Guardian, March 4, 2002.*

[37] In September 2001, Feingold redeemed himself somewhat, when his was the sole Senate vote against the USA Patriot Act.

[38] John Breaux (LA), Robert Byrd (WV), Kent Conrad (ND), Christopher Dodd (CT), Byron Dorgan (ND), Zell Miller (GA), Ben Nelson (NE), Russ Feingold (WI). Zell Miller's vote was not surprising, as he had a record of voting with the Republicans in the Senate (*see* **Miller, Zell**).

[39] Some of the Democrat defections may have been based on a reluctance to vote against a former Senate colleague. In other words, theirs may have been "courtesy votes."

[40] Of course, Jeffords might well have voted for him anyway.

That does not appear to have been Robert Byrd's finest moment.

Given that, in 1999, John Ashcroft had told students at Bob Jones University,[41] in South Carolina, "there is no king but Jesus," the members of the Senate Judiciary Committee (or at least those who believed strongly in the Establishment Clause[42] of the First Amendment) had good reason for concern. Of even greater concern was his statement, to those same students, that he believed that laws and civil authority cannot take the place of a religious order founded upon faith.[43] As American law is based, not on holy writ, but on the Constitution, it was extremely disturbing that a nominee for the very position that has a specific duty to uphold the law and defend the clearly secular U.S. Constitution should espouse such a radical view. In effect, he was calling for the United States to be a theocracy. Senator Patrick Leahy, who was Chairman of the Judiciary Committee until the Republican takeover on January 19, 2001, said, *"The committee will want to explore whether Senator Ashcroft's views have changed since he proudly accepted the university's honorary degree."* Given Ashcroft's history, it is unlikely, of course, that Leahy believed there was even the remotest possibility of that being the case.

> *"Atty. Gen. John Ashcroft's announced desire for camps for U.S. citizens he deems to be 'enemy combatants' has moved him from merely being a political embarrassment to being a constitutional menace."*
>
> *—Los Angeles Times, August 2002*

---

[41] Then-Senator Ashcroft was at Bob Jones University to receive an honorary degree in recognition of his being the first member of Congress to call for Clinton's impeachment following the Monica Lewinski scandal. Vindictiveness has its own rewards, it would appear.

[42] *See **Bill of Rights**.*

[43] In a masterpiece of understatement, historian Arthur Schlesinger, Jr. has characterized John Ashcroft as a "religious nut." Ashcroft's narrow views on what constitutes acceptable behavior have led some wags to suggest that he is opposed to couples indulging in sex while standing, because it might lead to dancing. His religion does, indeed, prohibit dancing.

Regarding terrorism, which Ashcroft claimed to be fighting assiduously, and counterterrorism, neither was a priority from the time of his appointment until September 11, 2001. It was not even in a list of 68 programs for which he requested a budget increase on September 10, 2001. At that time, he also sent a memorandum outlining his top seven priorities to the heads of his departments. Those priorities did not include counterterrorism. It gets worse; he also drastically cut an FBI request for equipment and two thousand more agents to track down terrorist threats.[44] Specifically, he cut their request for items such as computer networking and foreign language intercepts by half, cut a cyber-security request by three quarters and eliminated entirely a request for "collaborative capabilities."[45] It gets worse still; on July 12, 2001, acting FBI Director Tom Pickard tried to brief Ashcroft on terror threats within the U.S. Ashcroft's response was to tell him that he didn't want to hear any more about that subject. Pickard described the meeting, in June 2004 testimony, under oath, before the *9/11 Commission*. Another senior FBI official, who is now retired, corroborated his report, as did Ruben Garcia, of the FBI's Criminal Division (who was, apparently, at the meeting), in testimony before the 9/11 Commission. In his own sworn testimony before the Commission, Ashcroft denied having dismissed Pickard's warnings. At subsequent meetings, prior to September 11, 2001, Pickard felt compelled to avoid the issue.[46]

Notwithstanding his absence of focus on counterterrorism, Ashcroft wasted no time agitating for powers he had wanted from his first day on the job. Within 45 days of September 11, his department introduced the **USA PATRIOT Act**, a document whose enormousness was exceeded only

---

[44] Source (one of many): *Julian Borger, "Ashcroft drawn into row over September 11," Guardian Unlimited, May 21, 2002, http://www.guardian.co.uk/september11/story/0,11209,719231,00.html.*

[45] Source: *Internal administration document, dated September 12, 2001, cited at http://atrios.blogspot.com/107993116069306753.*

[46] *"Did Ashcroft brush off terror warnings?" MSNBC, June 23, 2004, http://msnbc.msn.com/id/5271234.*

by the enormity of many of the measures it contained. Congress passed it without debate and, for most of those who voted for it, without even reading it. Although many of the draconian measures in the Act are, ostensibly, only to be used in response to suspected terrorist activity, the Act does not, in fact, restrict their use to such occasions. No warrants and no probable cause are required for the FBI to gain access to anyone's private medical records, library records, student records, and so on.[47,48]

On October 25, 2001, Ashcroft addressed the U.S. Mayors Conference. The following excerpt from his speech is very interesting:

> *"Let the terrorists among us be warned: If you overstay your visa—even by one day—we will arrest you. If you violate a local law, you will be put in jail and kept in custody as long as possible. We will use every available statute. We will seek every prosecutorial advantage. We will use all our weapons within the law and under the Constitution to protect life and enhance security for America."*

There's an implied assumption, there, that anyone who overstays his or her visa is a terrorist, but note the emphasis on using **any** means possible to catch terrorists. Less than two months later, Ashcroft refused to permit a search of the National Instant Criminal Background Check System (NICS) to determine whether a suspected terrorist had purchased guns. Around the same time, he said the following to the Senate Judiciary Committee:

> *"To those who pit Americans against immigrants and citizens against noncitizens, to those who scare peace loving people with phantoms of lost liberty, my message is this:*

---

[47] Source (one of many): *American Civil Liberties Union, http://aclu.org.*

[48] In March 2005, Congressman Bernie Sanders (I-VT) reintroduced a bill that failed to pass in 2003 because of a 210-210 tie vote (achieved by Republicans in the House by extending the normal 17-minute voting period long enough to coerce a small number of their fellow Republicans to vote against it). The bill was *H.R. 1157, The Freedom to Read Act.* It passed on June 15 by 238 votes to 187. If also passed by the Senate, it would reverse the corresponding part of the USA PATRIOT Act.

your tactics only aid terrorists, for they erode our unity and diminish our resolve. They give ammunition to America's enemies and pause to America's friends."

Apparently he was more concerned with the lost liberty of the NRA than with anyone else's.[49]

Even though counter-terrorism was supposedly Ashcroft's primary focus, his law enforcement priorities seem to have been decidedly skewed towards his narrow religious viewpoint, as exemplified by his actions regarding Oregon's Death with Dignity Act (assisted suicide law) and medical marijuana laws in California and elsewhere. In the former case, his attempt to block the law was strongly rebuked by the U.S. Ninth Circuit Court. Writing for the majority, Judge Richard C. Tallman said:

"The Attorney General's unilateral attempt to regulate general medical practices historically entrusted to state lawmakers interferes with the democratic debate about physician assisted suicide and far exceeds the scope of his authority under federal law."[50]

True to form, Ashcroft's Justice Department petitioned, on July 12, 2004, for an 11-judge panel of the same court to rehear the case.[51] His petition was turned down, with only one judge dissenting, on August 13, 2004.[52] On November 9, 2004, he appealed the decision to the U.S. Supreme Court, which agreed to accept the case[53] On June 6, 2005, the Supreme Court ruled 6 to 3 that federal law trumped state law

---

[49] An interesting polemic on this topic can be found at *The Angry Liberal*, *http://theangryliberal.com/12-08-01.htm.*

[50] *Federal Court Upholds Oregon's Assisted Suicide Law, New York Times,* May 26, 2004, *http://nytimes.com/2004/05/26/national/26CND-SUIC.html ?ex=1092024000&en=99b1db8c6c28c8cf&ei=5070&hp.*

[51] *Ashcroft seeks new hearing on Oregon suicide law. U.S. renews efforts to quash law passed by state's voters, San Francisco Chronicle/SFGate.com,* *http://sfgate.com/cgi-bin/article.cgi?f=/c/a/2004/07/13/MNG3A7KGI81.DTL.*

[52] *Appeals court rejects Ashcroft's fight against assisted suicide, Beth Casper, Statesman Journal, August 16, 2004,* *http://news.statesmanjournal.com/article.cfm?i=85215.*

[53] *High court takes medical marijuana case, CNN.com, http://cnn.com/ 2004/HEALTH/06/28/medical.marijuana.ap.*

and stated that the remedy, for medical marijuana users, lay with Congress, which can of course change federal law. On June 15, 2005, an attempt to get approval for a medical marijuana attachment to a federal agencies funding bill failed, in the House, by a vote of 264 to 161. No doubt Ashcroft felt very satisfied with the outcome.

Even within the field of terrorism, Ashcroft exhibited a troubling inconsistency. On May 8, 2002, Abdullah al Muhajir, more commonly known as José Padilla, was arrested at Chicago's O'Hare Airport as he arrived on a flight from Pakistan. He was charged with plotting to build and use a dirty bomb (a conventional bomb surrounded by radioactive material) on an unspecified U.S. target. Initially, no announcement was made of the arrest. Then, about one month later, while on a visit to Moscow, John Ashcroft went on TV to announce the arrest to the world and to declare that Padilla would be held as an *enemy combatant*. This last fact explains why Ashcroft didn't wait until his return to Washington, when a thirty-day deadline for either charging him in federal court or turning him over to the Defense Department would have expired. Despite gaining access to a lawyer, Padilla continued to be held, even though, on February 28, 2005, a federal judge ruled that he must be charged or released within 45 days. The Justice Department appealed the ruling, resulting in his lawyer being in the strange position of demanding that his client be indicted (or set free).

Bearing in mind the fact that Padilla had no actual bomb or the means to acquire or construct one, it's interesting to consider the case of an arms cache that was discovered in Noonday, TX, in April 2003.[54]

---

[54] *Outside View: Who is William Krar? Jim Kessler, UPI Outside View commentary, March 14, 2004, http://upi.com/inc/view.php ?StoryID=20040311-030156-8181r.*

The cache contained machine guns, half a million rounds of ammunition, remote controlled explosive devices disguised as briefcases, 60 pipe bombs and a cyanide bomb. William Joseph Krar, a white supremacist, was arrested. The discovery and arrest were not the result of an investigation, but of a mistake by Krar himself, who had mailed some phony government credentials to the wrong address—luckily that of an alert citizen. Ironically, the package contained a note, saying, *"We would hate to have these fall into the wrong hands."*

If Krar had not been caught, the damage his weapons could have done is staggering. Obviously, the Justice Department would want to triumphantly announce such a discovery, right? Well, no. There was no announcement and no press conference, in spite of Ashcroft's practice of announcing every triumph over terrorists, however small. In the year following Krar's arrest, Ashcroft issued hundreds of news releases (of about 2300 issued, up to that time, since his appointment), none of which mentioned Krar.[55] Krar pleaded guilty, on November 11, 2003, to possession of a chemical weapon.[56]

Apparently, Ashcroft considered a former street punk with Al Qaeda connections, who might possibly have had the potential to construct a dirty bomb if he could acquire the materials, to be much more dangerous (and newsworthy) than a white supremacist who had already stockpiled the means to kill thousands.[57]

Padilla was finally charged on November 22, 2005 and moved to Justice Department custody. The irony is that his charges, in the form of an eleven-count indictment, had

---

[55] Ibid.

[56] *The threat of domestic terrorism, Jane's Terrorism and Security Monitor, May 17, 2005, http://www.janes.com/security/law_enforcement/news/jtsm/jtsm050517_1_n.shtml.*

[57] Several sources, including *Outside View: Who is William Krar?, Jim Kessler, United Press International, http://upi.com/view.cfm?StoryID= 20040311-030156-8181r and Noonday in the Shade, Paul Krugman, New York Times, June 22, 2004, http://query.nytimes.com/gst/abstract.html?res=F00B16FC385D0C718EDDAF0894DC404482.*

nothing to do with the original purported reason for detaining him. The three main counts, under which four others were also charged, were conspiracy to murder U.S. nationals, conspiracy to provide material support to terrorists, and providing material support to terrorists. He may or may not be guilty. However, the position of the administration, and especially that of the former Attorney General, was repudiated, in that Padilla will now be tried, in full public view, in a civilian court. Whatever the outcome, there is a chance that justice will be seen to be done.

Apparently some people were disappointed to see John Ashcroft leave the Justice Department. It's hard to understand why.

assembly, freedom of: *See Bill of Rights.*

asshole: Any reporter[58] (apparently) who is critical of George Bush, as exemplified by Bush's remark to Dick Cheney during the 2000 campaign, *"There's Adam Clymer—major league asshole—from the New York Times."*[59,60] Cheney's thoughtful and analytical corner-of-the-mouth response was, *"Yeah, big time."* What did Bush learn from this experience? Very little, apparently, other than that it's not a good idea to call someone an asshole near a live microphone.

Attila the Hun: Fifth Century warlord, often used as a reference point in describing many of today's right-wing ideologues, who are described as being either "somewhat to the right" or "a long way to the right" of Attila the Hun. In fact, Attila was not really right wing (by today's definition) and could be more fairly described as a radical anarchist.

Atwater, Lee: Late Republican National Committee Chairman, presidential campaign manager, and master of vicious attack politics. Atwater died in 1991 of a brain tumor. He was

[58] Or possibly just Adam Clymer. Who knows?

[59] As reported by Jake Tapper, in *Salon.com, September 4, 2000.*

[60] Clymer is now with the Annenberg Public Policy Center of the University of Pennsylvania.

also an accomplished and well-known guitarist. In his campaign manager role, he was responsible for the infamous and misleading Willy Horton ad that was very instrumental (possibly decisive) in George H.W. Bush's defeat of Michael Dukakis in 1988. Republican strategists see Atwater as a role model.

Aznar, José María: Former Prime Minister of Spain and friend of George Bush. His defeat in the March 2004 Spanish elections was assured when, two days earlier, three Madrid commuter trains were bombed at a cost of about 190 lives, with a further 1000 or so people injured. He wanted to believe (and wanted the people to believe) that the bombings were the work of ETA (Euskadi Ta Askatasuna—the Basque Fatherland and Liberty Group), rather than Al Qaeda. Apparently the tide turned against him for two reasons—his decision to back George Bush (against overwhelming popular opposition) with Spanish troops in Operation Iraqi Freedom and his attempt to mislead the people about the perpetrators of the bombing. His successor, José Luis Rodríguez Zapatero, was opposed to Spanish participation in the Iraq war.

B

B is for Bring, as in *"My answer is 'Bring them on.'"*
—*George Bush, Washington, DC, July 3, 2003*
("You fight 'em and I'll hold your coat.")

Baker, James A. III: From 1975 to 1993, James Baker was, successively, Under Secretary of Commerce in the Ford administration, White House Chief of Staff, then Secretary of the Treasury in the Reagan administration, and Secretary of State in the George H.W. Bush Administration. For the final six months of that administration, he was White House Chief of Staff and Senior Counselor to the President. Since 1993, he has been Senior Counselor to the **Carlyle Group**. He is also a partner in the law firm, Baker Botts.

He has been involved in presidential politics since Gerald Ford's unsuccessful bid for election in 1976 (following his completion of the term of the disgraced Richard M. Nixon). He led Ford's campaign, both of Reagan's successful campaigns, and George H.W. Bush's successful first campaign and unsuccessful 1992 reelection campaign. Finally, he led George W. Bush's legal team in the 2000 Florida recount battle. Although George Bush and his allies claim to have won the election fair and square, Baker's own words betray that position. In a 2003 speech to what investigative journalist Greg Palast describes as "Russian bigwigs," Baker said, *"I fixed the election in Florida for George Bush."*[1]

> *"Baker's claim to have fixed the election was not a confession; it was a boast. He meant to dazzle current and potential clients about his Big In with the Big Boy in the White House."*
>
> —*Greg Palast, December 8, 2003*[2]

---

[1] *Baker Takes the Loaf: President's Business Partner Slices Up Iraq, December 8, 2003, http://www.gregpalast.com/detail.cfm?artid=300&row=0.*

[2] Ibid.

Baker has a long association with the Bush family and has sometimes been referred to as their consigliere, an obvious comparison with the close advisors to Mafia dons. He has certainly been a help to Bush father and son, having arranged for the Carlyle group to hire the son while the father was in office, and to hire the father after his defeat by Bill Clinton. Although, as President, George W. Bush cannot also work for the Carlyle Group (at least not openly), he has a strong fiduciary interest as the heir to the wealth his father is accumulating as a consultant to that organization.

Given Baker's very aggressive, some would say belligerent, involvement on behalf of George W. Bush in the 2000 Election controversy, it came as a surprise when, on March 24, 2005, he and former President Jimmy Carter announced the formation of the private *Commission on Federal Election Reform.*

Barbour, Haley: Governor of Mississippi, former lobbyist[3] and former Chairman, from 1993 to 1996, of the Republican National Committee. He was previously the executive director of the Mississippi Republican Party (1973 to 1976) and a top political advisor in the Reagan White House.

Both George Bush and Dick Cheney campaigned for Barbour in his run for the Mississippi governorship. Barbour is, not surprisingly, a strong Bush/Cheney supporter.

In May of 2004, Barbour and the Republican-controlled Mississippi State Senate made a stunning and unprecedented (anywhere) rollback of the state's Medicaid program, ending Medicaid eligibility for 65,000 senior citizens and people with severe disabilities, including paraplegics and quadriplegics, those with cerebral palsy, heart disease, Alzheimer's, and schizophrenia and other mental illness.[4,5]

---

[3] As Chairman and CEO of Barbour, Griffith and Roberts, a Washington, DC lobbying firm.

[4] The Mississippi House is Democrat-controlled. Democratic legislators claim they were coerced into voting for the measure and gave in at the last minute to avoid even worse cuts. In the absence of legislation (required annually) to renew the social services budget, Barbour, as Governor, could have made any cuts he wished.

The maximum annual income allowed for Medicaid eligibility was reduced from just under $12,600—already a near-starvation level—to just under $6,800. Barbour dismissed the plight of the majority of those affected by the cuts with a remark about taxpayers having to *"pay for free health care for people who can work and take care of themselves and just choose not to."* When it comes to so-called **compassionate conservatism**, Barbour and Bush seem to be reading from the same page.

Bartlett, Dan: White House Director of Communications. *See James, Daniel.*

Berlusconi, Silvio: Former Prime Minister of Italy and friend of George Bush. For a long time, his status was in some doubt, as he resigned on April 20, 2005. However, at the request of the Italian president, Carlo Azeglio Ciampi, who wanted him to serve out his full term, he immediately announced he would form a new government, which he managed to do eight days later. On April 11, 2006, his party was defeated in the general election by the center-left alliance led by Romano Prodi, the former president of the European Union.

Berlusconi became a successful business tycoon and Italy's richest man before entering politics. He formed his own political party, Forza Italia, in 1993, becoming Prime Minister in 1994, when he formed a coalition with the National Alliance and the Northern League, both of which are right-wing parties. His government collapsed just seven months later, after rivalries developed among the three parties, and his indictment, in a Milan court, for tax fraud. After several years of organizing, he became Prime Minister, once more, in 2001.[6]

In spite of clear opposition from the Italian people, Berlusconi agreed to join George Bush's *Coalition of the Willing* in support of the war against Iraq. He was, however, under intense pressure, within Italy, to withdraw that support. His life was

[5] *Punishing the Poor, Bob Herbert, New York Times, June 11, 2004,* (now available on the website of Congressman Bernie Sanders (I-VT) at *http://bernie.house.gov/documents/articles/20040611163728.asp).*

[6] *Profile: Silvio Berlusconi, BBC News, http://news.bbc.co.uk/1/hi/world/europe/3034600.stm.*

further complicated by charges of corruption (specifically bribery[7]). Italy's Constitutional Court thwarted his attempts to obtain immunity for as long as he remained in office, although he has yet to be called to account.

Whether his successor, Romano Prodi, who has said he wants to be cooperative with the United States, will be truly supportive of George Bush is an open question. Both before and after the election, he said he would withdraw the last of the Italian contingent from Iraq—a process already started by Berlusconi.

Biggs, Andrew: Associate Commissioner for Retirement Policy, Social Security Administration. Biggs is a political appointee to what should be an apolitical position. He was formerly the Cato Institute's point man on Social Security privatization. In the second week of January 2005, he appeared with George Bush at a campaign-style event to promote the privatization of Social Security—a very unusual thing for a senior civil servant to do, and something putting him squarely in the *fox guarding the hen house* category.

Bill of Rights: The first ten amendments to the U.S. Constitution, ratified as a single bill on December 15, 1791. Several other amendments (13th, 14th, 15th, 19th and 26th), subsequently ratified individually, enumerate additional rights and are included here for the sake of completeness.

> **CAVEAT**
>
> The author of this book is not a lawyer. You should regard any interpretations in this entry (Bill of Rights) as those of an informed layperson. A more thorough (if somewhat tedious) treatment can be found at websites such as FindLaw[8] (*http://findlaw.com*), the American Civil Liberties Union (*http://aclu.org*), and others.[9] If you are adversely affected by any violation of the amendments discussed here, you should consult a lawyer or contact an organization such as the ACLU.

---

[7] He is accused of bribing judges, in 1985, to block a business rival's takeover of a state-owned company.

[8] Most of the articles at FindLaw are written for lawyers. However, even reasonably well-informed non-lawyers (e.g., historians or history buffs) interested in case law may find them interesting.

[9] You may also want to try a Google search (e.g., on **first amendment**).

Article I (Freedoms)

Article I, otherwise known as the **First Amendment**, is clearly the most important, as so much of the freedom granted to "the people" depends on its preservation, intact. Here it is, in all its solemn and simple elegance:

Congress shall make no law respecting an establishment of religion, or prohibiting the free exercise thereof; or abridging the freedom of speech, or of the press; or the right of the people peaceably to assemble, and to petition the Government for a redress of grievances.

The actions of watchdog organizations like the American Civil Liberties Union, Americans United for Separation of Church and State and People for the American Way have, historically, kept most threats to the First Amendment under reasonable control. Bad legislation here and there, misinterpretations (some deliberate) at the local, state and national level, and so on, have been challenged, if necessary, all the way to the U.S. Supreme Court. Since January 2001 and, especially, since September 11, 2001, the resources of watchdog organizations have themselves been challenged as never before.

Religion and Religious Freedom

Congress shall make no law respecting an establishment of religion, or prohibiting the free exercise thereof ...

That first statement is commonly known as the Establishment Clause. It neither favors a specific religion, nor does it favor religion over non-religion. Those who insist that America is a *"Christian nation"* disagree. They believe (or claim to believe) that religion is, indeed, favored over non-religion. If the statement referred to "a religion," rather than just to "religion," their position might possibly be supportable. However, given the extreme care taken by the framers of the Constitution, the omission of the indefinite article was almost certainly a conscious one. Even more important is the omission, throughout the Constitution, of any mention of a deity.

Those who claim to speak for the Christian community (e.g., Rev. Jerry Falwell) point to the "Year of our Lord" reference in the paragraph preceding the signatures to the Constitution as evidence of religious intent. This is as fatuous as claiming that anyone who places AD (Anno Domini) after a date is expressing a religious belief. The former was common practice in the eighteenth Century and is still often used for proclamations and similar documents. The use of AD and BC is common in history texts and elsewhere.

The best response to the views of the *"Christian Nation"* advocates is a very old one. It is contained in Jefferson's famous January 1, 1802 letter[10] to the Danbury (Connecticut) Baptists, in which he said:

> '*I contemplate with sovereign reverence that act of the whole American people which declared that their legislature should "make no law respecting an establishment of religion, or prohibiting the free exercise thereof," thus building a wall of separation between Church & State.*'

Jefferson put a great deal of thought into his letter. After first writing a draft, he solicited input from three members of his cabinet, including his Attorney General, Levi Lincoln. Although writing the letter at all, in response to an address of the Danbury Baptists, was politically motivated, it appears to truly represent Jefferson's sincere sentiments. Most people were not aware of the letter until Jefferson's writings were published in 1853. Twenty-six years later, in 1879, his "wall of separation" statement was cited in a Supreme Court case (*Reynolds v. United States*[11]), in the following opinion, delivered by Chief Justice Waite:

---

[10] A good article, regarding things Jeffersonian and, in particular, the letter to the Danbury Baptists (both the draft and the final version), can be found on the Library of Congress website at *http://loc.gov/loc/lcib/9806/danbury.html*.

[11] George Reynolds was tried and convicted, in Utah, for bigamy *(98 U.S. 145 (1878))*. His defense was that, as a Mormon, he had a religious duty to have more than one wife. The Supreme Court upheld his conviction.

"... it may be accepted almost as an authoritative decla-ration of the scope and effect of the [first] amendment."

It was subsequently cited in 1947 (*Everson v. Board of Education*[12]) and 1948 (*McCollum v. Board of Education*[13]). A number of Supreme Court justices, including Potter Stewart and William Rehnquist, have taken issue with the use of Jefferson's statement. Stewart objected to the use of a metaphor that was *"a phrase nowhere to be found in the Constitution."* Rehnquist complained that the Establishment Clause *"has been expressly freighted with Jefferson's misleading metaphor for nearly 40 years."* Many more, of course, have vehemently defended that metaphor. The fact that the neither the Constitution nor any of the amendments contain any metaphors does not rule out the use of metaphors in describing intent.

Freedom of Speech

Congress shall make no law ... abridging the freedom of speech ...

Many kinds of speech are, often for good reason, not free. Just as one should not shout "Fire!" in a crowded theatre, one should also not incite a crowd to riot. Libel and its spoken equivalent, slander, are only condition-ally protected.[14] Although pornography (considered a form of speech) is protected, there are notable exceptions

---

[12] The case *(330 U.S. 1 (1947))* challenged a New Jersey law authorizing payment for transportation costs to and from, not only public schools, but also private schools, including parochial ones (e.g., Catholic). As it set a precedent for rulings in other cases, it is considered seminal.

[13] The case *(333 U.S. 203 (1948))* dealt with a complaint about voluntary religious education being provided in the public schools in Champaign, IL. The Supreme Court upheld the complaint by a 6-1 vote. In the major-ity opinion, Justice Hugo Black wrote: *"The Court must support the im-penetrable wall between church and state."*

[14] The United States accepts the truthfulness of allegedly libelous state-ments as a valid defense and, moreover, requires that the plaintiff prove that statements are false. The United Kingdom is a notable example of a country that puts the onus on the defendant(s) to prove the truth of al-legedly libelous statements.

with respect to its use in the broadcast media and where the exploitation of children is involved.

In the end, though, the most precious example of protected (i.e., free) speech is political speech—in particular, speech that is unpopular with either the community or the government currently in power.

Freedom of the Press

Congress shall make no law ... abridging the freedom of the press ...

The press is sometimes referred to as the Fourth Estate. Historically, that makes it an informal fourth branch (or estate) of government, although the original three branches were English ones—the nobility, the clergy and the commons.[15] Fourth Estate started as a fairly loose term that could even refer to a mob, but its use to refer to the press (and, now, the news media generally) rapidly became the accepted one.

The framers of the Constitution divided government into three branches—legislative, executive and judicial—in order to provide checks and balances. Although this sounds good in theory, it depends in practice on a reasonable diversity of points of view and on the scrupulous independence of the judiciary. Where all three branches are motivated by a common ideology (as opposed to ideals), the checks and balances can be considerably weakened or even disappear altogether. This is why it is important that there be an influential "fourth branch" to shine a bright light on the malefactions and/or collusion of the first three.

Without freedom of the press, that fourth branch, the press itself (and, now, the broadcast news media) is rendered ineffective. In fact, it can no longer function as the Fourth Estate. Failure by the press to provide a strong counterbalance to collusion among the branches of gov-

---

[15] Represented today by the House of Lords, the Church of England and the House of Commons.

ernment puts its freedom, and ultimately the freedom of the people, at considerable risk. The craven compliance and even laziness of much of today's news media, in which they accept administration talking points, press releases and photo opportunities as credible points of reference, bodes ill for America. Since early 2004, there seems to be some slight reversal of this trend. We can only hope that it continues, although the performance of the media during the 2004 election campaigns, especially the one for president, provided little cause for optimism. On the other hand, by early 2006, the press appeared to have woken up somewhat.

Freedom of Assembly

Congress shall make no law ... abridging[16] *... the right of the people peaceably to assemble, and to petition the Government for a redress of grievances.*

A significant number of Americans, including those in the press, cheered when Lech Walesa mounted his massive Solidarity (Solidarność) demonstrations in Poland and ultimately brought about the change in the Polish Government. The press certainly provided wide coverage and the demonstrations were visible to all. Given the restrictions in Poland at that time, Walesa and the other members of Solidarity took a considerable risk.

In theory, the First Amendment guarantees that demonstrations (i.e., peaceable assemblies) in the United States will pose no risk, to the participants, of government retribution. It supposedly guarantees that demonstrations may be held in such a manner and place as to allow their message to be clearly visible (there being, in theory, no impediment to such a goal). Finally, it allows the people to petition the government (local, state or federal), either through peaceable assembly or by other non-violent means.

---

[16] As used here, the verb abridge means diminish, restrict or curtail.

"First Amendment zones" (corruption of Article I)

Even before the 2000 Election, certain groups had been compelled to limit their exercise of their First Amendment rights to a restricted zone. Both free speech and religious freedom were at issue. The most prominent group was the Hare Krishna movement,[17] which had gained a certain amount of notoriety as a result of impeding the progress of airline passengers to or from their departure or arrival gates at the nation's airports. Whether or not one agrees with the solution, which was to restrict their activities to an area to one side of the normal flow of passengers, it was an exercise in balancing competing rights, in this case the free speech rights of religious proselytizers and the rights of passengers and others to go about their business unimpeded.

Thus was created what has become known as the First Amendment zone. See the separate *First Amendment zones* entry for a discussion of the extent to which this already somewhat dubious artifact has been grossly perverted for purely political purposes.

Article II (Militia? What Militia?)

The **Second Amendment** says the following:

A well regulated Militia, being necessary to the security of a free State, the right of the people to keep and bear Arms, shall not be infringed.

This is one of the shortest Articles in the Bill of Rights. It is also the most controversial. The controversy is basically over whether the first thirteen words should be regarded as some kind of general comment or as a clear qualifier for what follows. The gun lobby, including of course the National Rifle Association (NRA), insists that the final state-

---

[17] Interestingly, the Hare Krishna movement is now going through the same tribulations as the Catholic Church, with lawsuits seeking and getting compensation for sexual abuse of members' children by those entrusted with their care. All of their U.S. boarding schools have now closed. This has nothing to do, of course, with the Bush administration or with right-wing organizations.

ment is unconditional. In fact, when they quote the Second Amendment in their advertising, they disingenuously omit the first thirteen words. Gun control advocates, on the other hand, insist that the first thirteen words clearly impose a limitation on the final statement; otherwise, why would they be there in the first place? The Supreme Court has repeatedly come down on the side of gun control, consistently ruling that the Second Amendment protects the rights of the well-regulated militias of the states, not individual citizens, to keep and bear arms.[18] What is now considered the definitive Supreme Court ruling was in United *States v. Miller (307 U.S. 174 (1939))*. In overturning the Arkansas conviction of Jack Miller and Frank Layton for carrying a sawn-off shotgun, the Western Arkansas District Court had ruled that the statute under which they were convicted violated their Second Amendment rights. Following an appeal by the Justice Department, the Supreme Court upheld the conviction and, in its opinion, stated:

> *"In the absence of any evidence tending to show that possession or use of a shotgun having a barrel of less than eighteen inches in length at this time has some reasonable relationship to the preservation or efficiency of a well-regulated militia, we cannot say that the Second Amendment guarantees the right to keep and bear such an instrument. Certainly it is not within judicial notice that this weapon is any part of the ordinary military equipment or that its use could contribute to the common defense."*

Given his well-known objection to any kind of gun control, it was unlikely that former Attorney General John Ashcroft would appeal a similar case to the Supreme Court. (*See Ashcroft, John.*) However, he resigned without having been put to the test on that issue.

The reference to common defense is important, because the Founders were opposed to the idea of a standing army, and

---

[18] Source: *http://usgovinfo.about.com/library/weekly/aa031900a.htm.*

regarded state militias as the best approach to the defense of the nation.[19]

In a very recent ruling (in *Seegars v. Ashcroft*, January 13, 2004[20]), which has been described as "one of the most thorough and thoughtful decisions on the Second Amendment ever rendered,"[21] U.S. District Judge Reggie B. Walton (surprisingly, a George W. Bush appointee) said:

> *"The Court must conclude that the Second Amendment does not confer an individual right to possess firearms. Rather, the Amendment's objective is to ensure the vitality of state militias."*

The court's ruling, which upheld the District of Columbia's 27-year-old ban on the sale of handguns, was obviously a great disappointment, not only to the NRA, but also to George Bush and especially to John Ashcroft. It is unconscionable, of course, that the Attorney General of the United States should have sought to overturn the lower court's ruling, especially when it would be contrary to the wishes of the majority of DC residents.

Article III (Quartering Soldiers)

So far, the Bush administration has taken no action in which the **Third Amendment** would be applicable—and the possibility of such action seems unlikely. However, for the sake of completeness, here it is:

> *No Soldier shall, in time of peace be quartered in any house, without the consent of the Owner, nor in time of war, but in a manner to be prescribed by law.*

---

[19] What they quite obviously did not have in mind are today's private militias, who seem to think they can protect themselves against the government by force of arms.

[20] The full 68-page ruling in this case may be found at *http://vpc.org/ graphics/SeegarsOpinion.pdf* (requires Adobe Reader).

[21] From a statement by Violence Policy Center Litigation Director and Legislative Counsel, Matt Nosanchuk.

Article IV (Security, Searches and Seizures)

Violations of the **Fourth Amendment**, on the other hand, are serious and, currently, real matters. Its intent could not be clearer:

> *The right of the people to be secure in their persons, houses, papers, and effects, against unreasonable searches and sei- zures, shall not be violated, and no Warrants shall issue, but upon probable cause, supported by Oath or affirmation, and particularly describing the place to be searched, and the persons or things to be seized.*

Since the invention of the telephone, searches have in- cluded wiretapping. The Internet has, in turn, immensely increased the possible scope of electronic scrutiny.

Elsewhere, we hint at the extent to which former Attorney General *John Ashcroft*, with the support of the draconian and perversely named **USA PATRIOT Act**,[22] effectively trashed the Fourth Amendment, along with the First and the Fifth. Ashcroft's successor, Alberto Gonzalez, indicated that he was willing to pursue some reasonable changes to the Act when it came up for renewal.[23]

One of the rights arising out of the Fourth Amendment is the right to privacy. In an encouraging decision, on June 26, 2003, the Supreme Court upheld, by a vote of 6 to 3, the privacy rights of consenting adults with respect to sexual activity, including anal intercourse. Although the decision

---

[22] USA PATRIOT takes the art of the acronym to ridiculous extremes. It is both contrived and ironic. Here it is in all its glory: **U**niting and **S**trength- ening **A**merica by **P**roviding **A**ppropriate **T**ools **R**equired to **I**ntercept and **O**bstruct **T**errorism. It's almost certain that the acronym came first, with the words being subsequently contrived to fit. One might very well call the technique "reverse acronymology."

[23] The Act came up for renewal in June, 2005. In spite of George Bush's call for it to be renewed in its entirety (not to mention his wish that it be made permanent), 38 House Republicans joined Democrats and Inde- pendent, Bernie Sanders (VT), to pass the Sanders Amendment to Sec- tion 215, requiring the government to obtain a traditional search warrant if they wish to gain access to people's reading records (usually at a pub- lic library). This was later modified to simply require the Director of the FBI to be personally involved in such decisions.

almost certainly did not please the Bush administration (given George Bush's allegiance to the Religious Right), there was no comment from the White House.

More recently (January 2006), a member of the Bush Administration revealed a startling misunderstanding of the Fourth Amendment's due process provision (*see* **Hayden, Michael**).

Article V (Taking the Fifth)

The influence of crime movies and the antics, in the 1950s, of the late unlamented Junior Senator from Wisconsin, Joseph McCarthy, have led to a popular belief that the **Fifth Amendment** is only about avoiding self-incrimination ("pleading ..." or "taking the Fifth"). However, that ("nor shall be compelled in any criminal case to be a witness against himself") is only one part of it. The full Article says:

> *No person shall be held to answer for a capital, or otherwise infamous crime, unless on a presentment or indictment of a Grand Jury, except in cases arising in the land or naval forces, or in the Militia, when in actual service in time of War or public danger; nor shall any person be subject for the same offence to be twice put in jeopardy of life or limb; nor shall be compelled in any criminal case to be a witness against himself, nor be deprived of life, liberty, or property, without due process of law; nor shall private property be taken for public use, without just compensation.*

Although the right to avoid self-incrimination is of vital importance, the USA PATRIOT Act and the excesses of the Justice Department (under former Attorney General John Ashcroft) lend special significance to the part about deprivation of liberty without due process of law. In 1866, Congress lent extraordinary emphasis to the Fifth Amendment by expanding on it in Section 1 of the Fourteenth Amendment, some of which deals with due process.

Article VI (Speedy and Public Trials, Counsel, and Confrontation)

Here's the **Sixth Amendment**:

In all criminal prosecutions, the accused shall enjoy the right to a speedy and public trial, by an impartial jury of the State and district wherein the crime shall have been committed, which district shall have been previously ascertained by law, and to be informed of the nature and cause of the accusation; to be confronted with the witnesses against him; to have compulsory process for obtaining witnesses in his favor, and to have the Assistance of Counsel for his defence.

Totalitarian states offer none of these protections. People can be arrested without formal charge, have no right to counsel, and can languish in jail indefinitely. For those who ran afoul of the authorities, colonial rule was no better — hence the rejection of British rule that led to the War of Independence (1775-1783), the Declaration of Independence (1776), the U.S. Constitution (1787) and, ultimately, the Bill of Rights (passed by Congress in 1789 and ratified in 1791).

With the exception of voting rights[24] and qualifications to run for office, the rights afforded by the Constitution and the Bill of Rights apply not just to citizens; they apply to everyone. The First, Second and Fourth Amendments, for example, refer to "people," not "citizens." The Fifth Amendment refers to "person," not "citizen." The Sixth Amendment refers to "the accused," not to "the accused citizen."

An April 2003 report on "The September 11 Detainees," released on June 2, 2003, by the Office of the Inspector General of the Department of Justice, dealt with the mistreatment and deprivation of the rights of non-citizens at facilities in Brooklyn, NY, and Passaic, NJ.[25]

---

[24] The US Constitution does not actually affirm the right of every citizen to vote. This weakness was cited (and, in the opinion of many, exploited) in the notorious *Bush v. Gore* decision of the U.S. Supreme Court on December 12, 2000.

[25] The 198-page report may be downloaded from the website of the Office of the DOJ Inspector General at *http://www.usdoj.gov/oig/special/0603/ full.pdf.* The file size is about 13 megabytes. Highlights of the report are

Article VII (Lawsuits and Right to Trial by Jury)

Here's the **Seventh Amendment**:

In suits at common law, where the value in controversy shall exceed twenty dollars, the right of trial by jury shall be preserved, and no fact tried by a jury shall be otherwise re-examined in any Court of the United States, than according to the rules of common law.

Based on this amendment, juries have, until now, been able to assess damages for corporate wrongdoing (and other torts), in either individual or class action cases, ensuring that the victims of such wrongdoing are adequately compensated. Moreover, by assessing a large enough penalty, they have been able (if imperfectly) to make corporations modify their behavior, rather than just treating a judgment as merely part of the cost of doing business.

For examples of how the individual and group rights hitherto protected by the Seventh Amendment are being eroded, see *tort reform.*

Article VIII (Bail, Fines and Punishment)

The **Eighth Amendment** is expressed concisely and elegantly:

Excessive bail shall not be required, nor excessive fines imposed, nor cruel and unusual punishments inflicted.

Excessive Bail

FindLaw's article[26] on the Eighth Amendment says that: *"Bail is 'excessive' ... when it is set at a figure higher than an amount reasonably calculated to ensure the asserted governmental interest. If the only asserted interest is to guarantee that the accused will stand trial and submit to sentence if found guilty, then 'bail must be set by a court at a sum designed to ensure that goal, and no more.'"*

---

provided in a press release, which can be viewed at *http://www.usdoj. gov/oig/special/0603/press.htm.*

[26] *http://caselaw.lp.findlaw.com/data/constitution/amendment08/01.html.*

Excessive Fines

With one exception, the Supreme Court has chosen to treat the excessive fines clause as applying only to fines paid to the government (which includes fines paid to a court), excluding compensatory damages paid as a result of a civil lawsuit (*see* **tort reform**). The exception relates to civil asset forfeiture, an issue that predates the Bush administration.

Cruel and Unusual Punishment

There are ongoing debates regarding what constitutes cruel and unusual punishment, especially with respect to three-strikes laws, mandatory minimum sentences (e.g., for drug offenses) and the death penalty. Nearly half the states are uncomfortable with the death penalty, including twelve where it does not apply, five where there have been no executions since the Supreme Court reinstated it in 1976, and six where there has been only one execution in that time.[27] Texas, where George W. Bush served two terms as Governor, holds the record for executions, which peaked during Bush's tenure. Even that state is now giving juries the option to use the sentence of life without parole, rather than death.[28]

Article IX (Enumerated Rights not Precluding Other Rights)

The **Ninth Amendment** makes it clear that rights are not limited to those spelled out in the Constitution:

The enumeration in the Constitution of certain rights shall not be construed to deny or disparage others retained by the people.

This was James Madison's approach to ensuring that, just because a right is not specifically enumerated in the first eight amendments, the government should not assume that

---

[27] *Death penalty debate finally produces useful result, USA Today, June 21, 2005, http://usatoday.com/news/opinion/editorials/2005-06-21-our-view_x.htm.*

[28] Ibid.

it has the power to deny such a right. An example would be the right to privacy. In a landmark case (*Griswold v. Connecticut*[29]), the Supreme Court ruled that the right to privacy derived, as an "associational right," from rights spelled out in the First, Third, Fourth and Fifth Amendments. However, in writing the majority opinion, Justice William O. Douglas invoked the Ninth Amendment, as also did Justice Arthur Goldberg in a concurring opinion.[30] The decision in *Griswold v. Connecticut* served as a precedent in the case of *Roe v. Wade*.

As the Bush administration has been denying rights explicitly protected by the Bill of Rights (e.g., the right to due process) and delaying implementation of Supreme Court rulings (e.g., with respect to detainees' right of access to a lawyer), derived and associational rights seem to be somewhat moot at the moment.

Article X (Powers reserved to the states)

The **Tenth Amendment** is often regarded as redundant, as it simply provides reassurance for what should be obvious. This has not stopped lawyers from citing it in cases involving "states' rights." Here it is:

> *The powers not delegated to the United States by the Constitution, nor prohibited by it to the States, are reserved to the States respectively, or to the people.*

Congress debated whether or not to qualify this amendment by saying "not expressly delegated," rather than simply "not delegated." The actual wording of the Amendment makes the outcome of that debate obvious.

*   *   *   *   *

The following Articles, although not part of the original Bill of Rights, deal with additional rights.

---

[29] *Griswold v. Connecticut* dealt, in 1965, with Connecticut's notorious 1879 law, banning the sale or use (even by married persons) of contraceptives. The Supreme Court ruled, on privacy grounds, that the ban was unconstitutional.

[30] Goldberg devoted several pages to the Ninth Amendment.

Article XIII (Abolition of slavery)

The **Thirteenth Amendment**, which trumped one of the rights of the southern states, seems clear enough. It would appear to prohibit, not only slavery, but also other forms of involuntary servitude,[31] with one apparently reasonable exception.

Section 1. Neither slavery nor involuntary servitude, except as a punishment for crime whereof the party shall have been duly convicted, shall exist within the United States, or any place subject to their jurisdiction.

Section 2. Congress shall have power to enforce this article by appropriate legislation.

Things are not always as they seem. Numerous exceptions to the Amendment's applicability have been found over the years.[32] The contracts of seamen, for example, were held to be valid, even though they involved the forfeiting of a certain amount of personal liberty.[33] The U.S. Supreme Court has also found compulsory military service (the draft) and jury duty to be exceptions.[34,35] A strange exception, which might be overturned if its enforcement were to be attempted today, upheld a state law that required every able-bodied man in its jurisdiction to labor "for a reasonable time," without direct compensation, on public roads near his residence.[36]

Whether George Bush or his Justice Department might be seeking further exceptions to the Thirteenth Amendment is something that is possibly open to speculation, especially as there could be some question about his interpretation of "duly convicted."

---

[31] Including Mexican peonage and the Chinese coolie trade.

[32] *Situations in Which the Amendment Is Inapplicable*, FindLaw, http://caselaw.lp.findlaw.com/data/constitution/amendment13/03.html.

[33] *Robertson v. Baldwin, 165 U.S. 275, 282 (1897).*

[34] *Selective Draft Law Cases, 245 U.S. 366 (1918).*

[35] *Butler v. Perry, 240 U.S. 328, 333 (1916).*

[36] Ibid.

Article XIV (Citizenship, due process, etc.)

Only Section 1 of the **Fourteenth Amendment** deals with rights, which it does in two sentences. The first sentence defines citizenship:

> *All persons born or naturalized in the United States, and subject to the jurisdiction thereof, are citizens of the United States and of the State wherein they reside.*

The second sentence deals, not only with the preservation of the privileges and immunities of citizens, but also with the protections that are applicable to all persons, whether citizens or not.

> *No State shall make or enforce any law which shall abridge the privileges or immunities of citizens of the United States; nor shall any State deprive any person of life, liberty, or property, without due process of law; nor deny to any person within its jurisdiction the equal protection of the laws.*

According to James Madison biographer Irving Brant, the Fourteenth Amendmentwas intended by Congress to make the first eight articles of the Bill of Rights applicable to state and local governments. Unfortunately, it took the Supreme Court until after World War II to begin to make the amendment really meaningful. The Court's 1947 ruling in *Everson v. Board of Education* definitively declared that the amendment applies the First Amendment "establishment" clause to state and local government.[37]

Article XV (Voting rights)

The **Fifteenth Amendment**, ratified in 1870, appears to have established the right of all races to vote. Unfortunately, the negative nature of its wording (*"shall not be denied or abridged ... on account of ..."*) does not overcome the fact that the U.S. Constitution does not guarantee anyone the fundamental right to vote. Here is what it says:

---

[37] *The Bill of Rights: Its Origins and Meanings (pages 318-343), Irving Brant, Signet, 1967, ISBN 0-45161-444-5.*

Section 1. The right of citizens of the United States to vote shall not be denied or abridged by the United States or by any State on account of race, color, or previous condition of servitude.

Section 2. The Congress shall have power to enforce this article by appropriate legislation.

It took 90 years for the appropriate legislation, the Civil Rights Act of 1964, to finally appear. Among the civil rights covered by the Act, the problem of racial discrimination with respect to voting (especially in the southern states) was addressed. Unfortunately, subtle and hard to prove kinds of discrimination still exist. In the 2000 election, Florida had its notorious *felon purge*, which affected African Americans disproportionately. In 2004, Ohio was reported to have provided vastly more facilities (polling stations and voting booths) in predominantly white areas, with the residents of other areas being forced to line up for hours to use very limited facilities (or, because time ran out, not use them).

Article XIX (Voting rights)

The **Nineteenth Amendment**, ratified in 1920, did the same for women as the Fifteenth Amendment did for male minorities. Its wording is similar, namely:

Section 1. The right of the citizens of the United States to vote shall not be denied or abridged by the United States or by any State on account of sex.

Section 2. Congress shall have power to enforce this article by appropriate legislation.

Women had had partial suffrage in some states and for some kinds of elections (e.g., school boards) since as early as 1838. Between 1869 and 1914, eleven states introduced universal suffrage. The suffragist movement finally pushed Congress into introducing the Amendment in 1919.

As with the Fifteenth Amendment, the Nineteenth does not actually confer a right to vote. Rather, it only establishes the right of women not to be discriminated against on the basis of their sex in setting voting qualifications.[38]

Article XXVI (Voting rights)

The **Twenty-Sixth Amendment**, ratified in July 1971, lowered the voting age to 18. Its wording is similar to that of the Fifteenth and Nineteenth Amendments:

> *Section 1. The right of citizens of the United States, who are eighteen years of age or older, to vote shall not be denied or abridged by the United States or by any State on account of age.*
>
> *Section 2. The Congress shall have power to enforce this article by appropriate legislation.*

Again, as with the two other voting rights amendments, it avoids establishing a general right to vote. However, there appears to have been no overt attempt since its ratification to specifically prevent or make it difficult for eighteen, nineteen and twenty-year-olds from doing so. Educating many of them to exercise their franchise is, of course, another matter.

Bin Laden, Osama: A member of the extremely wealthy bin Laden family of Saudi Arabia, born in 1955, the only son of the fourth of Mohammed bin Laden's wives. Mohammed bin Laden, a Yemeni, was the founder of the huge and immensely successful Binladin Group,[39] a financial empire that started as a construction company. Osama bin Laden's mother was Syrian.[40]

On his father's death in a helicopter crash in 1968, bin Laden inherited about $80 million. He completed his education, receiving a degree in civil engineering in 1979 from King Abdul-Aziz University. In his student days, he is said to have

---

[38] *FindLaw, U.S. Constitution, Nineteenth Amendment,* http://caselaw.lp.findlaw.com/data/constitution/amendment19.

[39] There are several ways to spell the bin Laden family name using the Roman alphabet. The choice of "Binladin" for English manifestations of the company name, Binladin Group, was presumably a corporate one.

[40] The source for the historical information on bin Laden is *Who is Osama bin Laden?* http://www.empereur.com/laden.html.

spent a great deal of time enjoying himself in bars in Beirut, Lebanon. Around the time of his graduation, he became interested in politics, especially in the wake of the Israeli-Egyptian peace treaty and the overthrow of the Shah of Iran. When the Soviet Union invaded Afghanistan, in 1979, his interest turned to rage.[41] He promptly left for Afghanistan.

Most politically well informed people became aware of bin Laden's existence during the Soviet-Afghan War (which lasted until 1989, when the Soviets withdrew in defeat).

To help bin Laden and the Mujahideen[42] fight the Soviets, he was provided with money and weapons, under the auspices of the CIA, to fight the Soviet invaders. To conceal American involvement (even from bin Laden himself), the CIA worked through Pakistan's Inter-Services Intelligence (ISI), providing money and weapons in what has been described as "the largest covert operation in the history of the CIA."[43] For much of the same period, and subsequently, the FBI considered bin Laden to be the world's foremost terrorist.

Two years after the end of the Soviet-Afghan War, the Gulf War started and bin Laden saw the United States establishing bases in his homeland of Saudi Arabia. He also had not forgotten his anger at the assistance of the U.S. Sixth Fleet in Israel's invasion of Lebanon in 1982.[44] He redirected the anger he had felt towards the Soviet Union against Saudi Arabia and the United States. He was, by this time, in Sudan, having been exiled from Saudi Arabia by the royal family for his criticism of their repressive and corrupt regime. While in Sudan (from 1991 to 1996), he made much of his fortune (by then, around $250 million) available to about a dozen militant Islamist groups. It was in the north

---

[41] As he related to an Arabic language interviewer some years later.

[42] One of a number of spellings of this word.

[43] *Centre for Research on Globalisation: Who is Osama bin Laden?* *http://www.globalresearch.ca/articles/CHO109C.html.*

[44] This is something he discussed in a videotaped speech he sent to Al-Jazeera at the end of 2004. The full transcript of his speech, published on November 1, 2004, can be found at *http://www.informationclearinghouse.info/ article7201.htm.*

of Sudan that he set up his first three terrorist training camps. Eventually, under pressure from Saudi Arabia and the United States, Sudan expelled bin Laden and he took up residence in Afghanistan, where he invested about $3 million helping the Taliban overthrow the post-war government. Neither at this time nor during the Soviet-Afghan War did he engage in the fighting, limiting his participation to organization, coordination and financing. He performs those functions through Al Qaeda ("the base"), which is an umbrella group and clearing house, not entirely dependent on bin Laden's survival. What exists and what will survive is a loosely connected group of networks, all determined to wreak havoc on the United States and its allies.

The significant Al Qaeda or Al Qaeda-related attacks, prior to 9/11, were the February 1993 bombing of the World Trade Center, the August 1998 suicide bombing of the U.S. embassies in Kenya and Tanzania, and the October 2000 suicide bombing of the USS Cole in the harbor at Aden. Whether or not bin Laden personally planned any of these, he certainly seems to have facilitated the bombing of the embassies and USS Cole, at the very least.

In August 1998, President Clinton authorized an attack on the Harkatul Jihad Al-Islami military training camp in Khost, Afghanistan. According to the available intelligence, bin Laden planned to visit the camp for dinner on August 20. The attack took place on that date, killing or wounding many of the people there. Bin Laden was not one of them, as he had decided at the last minute to postpone his visit. Also spared were some of his commanders, who were going to make the visit with him.[45]

After 9/11, George Bush indicated that the U.S. would get bin Laden, "dead or alive." Only six months later, that resolve seemed to have disappeared, as illustrated by his own statements:

---

[45] *Osama Bin Laden survived Missile Attack because he postponed, at the last minute, a planned trip to the Camp, Kamran Khan, http://www.anusha.com/ osamasur.htm.*

September 13, 2001: "The most important thing is for us to find Osama bin Laden. It is our number one priority and we will not rest until we find him."

March 13, 2002: "I don't know where bin Laden is. I have no idea and really don't care. It's not that important. It's not our priority."

What has become clear, since, is that Saddam Hussein, not Osama bin Laden, was and always had been Bush's foreign policy priority.

Midway between those two dates was the attempt to capture bin Laden at Tora Bora, Afghanistan. It failed miserably. U.S. commanders knew, based on definitive intelligence, that bin Laden was among hundreds of Al Qaeda and Taliban members who were fleeing across the mountains into neighboring Pakistan.[46] However, rather than using Special Forces teams, General Tommy Franks outsourced the job to the local Afghan commanders. Unfortunately many of the commanders were sympathetic to bin Laden. Moreover, Al Qaeda paid the commanders to help them flee. In the exodus, close to 900 Arabs fled to the Khyber tribal region of Pakistan, while senior Al Qaeda leaders went to Parachinar, which is very close to the Pakistan-Afghanistan border.[47,48]

Bin Laden later returned to Afghanistan, specifically to Khowst, which is in the Afghanistan tribal areas south of and fairly close to Parachinar. His host in Khowst was, not surprisingly, the local Taliban leader. Subsequently he returned to Pakistan. Judging by the failure of all who are

---

[46] *Exclusive: CIA Commander: U.S. Let bin Laden Slip Away*, Michael Hirsh, *Newsweek*, August 15, 2005, http://msnbc.msn.com/id/8853000/site/newsweek.

[47] In fact, the Afghanistan border is north, west and south of Parachinar, which is within a spur of Pakistani territory that, because of the geometry of the mountains, encroaches westward into what would otherwise be Afghan territory.

[48] *Afghans helped Bin Laden Flee Country, Official Says, Leaders who were sympathetic to Al Qaeda purportedly played a role in Tora Bora escape*, Reuters, September 15, 2005, http://www.latimes.com/news/nationworld/world/la-fg-osama15sep15,1,4446442.story?coll=la-headlines-world.

looking for him to find him, he appears to be quite secure. George Bush's March 13, 2002 remarks may, in fact, have been an acknowledgement of this fact.

As Al Qaeda has become quite sophisticated, with many university-trained members with both management and technical skills, the survival of bin Laden is no longer a significant factor in their effectiveness. He is, of course, no longer their main source of financing, although his financial contribution is, no doubt, still significant. Killing him may not be a good idea, as that would only create a martyr. Thus George Bush faces a dilemma (or, apparently, would just as soon not face it).

> The bin Laden and Bush families have very close personal and business ties. In *House of Bush, House of Saud*,[49] Craig Unger describes how members of the bin Laden family were flown on an American plane from the U.S. to Saudi Arabia on September 19, 2001—eight days after the 9/11 attacks. Interestingly, the Bush administration had decided, a few hours after the attacks on the World Trade Center and the Pentagon, that Osama bin Laden and Al Qaeda were the prime suspects, even though they didn't yet have any evidence. These and other factors have given rise to quite a few conspiracy theories, discussion of which is well beyond the scope of this book.

Blair, Tony: British Prime Minister, Leader of the Labour Party, and in spite of their very different views on the nature of the *social contract,* friend of George W. Bush.

Blair followed Bush's example and gave the British people the same rationale as Bush for participating in Operation Iraqi Freedom. This was in spite of considerable opposition from the people and from many in his own party. In the aftermath, many of his former party allies have abandoned their support for him.

---

[49] *House of Bush, House of Saud: The Secret Relationship Between the World's Two Most Powerful Dynasties, Scribner, 2004, ISBN 0-7432-5337-X.*

The authors of a report in *Renewal*, an influential quarterly Labour journal, say:

"As it stands, none of the major rationales for the war stand up. There are no weapons of mass destruction, the country, the region and the world are not safer places, the lives of the Iraqi people are not safer and it remains an open question whether they are or will be much better. And the debris has inevitably fallen primarily on Blair, given that he took an unwilling and unenthusiastic party and people into the conflict. Tragically, Blair still appears to believe that if he can only explain it one more time, we will get it. But Tony, we get the message — we just don't accept it."[50]

Tragically, Tony Blair and George Bush appear to be equally out of touch with reality.

Bloch, Scott J.: Special Counsel, U.S. Office of Special Counsel (OSC). Bloch, who was nominated by George Bush in June 2003 and confirmed by the Senate in December 2003, was previously Deputy Director and Counsel to the Task Force for Faith-based and Community Initiatives at the Department of Justice.

In February 2004, he took the very strange step of ordering the removal of gay rights information[51] from the OSC website.[52] One of the main purposes of the Office of Special Counsel is to protect the rights of whistleblowers. However, it also provides information on prohibited personnel practices, including a provision, in effect since 1978, prohibiting discrimination against employees for private behavior that does not affect their job performance. Bloch's order removed references to sexual orientation from a complaint form, training slides and a brochure, all of which are accessible on the site. Like so many other negative actions in the

---

[50] *Former Labour allies round on Blair, Patrick Wintour, The Guardian, August 9, 2004, http://politics.guardian.co.uk/labour/story/0,9061,1279153,00.html.*

[51] *Gay Rights Information Taken Off Site, Washington Post, February 18, 2004, http://www.washingtonpost.com/ac2/wp-dyn?pagename=article&node=&content Id=A49392-2004Feb17&notFound=true.*

[52] *http://www.osc.gov.*

Bush administration, this was the start, rather than the end, of a process. In a March 10, 2004, interview with *Federal Times*,[53] Bloch said, "People confuse conduct and sexual orientation as the same thing, and I don't think they are." His reading of the 1978 regulation is that his office can protect someone who is fired for attending a gay rights parade, but cannot protect someone who is fired for being gay.

In February 2004, Bloch had said he was acting on his own initiative, rather than on instructions from George Bush. Whether or not that is true, the fact is that, in his October 11, 2000, debate with Al Gore, Bush made a clear (or at least implied) pledge with his statement that homosexuals "ought to have the same rights as all other people."[54] Bloch's position is also at odds with that of the Office of Personnel Management (OPM), which has always interpreted the 1978 ruling to mean that government employees cannot be fired for their sexual orientation. Ironically, OPM directs employees facing such discrimination to the Office of Special Counsel to obtain redress.

Bodman, Samuel: Secretary of Energy for George Bush's second term and former Deputy Secretary of Commerce (under *Donald Evans*). Bush nominated him on December 10, 2004. He was confirmed unanimously by the Senate on January 31, 2005 and was sworn in the following day.

On the positive side, his management and technical qualifications are excellent. He is a former chemical engineering professor and has a doctorate in science from MIT. On the negative side, he has little policy-oriented experience, headed a company that was twice fined, during his tenure, for failing to report hazardous chemical spills and not complying with federal cleanup orders, and, finally, his job entails advancing Bush's energy agenda, which includes drilling in the Arctic National Wildlife Refuge (ANWR). In real-

---

[53] *OSC to study whether bias law covers gays, Federal Times Online, March 15, 2004, http://federaltimes.com/index.php?S=2727185.*

[54] *Bush Allows Gays to Be Fired for Being Gay, The Daily Mis-Lead, March 23, 2004, http://www.misleader.org/daily_mislead/Read.asp?fn=df03202004.html.*

ity, of course, America's energy policy is squarely in the hands of Vice President **Dick Cheney**, who continues to stonewall in the face of demands that he release information on his 2001 **Energy Task Force**.

Boehner, John: Republican Congressman from Ohio's 8th District and successor to **Tom DeLay** as House Majority Leader. He was elected by his House colleagues on February 2, 2006, beating his nearest rival, Roy Blunt (MO), in an upset, by 122 to 109 votes.

Boehner was supposedly a reform candidate who said that, if he were elected, there would no longer be a K Street Project or anything else like it[55] (see last paragraph of **Gingrich, Newt**). Many progressives were skeptical.

> "If Boehner becomes House majority leader, you can expect a continuation of the DeLay parade of horribles. Calling John Boehner a reform candidate is like calling Attila the Hun a nice guy."
>
> —Gary Ruskin, Congressional Accountability Project[56]

From the above and many other comments, it's evident that progressive organizations do not regard Boehner's accession to the Delay throne as a good thing. Rather, they expect more of the same.

Bolten, Joshua ("Josh"): White House Chief of Staff. George Bush appointed him on March 28, 2006 to replace **Andrew Card**, who resigned on the same day. Bolten was previously Director of the Office of Management and Budget (OMB). Prior to that, he was Andrew Card's deputy.

When Bolten was nominated, on June 22, 2003, to his OMB position, he said, "Mr. President, thank you. Thank you for your kind words and your confidence. If confirmed by the Senate, I'll be a tireless advocate for your agenda, and a tight-fisted custodian of the people's money." On September 16, 2005, Forbes Magazine,

---

[55] Boehner's PAC raises critics' questions, Jessica Wehrman, Dayton Daily News, January 15, 2006, http://citizensforethics.org/press/pressclip.php?view=1493.
[56] Ibid.

in naming Bolten *Dunce of the Week,* quoted John Fund of the *Wall Street Journal* as saying that Bolten, rather than being tight fisted, had been spending like a drunken sailor.[57]

Of course, it's very difficult to advocate for Bush's agenda and exercise fiscal restraint at the same time. No doubt, Bolten's probable successor at OMB, former Republican Congressman (from Ohio's 2nd district) and U.S. Trade Representative **Rob Portman**, will face the same challenge. Bush nominated Portman to the position on April 18, 2006.

Bush's choice of Bolten to replace Card seemed to be a prelude to a larger shake-up, which is an assumption since confirmed. It was most likely motivated by criticism from members of Bush's own party and Bush's sagging approval ratings (37% on the day of the change). As Chief of Staff, Bolten has the authority to choose the members of the White House staff (i.e., his own staff). He started by reducing **Karl Rove**'s responsibilities and removing **Scott McClellan** as Press Secretary.[58]

Bolton, John: George Bush's nominee for U.N. Ambassador. Secretary of State, **Condoleezza Rice**, announced his nomination on March 7, 2005. His hearing before the Senate Foreign Relations Committee, which started on April 11, ended on May 12 with a 10 to 8 vote, on party lines, to send his nomination to the Senate. One of the ten Republicans who voted for him, Senator George Voinovich (OH), expressed strong misgivings and stated that he would not be voting for him in the Senate.[59] Senator Lincoln Chafee (R-RI) also had reservations, but said he would vote for Bolton in the Senate.

---

[57] *Dunce of the Week: Josh Bolten, Rich Karlgaard, Forbes.com, September 16, 2005, http://www.forbes.com/columnists/management/2005/09/16/ dunce-of-the-week-cz_rk_0917bolten.html.*

[58] It was not entirely clear whether McClellan's departure was Bolten's decision or his own. Bolten had asked those who were considering leaving during Bush's remaining time in office to do so immediately, presumably so as to allow replacements to get up to speed well before the November 2006 midterm elections.

[59] Which raises the obvious question of why he was willing to vote him out of committee.

In Bush's first term, Bolton was Undersecretary of State for Arms Control and International Security.

> *"His job is to keep a hawk eye on dovish Colin Powell. And he's helped turn Bush foreign policy into an ideological hammer."*[60]
>
> —*Nicholas Thompson, Salon.com, July 16, 2003*

The Senate confirmed Bolton's appointment as Undersecretary in 2001, with a 57 to 43 vote that was mostly along party lines. Ideologically, he's in the same category as *George Bush, Dick Cheney, Donald Rumsfeld,* and the *neoconservatives* in (or formerly in) the Defense Department (*Paul Wolfowitz, Douglas Feith,* etc.). According to Nicholas Thompson, *Washington Monthly* Contributing Editor, he agrees with the neoconservatives on all of the country's fundamental foreign policy issues.[61] He has also strengthened the alliance between the Bush administration and the Christian right. He also has a reputation for extreme abrasiveness, a bad temper and, incredibly for someone nominated as U.N. Ambassador, a dislike of the United Nations. He was also involved in the deception regarding Niger's alleged agreement to sell yellowcake uranium to Saddam Hussein and in post-election activities in Florida, on behalf of George Bush, following the disputed 2000 election.

On May 26, 2005, the hearings for Bolton's new appointment stalled in the Senate, following a successful Democratic *filibuster,* on which the cloture vote fell four votes short of the required 60. The Democrats had demanded, unsuccessfully, that the Bush administration turn over documents they needed to make a decision. Subsequently, it was reported that Bolton was involved in the outing of Valerie Plame Wilson[62] and that he had lied to the Senate on a questionnaire during his confirmation hearings.[63]

---

[60] *John Bolton vs. the world, Nicholas Thompson, Salon.com, July 16, 2003, http://www.salon.com/news/feature/2003/07/16/Bolton.*

[61] Ibid.

[62] Valerie Plame Wilson is the wife of Ambassador Joseph Wilson. Her role as a CIA agent was leaked in apparent retaliation for her husband's New

> *"[T]his may be the first time a world superpower has used its top United Nations post as a spot for the remedial training of a troublesome government employee."*[64]
>
> —*New York Times editorial, August 2, 2005*

Those hearings were supposed to have resumed in September 2005. However, on August 1, 2005, the first day of the Senate's summer recess, George Bush made a recess appointment of John Bolton as U.N. Ambassador. By August 25, Bolton had made his mark in the U.N., by demanding 750 changes to U.N. reorganization plans just three weeks prior to a summit at which agreement on those plans was supposed to be reached. He called for immediate talks on his proposed amendments. According to the *Guardian*, the amendments *"seek to play down the emphasis given to alleviating poverty, and expunge all references to the millennium development goals, including the target for wealthy countries to donate at least 0.7% of national income to the developing world."*[65] The U.S. contribution is currently only 0.2% of national income.[66]

Brock, David: Former hack writer for the political right, who, by his own admission,[67] *"was a witness to, and a participant in, all of the scandals that gripped the capital city— Iran-Contra, the failed nomination of Robert Bork to the Supreme Court, the Thomas-Hill hearings, Troopergate, Paula Jones, Whitewater, and the secret scheming that led to the impeachment of President Clinton."* He ends the prologue to his book, *Blinded by the Right*, with, *"The need to shine light on the operations and agenda of the right wing has not*

York Times article discrediting George Bush's claim that Saddam Hussein sought to obtain yellowcake uranium from Niger.

[63] Bolton's lie was admitted by the State Department.

[64] Sen. George Voinovich (R-OH) said, on August 1, that he planned to send Bolton a book on how to be an effective manager.

[65] *Bolton throws UN summit into chaos: Bush's envoy demands 750 changes to reorganisation plans, Julian Borger, Guardian Unlimited, http://www.guardian.co.uk/usa/story/0,12271,1556790,00.html.*

[66] Some reports put it at only 1%.

[67] From the prologue to his book, *Blinded by the Right, David Brock, Crown Publishers, 2002, ISBN 0-8239-3099-1.*

abated in the wake of September 11. My intention is that the following political testament, offered in a spirit of full disclosure and reconciliation, will serve as a cautionary tale of lessons learned the hard way." His revelations in his book are consistent with and supportive of information available from other sources, although he provides a detailed insider's perspective not available elsewhere.

Brock has, not surprisingly, been vilified as a turncoat by the right. Some on the left view his change of heart with some skepticism, and some may, no doubt, find it hard to forgive him for his hatchet-job books on Hillary Clinton[68] and Anita Hill.[69] Regardless, he seems to have experienced a real epiphany—to the extent that he formed a not-for-profit organization, *Media Matters for America*[70], to correct the distortions published by the right-wing media (e.g., Fox News, *Washington Times*, Scarborough Country,[71] Rush Limbaugh, etc.).

Brown, Michael D.: Until his somewhat ignominious resignation on September 12, 2005, Brown was Undersecretary for Emergency Preparedness and Response (EP&R), in the ***Department of Homeland Security (DHS)***. Nominated by George Bush in January 2003 and confirmed without apparent controversy,[72] he was responsible for ***FEMA (Federal Emergency Management Agency)***, which is one of the agencies taken over by DHS.

Brown's first position in the Bush administration, starting in February 2001, was as General Counsel for FEMA, then led by Bush friend ***Joseph Allbaugh*** (who was alleged to have been Brown's college room mate).[73,74] From 1991 until Janu-

---

[68] *The Seduction of Hillary Rodham, David Brock, Free Press, 1998 (reprint), ISBN: 0-6848-3770-6*

[69] *The Real Anita Hill: The Untold Story, David Brock, Free Press, 1993, ISBN: 0-0290-4655-6*

[70] *http://mediamatters.org.*

[71] *Scarborough Country* is a right-wing talk show on MSNBC, hosted by Joe Scarborough, a former Republican congressman from Florida.

[72] Not unusual for sub-cabinet-level appointments.

[73] According to Brown, his own wife was his roommate in college (as told to Bill Maher on *Live will Bill Maher, HBO, March 3, 2006*).

ary 2001, Brown was the Judges and Stewards Commissioner of the now defunct International Arabian Horse Association (IAHA). He was asked to resign from that job, something that was confirmed on September 2, 2005, by Bill Pennington, who was president of the IAHA at the time.[75] As he is a qualified lawyer (JD), his initial appointment as General Counsel to FEMA is unsurprising. However, one could be forgiven for asking what it was about his IAHA experience that qualified him to head FEMA (or, prior to that appointment, to be deputy head of FEMA, followed by being acting head of FEMA).

Well, Brown's ten-year stint with IAHA does not appear in his White House biography[76] or the FEMA website biography,[77] nor does it appear in his profile on the FindLaw website,[78] although it did until September 8, 2005. (As of October 12, 2005, all three entries remained unchanged.) However, some interesting things, since revealed to be either untrue or gross exaggerations, do appear.[79] Let's look at some of the discrepancies:

1. Both biographies indicate that he served as an assistant city manager (in Edmond, OK, according to a 2001 White House press release), with emergency services oversight, and as a city councilman. The truth is that he was simply an assistant to the city manager, an intern position, with oversight probably limited to the stationery supplies. There is apparently no record of his ever having been a city councilman.

---

[74] *Talking Points Memo, Joshua Micah Marshall, http://www.talkingpoints memo.com/archives/week_2005_08_28.php#006397.*

[75] Ibid.

[76] *http://www.whitehouse.gov/government/brown-bio.html.*

[77] *http://www.fema.gov/about/bios/brown.shtm.*

[78] *FindLaw, Lawyer Directory, Lawyer Profile, http://pview.findlaw.com/ view/2507976_1.*

[79] *How Reliable is Brown's Resume? A TIME investigation reveals discrepancies in the FEMA chief's official biographies, Daren Fonda and Rita Healy, Time Online Edition, September 8, 2005, http://www.time.com/time/nation/article/0,8599,1103003,00.html.*

2. The FindLaw profile (as of October 12, 2005, but last updated on September 12, 2005) cites two interesting honors. Under "Education," he claims to have been "Outstanding Political Science Senior, Dean's and President's Honor Rolls" at Central State University, Edmond, OK. Under "Honors and Awards," he claims to have been "Outstanding Political Science Professor" at the same university. The first honor is possible, although a former political science professor, Carl Reherman, could not confirm Brown's either being an outstanding senior or appearing on the Dean's list. The second is false on the face of it, in that it takes several years to achieve a full professorship at any reputable university. FEMA's Deputy Strategic Director, Nicol Andrews, said that Brown had never claimed to have been a political science professor, the entry on the FindLaw website notwithstanding. She claimed that he was an adjunct professor of law at the Oklahoma City School of Law. As that appears in both biographies and the FindLaw profile, her statement is understandable, although it verifies nothing. The FindLaw entry dates his Adjunct Professorship as "1987 to present."

3. Brown claims to a Director of the Oklahoma Children's Home (1983 to present). An unnamed employee of the home since 1981 told Time reporters that Brown was never a director, never on the board, and that he had never heard Brown's name mentioned.

4. Brown claims, in his FindLaw profile, to be Chairman, Oklahoma Municipal Power Authority, in Edmond, OK (1980 to present). There is no mention of his name in their 2003 financial report. He has an entry in *Marquis Who's Who*,[80,81] in which his alleged tenure in that

---

[80] People listed in *Who's Who* provide the information for their own entries. Getting listed is apparently not difficult. Those who are listed get fre-

role is 1982 to 1988.[82] That same entry claims that a hydroelectric power plant and dam on the Kaw Reservoir in Oklahoma were named after him. A Google search reveals no other reference to such a power plant or dam than that in the *Who's Who* entry itself. It would be interesting to hear Mr. Brown try to explain both that situation and the obvious inconsistencies.

> *"Hiring this unqualified man to head this vital front-line agency, FEMA, is not a crime, but it is criminally stupid, negligent and contemptuous. It does not rise to the level of impeachable offense under our Constitution. But it should."*
>
> *—Michael Reynolds,*
> *The Mighty Middle, September 3, 2005*

FEMA's funding was drastically cut by the Bush administration, including a 44 percent cut in Army Corps of Engineers funds for flood control in New Orleans,[83] apparently exacerbating the disastrous effects of Hurricane Katrina. Presumably, Brown cannot be wholly blamed for that, although it's reasonable to expect him to be an advocate for his agency.

However, on Brown's watch, some FEMA funds seem to have been disbursed for purely political reasons.[84] In 2004, a federal consultant had advised that George Bush's re-election (*sic*) staff be brought in to minimize any political li-

---

quent requests to verify their entry, along with solicitations to buy the book (for several hundred dollars). This statement is based on the author's own experience.

[81] *http://www.marquiswhoswho.com/biogs/inthenews3.asp.*

[82] The first rule of successful lying is to be consistent. However, even consistency would not have saved him from the background check being done by the media and others—and which should have been done by the White House before he was even nominated for his job.

[83] *"No one can say they didn't see it coming,"* Sidney Blumenthal, Salon.com, August 31, 2005, *http://salon.com/opinion/blumenthal/2005/08/31/disaster_preparation.*

[84] *State records show Bush re-election concerns played part in FEMA aid,* Megan O'Matz & Sally Kestin, South Florida Sun Sentinel, March 23, 2005, *http://www.sun-sentinel.com/news/local/florida/sfl-fema23mar23,0,5221240.story?page=1.*

ability that might result from the "mess" created by Frances, the second hurricane in less than a month.

As it turned out, Frances was a lot less severe than expected and, apparently, didn't even touch Miami-Dade County. Nonetheless, it was reported in October 2004 that FEMA was awarding millions of dollars in disaster relief funds to residents of that county. By March 15, 2005, the amount was about $31 million, paid to almost thirteen thousand applicants, of whom only fourteen had, so far, been indicted on fraud charges.[85] In investigating the story in October 2004, the *South Florida Sun Sentinel* requested hundreds of pages of Governor Jeb Bush's storm-related email messages, which the Governor's office refused to produce. They were finally handed over in March 2005, after the paper threatened a lawsuit. Although there's a need to respond quickly to claims (and sometimes ask questions later), there is no apparent explanation for honoring claims, willy nilly, from a county that was known to be unaffected by the hurricane.

The story, as later revisited by the *Sun Sentinel,* gets worse. Florida coroners reported that FEMA aid money paid the funeral expenses of at least 203 Floridians whose deaths were not caused by Hurricane Frances or the earlier Hurricane Charley.[86] Referring to cases in Lee County, medical examiner Rebecca Hamilton said that none of the deaths for which hurricane-related claims were paid was even remotely associated with any kind of a hurricane. Ten people from other counties were not even in Florida at the time of their deaths. One was a driver who died in a head-on collision in Ashburn, GA.

Returning to September 1, 2005, we find Michael Brown in a CNN interview about the aftermath of Hurricane Katrina, in which he said, "Things are going relatively well." As that was

---

[85] As a result of an investigation conducted, by the Senate Homeland Security and Governmental Affairs Committee, at the urging of Senator Bill Nelson (D-FL).

[86] *FEMA paid for at least 203 funerals not related to 2004 hurricanes, Sally Kestin, Megan O'Matz & Jon Burstein, South Florida Sun Sentinel, August 10, 2005, http://www.sun-sentinel.com/news/local/florida/sfl-fema10aug10,0,2403181.story?track=mostemailedlink.*

the third day of grueling and grossly understaffed rescue and recovery operations, with dead bodies showing up, and with refugees in the New Orleans Superdome living in a sweltering atmosphere, one might be forgiven for asking what planet he was living on. He also claimed that those New Orleans residents who did not evacuate before the hurricane arrived bore some responsibility for their fates, thus showing a monumental insensitivity to the fact that some of the poorest people in the country live in the area, have no personal transportation, could not afford to pay for other means of travel, and in some cases might be too frail to travel.[87]

On September 9, 2005, Brown's boss, **Michael Chertoff**, Director of Homeland Security, held a press conference to announce that Brown was returning to Washington from the hurricane disaster area, and that he would be replaced, in the field, by Vice Admiral Thad Allen, chief of staff of the U.S. Coast Guard. Although Brown was also at the press conference, Chertoff did not provide him with an opportunity to answer questions.

On December 27, 2002, a Reuters headline said, referring to Joseph Allbaugh, *"FEMA Head Becomes Latest Bush Team Departure."*[88] They could have dusted it off and reused it on September 12, 2005, but went with the more specific, *"FEMA chief Brown resigns in wake of Katrina."*[89]

> *"We don't want to sacrifice the real ability to get a full picture of Mike's experiences; we don't want to sacrifice that ability simply in order to make an image point."*[90]
>
> —*Michael Chertoff, DHS Secretary, October 26, 2005*

---

[87] *FEMA Chief: Victims bear some responsibility, CNN, September 1, 2005, http://cnn.com/2005/WEATHER/09/01.katrina.fema.brown.*

[88] *FEMA Head Becomes Latest Bush Team Departure, Reuters, December 27, 2002, http://indymedia.ie/newswire.php?id=22619.*

[89] *FEMA chief Brown resigns in wake of Katrina, Reuters, September 12, 2005, http://today.reuters.co.uk/news/newsArticle.aspx?type=globalNews&story ID=2005-09-12T193032Z_01_DIT267240_RTRUKOC_0_US-BROWN.xml.*

[90] *FEMA Extends Brown's Contract by 30 Days, Associated Press, October 26, 2005, http://truthout.org/docs_2005/102605R.shtml.*

Astonishingly, shortly after his resignation, it was announced that Brown was providing consulting services to FEMA for a further 30 days at his full $148,000 per year salary. Possibly they wanted to anticipate the need to save Arabian horses in disaster areas. Incredibly, on October 26, it was announced that the use of his consulting services had been extended by a further thirty days, so that he could provide advice on his experience with Hurricane Katrina.[91] One could only assume that he would take thirty days to describe how he humiliated himself at every turn. What else could be learned is something of a mystery.

On November 10, 2005, sixteen days into his 30-day extension, it was announced that Brown was no longer on FEMA's payroll.

Brown's last appearance was three months later, on February 10, 2006. He appeared before a Senate hearing (as also did his former boss, Michael Chertoff), at which he claimed to have been a scapegoat for FEMA's hopelessly inept response to Katrina.[92] A White House videotape subsequently revealed that he had, indeed, attempted to alert both George Bush and Michael Chertoff to the seriousness of the situation, with Bush showing very little interest.[93]

bunker buster: A tactical weapon designed to penetrate very thick fortifications, such as those used to protect underground bunkers. Secretary of Defense *Donald Rumsfeld* and his *neocon* friends have become enamored of nuclear versions of this weapon, so much so that they regard their development as essential. Unlike the conventional versions, the nuclear versions can contaminate the area around the explosion for years, causing cancer, other radiation-triggered diseases and birth deformities. A report to Con-

---

[91] Ibid.

[92] *Brown says he's been made Katrina scapegoat: Ex-FEMA chief blames Homeland Security for slow response, CNN Politics, February 13, 2006, http://www.cnn.com/2006/POLITICS/02/10/katrina.brown.*

[93] *Katrina Video Refuels Debate Over Response, Peter Baker and Spencer S. Hsu, Washington Post, March 3, 2006, http://truthout.org/docs_2006/030306L.shtml.*

gress stated that casualties from a single nuclear bunker buster could range from several thousand to over a million. The manufacture and use of such weapons is quite clearly contrary to the spirit of Article VI of the Nuclear Non-proliferation Treaty (NPT),[94] of which the United States is a signatory, which says the following:

> *"Each of the Parties to the Treaty undertakes to pursue ne-gotiations in good faith on effective measures relating to cessation of the nuclear arms race at an early date and to nuclear disarmament, and on a Treaty on general and com-plete disarmament under strict and effective international control."*

Bush Baby: Nickname for George W. Bush, often used by co-median Bill Maher on his *Politically Incorrect* program on ABC during the 2000 presidential campaign.

Bush, Barbara (1): Wife of George H.W. Bush and, therefore, former First Lady. Mother of George W. Bush and his sib-lings. Grandmother of Barbara and Jenna Bush and their cousins.

> *"… she knows how to hate."*
>
> —*Richard Nixon, saying why he admired Barbara Bush (date unknown)*

Mrs. Bush has a reputation for insensitivity. In an interview, with her husband, on Good Morning America on March 17, 2003, she stated, as part of a response to a question by Diane Sawyer, *"But why should we hear about body bags, and deaths, and how many, what day it's gonna happen, and how many this or what do you suppose? Or, I mean, it's, it's not rele-vant. So, why should I waste my beautiful mind on something like that?"*[95]

More recently, on September 5, 2005, she said the following about the victims of Hurricane Katrina who had been

---

[94] Not to mention being intrinsically criminal.

[95] The statement can be viewed in its full context at *http://www.snopes.com/politics/quotes/barbara.asp.*

evacuated to the Houston Astrodome: *"What I'm hearing which is sort of scary is they all want to stay in Texas. Everyone is so overwhelmed by the hospitality. And so many of the people in the arena here, you know, were underprivileged anyway, so this—this (she chuckles slightly) is working very well for them."*[96]

Barbara Bush is not, of course, one-dimensional. She has a reputation as the tougher partner in her relationship with her husband. She has also been rumored, for years, to be pro-choice and to have been disturbed by her husband's transition to the "pro-life"[97] camp during his terms as Vice President and President. Her son, George, might have been pro-choice in his youth. Who knows? He is certainly not pro-choice now.

On the subject of Bush sons, all four seem to have serious ethical flaws (*see* **Bush, George W.**; **Bush, Jeb**; **Bush, Marvin**; *and* **Bush, Neil**). This has possibly more to do with the Bush legacy than with Barbara Bush's qualities as a mother (*see* **Bush, Prescott**; **Bush, Prescott, Jr.**; *and* **Bush, William**).

Bush, Barbara (2) and Jenna: George Bush's twin daughters, now adults. These are the children whom Bush was supposedly protecting by concealing his 1976 arrest for driving under the influence of alcohol in Kennebunkport, Maine. Had he admitted long ago to the arrest, rather than risking what actually happened—a pre-election revelation, followed by his lame excuse—it's possible that the press would have gone a little easier[98] on his daughters when they were caught drinking (and drunk) while under age. It appears that the

---

[96] *Editor and Publisher, Barbara Bush: Things Working Out 'Very Well' for Poor Evacuees from New Orleans, September 5, 2005, http:// editorandpublisher.com/eandp/news/article_display.jsp?vnu_content_id=1001054719.*

[97] Pro-life is in quotes, simply because it is a misleading term. Most people who call themselves "pro-life" are in favor of the death penalty. A significant number of them (the religious right) are also opposed to comprehensive sex education, which, among other things, seeks to avoid unwanted pregnancies and thus forestall the need for abortion. To its partial credit, in this respect, the Catholic Church is officially opposed to the death penalty, which is at least consistent with its anti-abortion position.

[98] Well, maybe not the supermarket tabloids.

temptation to call attention to his hypocrisy overcame any consideration of keeping news of presidential offspring off limits. As for Barbara and Jenna themselves, they seem to be neither better nor worse than most other people in their age group.

In May 2004, it was announced that they would be participating in their father's election campaign. They did that, including introducing him in a somewhat bizarre manner at the Republican Convention. After the convention and the November 2004 election, they appeared once more to have a fairly low profile. However, they have since been traveling abroad, particularly to Africa, as informal goodwill ambassadors for their father's administration. Given that reports of their trips have been mostly of the puff-piece variety, it's somewhat hard to determine how effective they are and how they are seen in the countries they have visited.

Bush, Columba: Jeb Bush's wife and, therefore, Florida's First Lady.

A web search on the name, Columba Bush, reveals her involvement in many activities traditionally associated with first ladies—mostly of a charitable nature. However, there is one story,[99] from 1999, that is consistent with what would appear to be the somewhat diminished ethical standards of members of the Bush family.

Mrs. Bush was going through Customs at Atlanta's Hartsfield International Airport on arrival from a trip to Paris. On reading her customs declaration form, the customs agent asked her if the $500 declared value of her purchases was correct. She said it was. Not satisfied, the customs agent searched her purse and found shopping receipts that were inconsistent with the declaration.[100] Mrs. Bush was

---

[99] *St. Petersburg Times, June 22, 1999, "Bush: Wife meant to hide shopping spree from me", http://www.sptimes.com/News/62299/State/Gov_Bush_says_his_wif.shtml.*

[100] Had she left any of her purchases in France (as gifts for friends residing there, for example), it would be possible for the total of her receipts to legitimately exceed the amount of her declaration. However, if you read on, you'll find that was not the case.

given a chance to revise her first statement, but declined to do so. Still not satisfied, the customs agent searched her luggage and found merchandise (mostly jewelry) that matched her receipts, for a total of about $19,000. She could have been arrested, but was allowed to pay a civil fine of about $4,100, which was about three times the amount of duty she would have had to pay if she had made an honest declaration. U.S. Customs could also have confiscated all of her purchases, but allowed her to keep them, which is normal procedure.[101] Mrs. Bush was also faced with having to pay $1,140 in Florida sales tax (6%).

Although there's no report of a repeat of the incident (or of any similar incidents), it does seem a little unseemly for the First Lady of Florida to be evading both customs duty and state sales tax. (*See, also, **Bush, Jeb**.*)

Bush Doctrine: This is apparently the doctrine whereby the United States considers itself to be the only remaining superpower and reserves the right to attack other nations preemptively in order to thwart the ambitions of those whom George Bush considers to be "evildoers." It is quite clearly based on the principles stated in the *Project for the New American Century* (PNAC). Operation Iraqi Freedom appears to have taught us that, in practical terms, the Bush Doctrine can be reduced to three simple statements: lie; attack; and cover up. Much of the cover-up involves historical revisionism (regarding the original purported reasons for going to war).

The Bush Doctrine is in clear violation of the U.N. Charter, of which the United States is a signatory.

Bush, George Herbert Walker: 41st President of the United States and, before that, Ronald Reagan's Vice President. From 1967 to 1970, he was a Texas congressman and, from 1976 to 1977, the Director of the CIA. Other government and

---

[101] Patrick Jones, a Customs spokesman, said, "The way it is typically done is to use the three-times-the-loss-of-revenue formula. Get the revenue, get the penalty and get these folks on their way."

non-government political roles included U.S. Ambassador to the U.N. (1971-1974), Special Envoy to China (1974-1975) and Republican National Chairman (1975-1976).[102]

Bush has often been compared to his son, George W. Bush, to the latter's disadvantage. Because of his sheer recklessness, the son's presidential record is indeed far worse than the father's. However, that doesn't mean Bush Senior has a clean record, either during the time he was President or earlier.

For example, two years before his 1966 election to the House of Representatives, he mounted an unsuccessful bid for Congress in which he campaigned against the Civil Rights Act.[103] A year before running against Ronald Reagan in the 1980 presidential primaries, he claimed that a nuclear war was "winnable," a position that might be seen to increase the risk of starting such a war.

During his tenure as CIA Director, Bush cultivated Manuel Noriega as a source of intelligence. Noriega, who was in charge of Panama's military intelligence, had been working with the CIA since 1960. In spite of evidence that Noriega was involved in drug trafficking, Bush kept him on the CIA payroll, going so far as to increase his salary to $100,000 per year. At the same time, he eliminated a requirement for intelligence reports from Panama to include information on drug trafficking.[104] Bush's CIA successor, Admiral Stansfield Turner, took Noriega off the payroll. However, when Bush became Vice President in 1981, he reversed that, providing Noriega, once more, with a six-figure salary.

In 1981, the Reagan/Bush administration started providing covert aid to the Nicaraguan Contras, who were trying to overthrow the democratically elected Sandinistas. This was made more difficult, but not impossible, by the 1982 Boland Amendment, which prohibited such aid from December

---

[102] *George H.W. Bush, http://famoustexans.com/georgebush.htm.*

[103] Ibid.

[104] *The Panama Deception, http://addictedtowar.com/panama.htm.*

1983 to September 1985.[105,106] Because the amendment did not explicitly apply to the National Security Council, the administration gave it the task of supervising the covert support.

Meanwhile, in Panama, Noriega had engineered the 1981 death, in a plane crash, of President Omar Torrijos.[107] The 1984 elections put Noriega in control of the country, almost certainly through fraud.

Returning to the United States, we find the Reagan administration setting up an "arms for hostages" deal with Iran, first with Israel acting as the intermediary, then with international arms dealer, Manucher Ghorbanifar, taking over Israel's role in the deal. Then Colonel **Oliver North**, who reported to National Security Advisor **John Poindexter**, had the brilliant idea to use the proceeds of the arms sales to fund the Nicaraguan Contras. Manuel Noriega was enlisted to assist the United States in this effort and if, at the same time, he was flying cocaine into Nicaragua, the CIA and the DEA turned a blind eye.

Eventually, it appears that Noriega became somewhat ambivalent about his support for the U.S. campaign against the Sandinistas. Apparently this angered his CIA handlers and, lo and behold, he was suddenly wanted by the DEA for drug smuggling. By this time, Reagan's two terms were over and George H.W. Bush was in the White House. In December 1989, claiming that Noriega was a threat to the security of the United States, Bush ordered the invasion of Panama in order to arrest him. Under the code name, *Operation Just Cause*, U.S. troops moved in and bombed 27 targets, including sections of Panama City and the headquarters of the Panamanian Defense Force, resulting in something between 2000 and 4000 civilian deaths—all to arrest one man. The administration's official death toll was something between 200 and

---

[105] This was an amendment to the 1982 House Appropriations Bill, affecting the Defense Appropriations Act of 1983. The amendment's wording was somewhat ambiguous and, thus, provided a number of loopholes.

[106] *Iran-Contra Affair, Wikipedia, http://en.wikipedia.org/wiki/Iran-Contra_Affair.*

[107] Noriega's involvement was only suspected at the time, but was later confirmed.

300 civilians, plus a small number of U.S. troops. A subsequent unofficial investigation, which documented the larger number of deaths, culminated in the 1992 documentary film, *The Panama Deception,* which won its director, Barbara Trent, the 1993 Academy Award for Best Documentary.

There were possibly some good reasons, including attacks on U.S. military personnel and others by Noriega's so-called *Dignity Battalions,* for some kind of intervention in Panama.[108] However, the invasion and attack, which lacked the support of the international community,[109] appears to have been a violation of international law and to have represented massive overkill in both the literal and the usual figurative sense.

Bush's next adventure was in Iraq.

On August 2, 1990, Saddam Hussein's troops invaded Kuwait, ostensibly because the Kuwaitis were slant drilling into Iraqi oilfields.[110] Prior to the invasion, Saddam met with April Glaspie, the U.S. Ambassador to Iraq. The Iraqi transcript of the meeting shows Glaspie telling Saddam that the U.S. had no opinion on Iraq's Arab-Arab conflicts, *"such as your dispute with Kuwait."* In testimony before Congress, Glaspie repudiated the Iraqi version, denouncing it as a "fabrication," although she admitted that it contained "a great deal" that was accurate. The immediate outcome of the invasion was the declaration, by Iraq, that it had annexed Kuwait and made it the Iraq's 19th province.[111]

---

[108] A U.S. soldier, who was killed shortly before the invasion, was said by the Panamanians to have been a member of the "Hard Chargers," a group whose goal was to incite reactions that could be used to justify U.S. military retaliation (*Operation Just Cause, http://absoluteastronomy.com/encyclopedia/o/op/operation_just_cause.htm*).

[109] The United Nations and the Organization of American States both issued statements, after the invasion, deploring the U.S. action and calling for the immediate withdrawal of troops.

[110] Kuwait had gained independence from Britain and Iraq in 1961, leading to Iraq claiming sovereignty over Kuwait. Under pressure and without enthusiasm, Iraq officially accepted Kuwait's sovereignty in 1963.

[111] For brevity, this account omits the negotiations, prior to the invasion, that eventually broke down.

President George H.W. Bush quickly set about recruiting allies and, with the backing of a U.N. resolution, started *Operation Desert Shield*, which involved a demand that Iraq withdraw from Kuwait. Iraq's refusal led, on January 17, 1991, to *Operation Desert Storm*, otherwise known as the *Persian Gulf War*. However, nothing is ever as simple as it seems. A major justification for launching *Operation Desert Shield* was, according to the Pentagon, a massive build-up, on the Iraq side of the border with Saudi Arabia, of an estimated 250,000 Iraqi troops and 1,500 tanks, ready to roll into Saudi Arabia at a moment's notice. There was only one problem; it wasn't true. The *St. Petersburg Times* (in Florida) acquired two commercial Soviet satellite images of the area of the alleged build-up, obtained at the same time as the Pentagon's images (which have never been declassified).[112] Two experts, including a former Defense Intelligence Agency (DIA) analyst, who specialized in desert warfare, were able to easily identify the U.S. build-up of fighter planes, standing wingtip to wingtip, at Saudi bases. However, they found no sign whatsoever of any build-up on the Iraq side of the border. Jean Heller, the *St. Petersburg Times* journalist who broke the story, contacted the office of then Secretary of Defense **Dick Cheney**, asking for evidence that would refute what the *Times* had found out. The official response was, *"Trust us."*

There are many accounts on the Internet of major incidents during the Gulf War that could be described as war crimes, including the merciless bombing of Iraqi troops as they retreated, at that point defenseless, from Kuwait City to the Iraq border. Whatever decisions were made by military commanders, the final responsibility for such acts rests with the Commander in Chief.

In 1997, the University of Toronto announced it was going to award Bush an honorary doctor of laws degree in November of that year. They ran into an enormous amount of opposition from people both within and without the Uni-

---

[112] *In war, some facts less factual: Some US assertions from the last war on Iraq still appear dubious, Scott Peterson, Christian Science Monitor, September 6, 2002, http://csmonitor.com/2002/0906/p01s02-wosc.html.*

versity. In spite of a spirited defense of the proposed award, the University reversed itself.[113]

> *'[T]hat the use of such overwhelming force inevitably led to the deaths of thousands of Iraqi civilians and tens of thousands of Iraqi troops, many of whom had already surrendered, was of no concern to Bush, who boasted about "Operation Desert Storm" as a triumph of his "New World Order"...'[114]*
>
> *—David Raby, History Professor, University of Toronto*
> *October 27, 1997*

Bush's popularity peaked during and immediately after the Gulf War, and then went into decline, culminating in his defeat by Bill Clinton in the 1992 Election. It didn't help with his base, of course, that he had violated his *"Read my lips. No new taxes"* pledge, made in his 1988 election campaign.

In one of his final acts as president, Bush granted full pardons to six people, including Ronald Reagan's former Defense Secretary, Caspar Weinberger,[115] who had been involved in the secret shipment of arms to Iran ("Arms for Hostages") and the related Iran-Contra affair (which used the money from the arms sales to support the Nicaraguan Contras in their campaign to overthrow the Sandinista government).[116] Pardons are usually for the already convicted. In Weinberger's case, he was about to be tried for lying to Congress about his knowledge of the arms sales. A key element of the case was Weinberger's private notes, containing references to Bush's endorsement of the secret shipments to Iran. Bush had claimed, when the arms shipments and Iran-Contra affair first

---

[113] The University of Toronto on-line publication, *The Bulletin,* published a defense (*Worthy Recipient, by Jack Cunningham*) and a statement of opposition (*Undeserved Honour, by David Raby*), by two faculty members, in the Commentary section of their October 27, 1997 edition, *http://news.utoronto.ca/bin/bulletin/oct27_97/comment.htm.*

[114] Ibid

[115] Weinberger died on April 4, 2006 at the age of 88.

[116] *Bush Pardons 6 in Iran Affair, Aborting a Weinberger Trial; Prosecutor Assails 'Cover-Up,' David Johnston, New York Times, December 25, 1992, reprinted at http://nytimes.com/learning/general/onthisday/big/ 1224.html#article.*

came to light, that he had been *"out of the loop."* That wasn't credible at the time and is less so with the passage of time and the increase in knowledge about both affairs.

Since he left the presidency, George H.W. Bush has been very involved with the Carlyle Group,[117] which was founded by David Rubenstein, a Carter White House aide, to buy, sell and invest in the arms industry. It owes much of its success, at least initially, to Ronald Reagan's former Secretary of Defense, Frank Carlucci. By March 2002, investors, including four members of the bin Laden family, had put at least $14 million into the company.[118] Not only does Bush appear to have an extremely large financial stake, but he also travels and makes speeches, along with such highly placed luminaries as **James A. Baker, III,** his former Secretary of State, and John Major, Britain's former Prime Minister, helping to grease the skids for government contracts for companies in which the Carlyle Group is heavily invested.

> *"George [H.W.] Bush is getting money from private interests that have business before the government, while his son is president. And, in a really peculiar way, George W. Bush could, some day, benefit financially from his own administration's decisions, through his father's investments. The average American doesn't know that and, to me, that's a jaw-dropper."*[119]
>
> *—Charles Lewis, Center for Public Integrity*

Bush is currently an adviser to Carlyle and serves on their board. When he's traveling on their behalf, he earns from $80,000 to $100,000 per speech, which he apparently invests in the company's privately traded stock.[120]

---

[117] *Investing in War: The Carlyle Group profits from government and conflict,* M. Asif Ismail, The Center for Public Integrity, http://publicintegrity.org/pns/report.aspx?aid=424&sid=200.

[118] *The Big Guys Work For The Carlyle Group. What exactly does it do?* Melanie Warner, Fortune, March 18, 2003, http://carlylegroup.net/thebigguys.htm. (CarlyleGroup.net is not the Carlyle Group's website.)

[119] *Bush Watch ... Bush Money,* http://bushwatch.com/bushmoney.htm.

[120] Ibid.

Bush, George Walker: 43rd President of the United States, formerly Governor of Texas.

Since his very dubious ascendancy to the presidency in 2000 (*see chad, felon purge* and **Harris, Katherine**), George Bush has turned a massive budget surplus into a record deficit, given enormous tax breaks to the wealthiest Americans and his corporate contributors, almost eliminated science as a factor in making policy decisions, assaulted the environment, reneged on long-standing international treaties, severely damaged the wall of separation between church and state, conducted a catastrophic war of choice with Iraq, neglected danger (initially) in Iran and North Korea, run the most secretive administration in living memory, locked up thousands of people in *Camp Delta* and elsewhere as *"enemy combatants,"* and on and on.

> *The catastrophic mistake of the Bush administration was to allow the war on Iraq to supplant the war on terror. They are two completely different entities.*[121]
>
> —*Gerald Warner, The Scotsman, July 10, 2005*

The Iraq war has cost the lives of over 2,400 American service men and women and, through injuries, has drastically diminished the lives of between ten and twenty thousand more. This does not take into account the tens of thousands[122] of innocent Iraqis who have been killed or maimed, or their families, or the families of U.S. soldiers. As of June 2006, over three years after Bush declared *Mission Accomplished*, it continues to cost lives at an alarming rate.

---

[121] *Disastrous Iraq adventure is a sideshow to the long haul war on terror, Gerald Warner, The Scotsman, July 10, 2005, http://news.Scotsman.com/opinion.cfm?id=765912005.*

[122] According to a survey conducted by researchers from the Johns Hopkins Bloomberg School of Public Health, the Columbia University School of Nursing and Al-Mustansiriya University in Baghdad, and published in The Lancet, the highly esteemed British medical journal, the civilian death toll is **conservatively** estimated to be 100,000 or more. Source: *Iraqi Civilian Deaths Increase Dramatically After Invasion, October 28, 2004, http://www.jhsph.edu/PublicHealthNews/Press_Releases/PR_2004/Burnham_Iraq.html.*

> *"America will never succeed in Iraq, if we once again naïvely expect democracy to take root there and flourish. What can possibly occur next week to transform that society that has not occurred for 7,000 years?"* [123]
>
> —*Edwin Black*

Iraq does now have some sort of government, although it has taken a long time and much compromise to get there. It took until mid-May, 2006, for the new prime minister, Nouri al-Maliki, to form what is at best a partial cabinet, lacking interior, national security and defense ministers. Unfortunately, the government still faces a split among Sunnis, Shiites and Kurds, who were only kept in check before by the strictures of Saddam Hussein's brutal regime. There is now talk of splitting Iraq into three countries, one for each of the three major groups. The supporters of that approach argue that it will avoid a civil war. Its detractors argue that it would make it easier for Al Qaeda to build a new base of operations.

> *"The invasion of Iraq, I believe, will turn out to be the greatest strategic disaster in U.S. history."* [124]
>
> —*Lt. Gen. William Odom (Ret.)* [125]

In the meantime, a $592 million U.S. Embassy is, with George Bush's approval, being built in Baghdad. The Embassy, which is big enough to accommodate a staff of 8000, is seen as evidence of Bush's intention to maintain a major U.S. presence in the region, even if most of the troops are eventually withdrawn. [126]

Bush is the first president since Herbert Hoover to oversee a net job loss (in his first term). Even in the months during which employment rose, the increase was insufficient to ac-

---

[123] *Edwin Black, Banking on Baghdad, Inside Iraq's 7,000-Year History of War, Profit, and Conflict, John Wiley and Sons, 2004, ISBN 0-4716-7186-X.*

[124] *Retired general: Iraq invasion was 'strategic disaster', Evan Lehmann, Lowell (MA) Sun Washington Bureau, September 30, 2005, http://lowellsun.com/ci_3075570.*

[125] Odom is now a scholar at the Hudson Institute.

[126] *In the Chaos of Iraq, One Project Is on Target: A Giant US Embassy, Daniel McGrory, The Times on Line UK, May 3, 2006, http://truthout.org/docs_2006/050306D.shtml.*

commodate those who were newly entering the workforce. He cited, in his apparent favor, a decrease in the unemployment rate, while neglecting to mention that the reduction was the result of many thousands giving up on their search for work and thus no longer being included in the statistics. The "official" rate was 5.4%. If those who gave up looking are included, the rate was 6.4%.[127]

He opposed the formation of the 9/11 Commission,[128] but later took credit for establishing it. He opposed testifying under oath and in public to the 9/11 Commission and refused to provide them with many of the documents they needed, then claimed to have been cooperative. His eventual testimony was not under oath or in public. Instead, he and Dick Cheney testified together (presumably to ensure that their stories would be consistent) at the White House, with the Commission members present not being allowed to take notes. He opposed the consolidation of a number of government departments into a *Department of Homeland Security (DHS)* (something that had been proposed, first, by the *Hart-Rudman Commission* and subsequently supported by Democrats), then, after it had been created, took credit for it.

> *"Mr. Bush is right when he says he cannot be blamed for everything that happened on or before Sept. 11, 2001. But he is responsible for the administration's actions since then. That includes, inexcusably, selling the false Iraq-Qaeda claim to Americans. There are two unpleasant alternatives: either Mr. Bush knew he was not telling the truth, or he has a capacity for politically motivated self-deception that is terrifying in the post-9/11 world."*
>
> *—New York Times, June 17, 2004*[129]

---

[127] *The missing million, Baltimore Sun, September 6, 2004, http:// baltimoresun.com/news/opinion/bal-ed.econ06sep06, 1,7750575.story?coll=bal-opinion-headlines.*

[128] Officially known as the *National Commission on Terror Attacks.*

[129] *From "The Plain Truth," New York Times Op-Ed, June 17, 2004, http://nytimes.com/2004/06/17/opinion/17THU1.html?ex=1088473509&ei=1&en=cb113d1e028b1462.*

As the foregoing quotation indicates, Bush seems to lack even a nodding acquaintance with the truth, whether or not his prevarications are deliberate.

George Bush or one or more of his positions, views, policies or actions (e.g., nominations, appointments, etc.) is a major topic or subtopic in the following entries:

affirmative access; Abrams, Elliott; Alito, Samuel; Allbaugh, Joseph; Ashcroft, John D; asshole;[130] Bloch, Scott J; Bodman, Samuel; Bolten, Joshua; Bolton, John; Brown, Michael D; Bush Doctrine; Bush Pioneers; Bybee, Jay S; C students; Camp Delta; Chertoff, Michael; Children's Environmental Health Network (CEHN); Christian Nation; Clear Skies Initiative; coalition of the willing; compassionate conservative; Cooney, Philip; Cox, Christopher; disassemble; distortion; dubyanomics; enemy combatant; estate tax; extraordinary rendition; Fascism; FEMA; First Amendment zones; gay marriage and civil unions; Geneva Conventions; global warming; Goat story; Gonzalez, Alberto; Goss, Porter; Hadley, Stephen J; Hayden, Michael; Healthy Forests Initiative; Hughes, Karen; ideological certainty; impeachment; James, Daniel; Johnson, Stephen L; Kempthorne, Dirk; Kerik, Bernard; Leavitt, Michael O; lies; mandate; Marriage Amendment; Miers, Harriet; Mis-Leader of the Free World; Mission Accomplished; Negroponte, John; Nicholson, Jim; No Child Left Behind; partial-birth abortion ban; photo op; Poindexter, John, Admiral; Portman, Rob; quid pro quo; Racicot, Marc; recess appointments; Rice, Condoleezza; Roberts, John G., Jr.; Rove Karl; Safavian, David H; secrecy; sex education; Smirking Chimp; Snow, Tony; tax giveaway; Tobin, James; Towey, Jim; trifecta; Village Idiot; Walters, John; War on Terrorism; War President; warmonger.

Bush, Jeb: Governor of Florida and George W. Bush's younger brother. His full name is John Ellis Bush, hence Jeb.

---

[130] Bush's characterization of someone else.

Prior to the 2000 election, Jeb Bush bragged that he would deliver Florida for his brother. For the politically naïve, it could be supposed he was planning to do that through aggressive campaigning. However, in response to the investigation by the U.S. Civil Rights Commission that, in 2001, looked into the conduct of the election in Florida, he said that he bore no responsibility to investigate how black districts were left without technology to handle the sea of voters. Also, even though he knew there would be a high turnout, he vetoed $100,000 for a voter education campaign.[131]

The Civil Rights Commission's investigation, which examined, among many other irregularities, the notorious *felon purge*, laid a great deal of blame at the doorstep of both Jeb Bush and his Secretary of State, *Katherine Harris*. Unfortunately, the Commission had no power to implement changes recommended or implied in its report. The incoming U.S. Attorney General, *John Ashcroft*, would in any case have been unlikely to act on even the strongest recommendations.

In some ways, Jeb Bush appears to be much less extreme than his brother. For example, he has a good environmental record, having signed legislation to protect the Everglades and having opposed offshore oil drilling. However, he has been involved in the neoconservative *Project for the New American Century*, which promotes and attempts to project American global leadership. He has also called for fewer death-row appeals and faster executions.

Like his brother George, Jeb Bush also panders to his right wing base, to the extent that he is even willing to stoop to the vilification of the innocent. This is exemplified by his involvement in the sad case of Terri Schiavo, who had a heart attack in 1990, almost certainly caused by a severe eating disorder, that left her in a permanent vegetative state. Her husband Michael spent the next several years trying to help her, going as far as studying to be a nurse. Finally, re-

---

[131] *Boston Globe, January 17, 2001, Bush in Denial on Florida's Voting Scandal, by Derrick Z. Jackson, http://commondreams.org/views01/0117-02.htm.*

alizing that her case was hopeless,[132] he asked for her feeding tube to be removed. Terri's parents and other family members disagreed, leading to a series of court battles, including appeals, in which Michael Schiavo prevailed, even after the attempted intervention of Congress, which passed a special law requiring a ruling by a federal appeals court.

Siding with Congress, Jeb Bush initiated plans to use state police to enter the hospice where Terri Schiavo's feeding tube had, by then, been removed and re-insert it. Reason prevailed, in the form of the head of the county police, who warned that there would be an armed confrontation if Bush went ahead. Bush backed down; however, in doing so, he angered the far right. Had he gone ahead, he would have violated the law, which could have led to his prosecution.

Nothing daunted, Bush tried one final ploy, which was to call for an investigation (on no evidence) by a state attorney into whether Michael Schiavo had, fifteen years previously, left Terri to die by deliberately delaying his call for help.[133]

> *... because the public is now tired of the Schiavo case, [Jeb] Bush will get away with trying to ruin an innocent man and will likely see his stature rise among certain extremists.*[134]
>
> —*Jonathan Alter, Newsweek, June 20, 2005*

The state attorney's report, issued on June 30, 2005, but not released to the press until July 7, found Michael Schiavo's 1990 testimony consistent with that of other interested parties and that any discrepancies in subsequent statements were not indicative on any criminal activity. Left with no choice, Bush said, in a letter, that he would follow the state attorney's recommendation that the inquiry be closed.[135]

---

[132] Based on qualified medical opinion.

[133] *Sliming the Innocent: How the latest in the Schiavo case has made Jeb Bush into the Al Sharpton of the right, Jonathan Alter, June 20, 2005,* http://msnbc.msn.com/id/8292690/site/newsweek.

[134] *Ibid.*

[135] *Gov. Bush Ends Schiavo Inquiry, Associated Press, July 9, 2005,* http://truthout.org/docs_2005/070905F.shtml.

Jeb Bush's involvement in the Schiavo case may not have been the worst thing he did in 2005. On October 1, he signed off on Florida's "Shoot First Law," which allows someone to shoot someone else, based solely on a "reasonable belief" that he or she is in danger of bodily harm. *For details of this draconian law, see* **NRA**.

Bush, Jonathan: Son of Prescott Bush, brother of George H.W. Bush, and uncle of George W. Bush. *See* ***Bush, Marvin.***

Bush, Laura: First Lady of the United States, former First Lady of Texas, and (obviously) wife of George W. Bush. During most of Bush's first term, other than fairly routine campaign speeches, Laura Bush (formerly Laura Welch) had minimal involvement in her husband's political life. As for other speeches, a page devoted to her speeches and news releases, on the White House website, listed none of either. However, starting with the 2004 campaign, she became very visible and very involved, including making a speech at the Republican National Convention. In general, however, she has stayed clear of controversial topics and is involved in issues more traditionally associated with first ladies. What is not typical is the extent to which she has traveled abroad.[136]

A noteworthy exception to the first lady's usual style was her speech at the 2005 annual dinner of the sickeningly sycophantic White House Correspondents' Association (WHCA). Following a contrived takeover from her husband at the microphone, she launched into a stand-up comedy act in which she ribbed him mercilessly. The sad part is that many of her characterizations rang true. The very interesting part is what the WHCA did not report—namely the following joke: *"He's learned a lot about ranching since that first year when he tried to milk the horse. What's worse, it was a male horse."* The crowd roared and, the following day, the press gave her a great review, which her delivery certainly de-

---

[136] For recent news on Laura Bush, see *http://whitehouse.gov/firstlady/ flpress.html.*

served. (The words were, of course, someone else's.) On the other hand, the "moral values" crowd, who would normally object to such a joke, was mostly silent. One can only imagine the reaction from the Religious and Republican Right if John Kerry were in the White House and Teresa Heinz Kerry had told the same joke (or if Hillary Clinton had done so during her husband's presidency).

Bush, Marvin: George W. Bush's youngest brother. Marvin Bush is not as well known as the other Bush brothers. However, he does seem to benefit from the same Bush family contacts.

At the time of the attack on the World Trade Center, he was a director of Stratasec (previously called Securacom), which provided electronic security for the World Trade Center, Dulles International Airport and United Airlines. The company also has contracts with the Department of Defense and what is described as an "ongoing line" with the General Services Administration (GSA), allowing it to secure government business on the basis of noncompetitive bids. Securacom was capitalized by the Kuwaiti-American Corporation (KuwAm), which has been linked to the Bush family since the Gulf War. Marvin Bush joined Securacom at the time of that capitalization and was listed in SEC filings as a significant shareholder.[137] The company's board chairman, Wirt D. Walker III, is Marvin Bush's (and, therefore, George W. Bush's) cousin. The Bushes' uncle Jonathan is on the board of KuwAm.

In spite of the possible associations with the events of 9/11 (and, other than propinquity, there may be none), there is no mention of Marvin Bush, Securacom or Stratasec in the 9/11 Commission Report. There has also been no public statement from the White House, on this subject, since 9/11.

---

[137] *Bush-Linked Company Handled Security for the WTC, Dulles and United, Margie Burns, Prince George's Journal (Maryland), February 4, 2003, available at http://www.commondreams.org/views03/0204-06.htm.*

Bush, Neil: George W. Bush's second youngest brother. For those who followed the savings and loan scandals of the late 1980s, Neil Bush is well known as director of Silverado Savings and Loan, which collapsed in 1988, at the end of the Reagan era, at a cost to taxpayers of over $1 billon. For Neil Bush, the outcome was that he was banned from banking. A secondary outcome was that he set aside his plans to run for Governor of Colorado.

If we fast-forward to October 2001, we find Neil Bush heading up a company called Ignite and attending an international technology conference in Dubai, where he was fishing for investors in his company. It's of only passing interest that the U.S. had just started bombing Afghanistan.[138] It's of much greater interest that Congress had recently passed his big brother's *No Child Left Behind* Act. That's because Ignite sells software to help schoolchildren prepare for the tests mandated by the Act. Where sufficient children fail the test, their school is deemed also to have failed, with the consequent loss of funding. Thus, they are willing to spend whatever is necessary to avoid failure, leading to very high profits for companies like Ignite. Based on the evaluation of a pilot program at a middle school in Orlando, FL (where *Jeb Bush* is the Governor), Ignite has a real possibility of selling its software throughout the state at an annual price of $50 per pupil—and that's only one state.

Bush Pioneers: Republicans who raised $100,000 or more for the Bush presidential campaign. Those who raised $200,000 or more were promoted to a category known as Rangers. Those raising $300,000 or more became Super Rangers. All three categories are, of course, granted considerable access to George Bush.

Bush, Prescott: Paternal grandfather of George W. Bush. He managed companies that were fronts for the Nazi industrialist, Fritz Thyssen, until well into World War II, when the

---

[138] Although much is possible when people are distracted by such things.

U.S. government intervened and seized the companies under the Trading with the Enemy Act.

Bush, Prescott, Jr.: Son of Prescott Bush, older brother of George H.W. Bush, and uncle of George W. Bush. He ran the only company, an exporter of communications satellites, allowed to do business with the People's Republic of China at a time when the U.S. had an embargo on all trade with that country.

Bush, William H.T. "Bucky": Son of Prescott Bush, youngest brother of George H.W. Bush, and uncle of George W. Bush. George Bush calls him "Uncle Bucky."

He is a director of Engineered Support Systems, Inc. (ESSI),[139] a company that has profited mightily from his nephew George's war in Iraq, and which he joined eight months before nephew George became president. On January 18, 2005, he cashed in $450,000 worth of stock options, far more than he would have received had there been no Iraq war. Because of the war, ESSI was able to boost its projected annual revenue by about $1 billion. The fact that it had a number of no bid and/or sole-source contracts didn't hurt, of course. As of February, 2005, a number of ESSI contracts were being reviewed by the Pentagon's Inspector General.

Bushism: Formerly, any of George H.W. Bush's syntactically and/or grammatically challenged utterances.

The frequent nonsensical utterances of George W. Bush are distinguished from his father's somewhat less egregious malformations by the term *George W. Bushisms.* However, they are more commonly referred to simply as *Bushisms.* A (*George W.*) *Bushism* appears, along with a brief comment, above the first entry for most of the initial letters (all but X, Y and Z) in this book. There are several websites and quite

---

[139] *Company's Work in Iraq Profited Bush's Uncle: William H.T. 'Bucky' Bush earned $450,000 on stock options with defense contractor ESSI, Walter F. Roche Jr., Los Angeles Times, February 23, 2005, http://www.commondreams.org/headlines05/0223-05.htm.*

a few published books containing either *Bushisms* or *George W. Bushisms.*

butterfly ballot: Ballot used in punch card voting machines in Palm Beach County, FL, during the 2000 election. Because the ballot used a two-page spread, with candidate's names either side of the column of holes into which voters pushed a stylus to cast their vote, several thousand voters inadvertently cast votes for Patrick Buchanan, rather than Al Gore.[140] The ballot's confusing nature also resulted in a large number of overvotes (inadvertently voting for more than one candidate or ticket). Although the ballot violated Florida election law (which requires the names of all candidates for an office to be on the same page), a court ruled against a group that appealed the count.[141] A correctly designed ballot would have ensured a margin of victory for Al Gore of well over 5000 votes.

Bybee, Jay S.: Former Assistant Attorney General[142] under John Ashcroft. In 2002, he co-wrote (with his deputy, *John Yoo*) and signed[143] a 50-page memo[144] that redefined torture.

---

[140] The Bush/Cheney ticket was the first one on the left page and the Gore/Lieberman ticket was the second one on the same page. The Buchanan/Foster ticket was the first one on the right page. Successive holes corresponded to alternating left-page and right-page entries. Many voters intending to vote for Gore/Lieberman simply assumed that, as that ticket was the second of the only two tickets that interested them on the page they were looking at, the second hole was the one into which to insert the stylus. Unfortunately, the correct hole was the third one.

[141] John Nichols relates this story in entertaining detail in his 2001 book, *"Jews for Buchanan: Did You Hear the One About the Theft of the American Presidency?", The New Press, NY, ISBN 1-56-584717-2.* The name of the book derives from the fact that a significant proportion of Palm Beach County voters are Jewish (typically Reform Jewish retirees from the New York area), and are not the kind of people likely to knowingly vote for the very conservative Patrick Buchanan—a fact he was, himself, quick to point out.

[142] Specifically, he was head of the Office of Legal Counsel, a very exciting place for any lawyer whose primary interest is Constitutional law.

[143] As the sole signatory, giving him no choice but to accept total responsibility for the memo's content.

[144] Now known as the "Bybee memo." A full discussion of the memo can be found at *http://discourse.net/archives/2004/06/olcs_aug_1_2002_ torture_memo_the_bybee_memo.html.* The full memo, in portable

Among other horrors, the memo expressed the view that physical torture *"must be equivalent in intensity to the pain accompanying serious physical injury, such as organ failure, impairment of bodily function, or even death."* In other words, we are to regard anything less than that (even slightly) as not being torture. Such a view is, of course, severely at odds with the **Geneva Conventions**. Quite apart from the extreme immorality of such a position, implementing it endangers U.S. service personnel and others who may be captured by an enemy, as calling an enemy to account for similar behavior would, in the circumstances, be very difficult.

On January 7, 2003, George Bush nominated Bybee to serve on the Ninth Circuit Court of Appeals, for which the Senate confirmed him on March 13, 2003. The Senate was unaware of the torture memo at the time of his confirmation. It seems reasonable to suppose that George Bush was very aware of the memo or, if he was not, he should have been. White House Counsel **Alberto Gonzalez** was certainly aware of it, as it was addressed to him and was the basis for his advice to George Bush and Defense Secretary **Donald Rumsfeld**. According to John Dean, there is a good case for Bybee's impeachment,[145] because he counseled President George W. Bush to break the law (as, also, did Alberto Gonzalez).

From 1989 to 1991, Bybee was associate counsel to President George H.W. Bush.

---

document format (PDF) is available at *http://www.washingtonpost.com /wp-srv/nation/documents/dojinterrogationmemo20020801.pdf.*
[145] *http://edition.cnn.com/2005/LAW/01/03/dean.judges.*

C

> C is for Child, as in *"You teach a child to read, and he or her will be able to pass a literacy test."*
> —George Bush, Townsend, TN, February 21, 2001
> (Which him may also be able to do one day.)

C students: On May 21, 2001, George Bush gave the commencement address, ironically titled "Light and Truth," at Yale University. Less than a minute into that address, he said, *"And to the C students—I say, you, too, can be President of the United States."*[1] He failed to mention that it helps somewhat to have a father who was, himself, the President of the United States (plus, of course, his father's friends in high places).

Cabinet (first term only): Here are former senior Cabinet members (and others with cabinet level status) in the Bush administration. Most of them have or had corporate connections (either as former directors, executives or employees, or as major shareholders, or involving contributions). The connections are shown under their names.[2] Those shown in bold italics have their own entries in this book. Although they have now left, they are still of interest as examples of Bush appointees:

- Secretary of Agriculture: ***Ann Veneman.***
  Calgene, Monsanto, Pharmacia

- Secretary of Commerce: ***Don Evans.***
  Tom Brown, Inc. (oil and gas)

- Secretary of Education: ***Rod Paige.***

---

[1] From the official transcript.

[2] Source of most of the corporate connection information: *Center for Responsive Politics, http://opensecrets.org.*

- Secretary of Energy: *Spencer Abraham.*[3]
  General Motors, Ford, Lear Corporation, DaimlerChrysler

- Attorney General (Department of Justice [DOJ]): *John Ashcroft.*
  AT&T, Enterprise Rent-a-Car, Microsoft

- Secretary of Health and Human Services (HHS): *Tommy Thomson.*
  Abbott Laboratories, America Online (AOL), Amtrak, GE, Merck, Philip Morris, Time Warner

- Secretary of Homeland Security: Tom Ridge.

- Secretary of State: *Colin Powell.*
  America Online (AOL), Gulfstream Aerospace

- Secretary of Veterans Affairs (VA): Anthony Principi.
  Lockheed Martin, Microsoft, Qualcomm

- Director, National Economic Council: Stephen Friedman.
  Fannie Mae, Goldman Sachs, Marsh & McLennan, Wal-Mart

- U.S. Trade Representative:[4] *Robert Zoellick.*

Cabinet (second term): Here are the senior Cabinet members in the Bush administration. Most of them have or had corporate connections (either as former directors, executives or employees, or as major shareholders, or involving contributions). The connections are shown under their names.[5] Those shown in bold italics have their own entries in this book.

- Vice President: *Dick Cheney.*
  Halliburton

---

[3] In the 2000 election, Abraham was the top recipient of contributions ($700,000) from the automotive industry. His bid for re-election failed, making him available for appointment to a cabinet position.

[4] Although this is not a cabinet position, it has cabinet-level rank.

[5] Source of most of the corporate connection information: *Center for Responsive Politics, http://opensecrets.org.*

- Secretary of Agriculture: *Mike Johanns.*
  Archer Daniels Midland, ConAgra Foods, Kraft Foods, Tyson Foods

- Secretary of Defense (DOD): *Donald Rumsfeld.*
  Gilead Sciences, Pharmacia, Motorola, Sears

- Secretary of Education: *Margaret Spellings.*

- Secretary of Energy: *Sam Bodman,* former Deputy Secretary of Commerce and former Deputy Secretary of the Treasury.

- Secretary of Health and Human Services: *Michael O. Leavitt* (formerly EPA Administrator) .
  Medtronic, Merck

- Secretary of Homeland Security: *Michael Chertoff.*

- Secretary of Housing and Urban Development (HUD): Alphonso Jackson (Deputy Secretary and Acting Secretary) .
  American Electric Power

- Secretary of the Interior: *Gale Norton.*
  Brownstein Hyatt and Farber, Delta Petroleum, NL Industries, BP Amoco, Ford Motor Company

- Attorney General (Department of Justice): *Alberto Gonzalez.*
  Vinson & Elkins

- Secretary of Labor: *Elaine Chao.*
  Bank of America, C.R. Bard, Inc., Clorox, Dole Food, HCA, Northwest Airlines

- Secretary of State: *Condoleezza Rice* (formerly National Security Advisor).
  Chevron, Charles Schwab, Transamerica Corp.

- Secretary of Transportation: Norman Mineta (the only Democrat in the Cabinet).
  Boeing, Lockheed Martin, United Airlines

- Secretary of the Treasury: John Snow.
  CSX (as Chief Executive Officer)

- Secretary of Veterans Affairs: *Jim Nicholson*.

There are also three who are not formally cabinet members, but who have cabinet level rank:

- Administrator, Environmental Protection Agency (EPA): *Stephen L. Johnson*.

- Director, Office of National Drug Control Policy (ONDCP): *John P. Walters*.

- U.S. Trade Representative: Rob Portman (until his confirmation as Director, Office of Management and Budget).

Finally, there are four presidential advisors:

- White House Chief of Staff: Until March 28, 2006, *Andrew Card*.
  General Motors (chief lobbyist)
  After March 28, 2006, *Joshua Bolten*
  Goldman Sachs

- Director, Office of Management and Budget (OMB): *Rob Portman*, subject to Senate Confirmation. (Joshua Bolten, now White House Chief of Staff, formerly held the position).

- National Security Advisor: *Stephen J. Hadley* (formerly Deputy National Security Advisor).

- Director, National Economic Council: Steve Friedman.
  Fannie Mae, Goldman Sachs, Marsh & McLennan Capital, Wal-Mart

Camp Delta: The U.S. prison camp at Guantánamo Bay, Cuba, used for the detention of *"enemy combatants."* As of the end of September 2005, there were about 520 prisoners remaining, with more than 230 having been released prior to that date.[6] Most were captured in Afghanistan after 9/11. Very few have actually been charged with a crime, which is not surprising, as many of the prisoners were reported to have been simply "rounded up"—a case of being in the wrong place at the wrong time.

> 'This woman had come down and she plays me the video. I say: "Are you blind? That doesn't look anything like me." But it makes no difference. I'd got to the point where I just couldn't take any more. "Do what you have to do," I told them. I'd been sitting there for three months in isolation, so I say, "Yes, it's me. Go ahead and put me on trial."'[7]
>
> —Shafiq Rasul, British detainee, who was working at a Currys[8] store in the U.K., at the time he was alleged to have posed for a video with Osama bin Laden[9]

On June 28, 2004, the U.S. Supreme Court held, 6 to 3, in *Rasul et al v. Bush, President of the United States, et al*, that "United States courts have jurisdiction to consider challenges to the legality of the detention of foreign nationals captured abroad in connection with hostilities and incarcerated at Guantánamo Bay."[10] The court didn't address the merits of the challenges being made by Rasul and others,[11] leaving that process to

---

[6] *Gitmo Judge Rejects Claim He's Interfering*, Larry Neumeister, Associated Press, http://news.yahoo.com/s/ap/20050926/ap_on_re_us/guantanamo_lawsuit.

[7] *The real truth about Camp Delta*, an excerpt from the book, "Guantanamo Bay: America's War on Human Rights," by David Rose, The Observer, October 3, 2004, http://www.guardian.co.uk/guantanamo/story/0,13743,1318654,00.htm.

[8] Currys is a large chain store in the UK. According to Rasul, he had told his interrogators that he hadn't even left the UK in the year in question and that the store's employment records would show that he was telling the truth. However, rather than checking those records or talking to the store's management, they simply alleged that the records could have been falsified. They also claimed he could have traveled to Afghanistan on a false passport.

[9] The video was supposedly made at the time bin Laden was planning the 9/11 attack.

[10] *Legal Information Institute, Supreme Court Collection, Rasul v. Bush, Syllabus*, http://straylight.law.cornell.edu/supct/html/03-334.ZS.html.

[11] They were not (and could not have been) asked to do so. They may, of course, be asked to rule on whatever decision a lower court subsequently makes in the individual cases.

the lower courts. However, Rasul and two others, Ruhal Ahmed and Asif Iqbal, had already been transferred to British authorities three months earlier. On their return to England, they were placed in custody, but released without charge the following day.[12]

It would seem that the Supreme Court wrapped the matter up quite nicely. But things are not always as they seem. Seventeen months later, on November 9, 2005, apparently not satisfied with the decision, Senator Lindsay Graham (R-SC) initiated an end-run around it by way of an amendment to the pending Defense Department Appropriations bill that would strip detainees designated by the administration as "enemy combatants" of habeas review.[13] In other words, he wanted the rights upheld by the Supreme Court to be taken away. Of course, such an amendment had no chance of passing (so one might naïvely think). Unbelievably, on November 10, the amendment did pass, 49 to 42. Had five Democrats[14] not voted for the amendment, it would have failed, 44 to 47. The bill, as a whole, passed unanimously on November 15, 2005, and became law on January 6, 2006.

The issue does not end there, as it will almost certainly resurface in the U.S. Supreme Court. According to FindLaw, the amendment, as written, does not conflict with the U.S. Constitution, as written; however, it does raise issues relating to the "unwritten constitution" (i.e., precedent).[15]

---

[12] *'Delight' at release of Guantanamo men, Lawyers and families of the Freed Guantanamo Bay detainees say the are "absolutely delighted" at the men's release from British custody, BBC News, March 11, 2004, http://news.bbc.co.uk/1/hi/uk/3500156.stm.*

[13] *TalkLeft: the politics of crime, Senate Passes Amendment to End Habeas for Detainees, November 10, 2005, http://talkleft.com/new_archives/013056.html.*

[14] Kent Conrad (ND), Mary Landrieu (LA), Joe Lieberman (CT), Ben Nelson (NE), and Ron Wyden (OR).

[15] *The Senate Votes to Curb Habeas Corpus Petitions by Guantanamo Bay Detainees: How the Bill Threatens the "Unwritten Constitution," Michael C. Dorf, FindLaw Legal News and Commentary, http://writ.news.findlaw.com/dorf/20051121.html.*

In the meantime, on May 19, 2006, the United Nations Committee Against Torture asked the United States to close Camp Delta and any secret prisons under its control (*see Gulag*), and to eschew the use of psychological torture by its "investigating agencies."[16]

Card, Andrew H., Jr.: White House Chief of Staff, until his resignation on March 28, 2006. George Bush announced his replacement, *Josh Bolten,* on the same day. White House press secretary Scott McClellan said Bolten would have the authority to make personnel shifts if he deems them necessary.[17]

> "*Simply rearranging the deck chairs on the Titanic by replacing Andy Card with Josh Bolten without a dramatic change in policy will not right this ship.*"[18]
>
> — *Senator Charles Schumer, March 28, 2006*

A onetime Massachusetts state legislator, Card also served in the George H.W. Bush administration as Assistant to the President and Deputy Chief of Staff, and in the Reagan Administration as Special Assistant, then Deputy Assistant to the President for Intergovernmental Affairs.

George Bush appointed Card at the beginning of his first term and, since then, Card mostly kept a fairly low profile. Given at least one of his activities, that seems to have been both deliberate and judicious.

In 2002, he and *Karl Rove* formed the White House Iraq Group (WHIG) with the objective of creating disinformation, using hyped intelligence, to be used in Bush's efforts to gain support for attacking Iraq. The other White House members were *I. Lewis Libby,* Dick Cheney's now-indicted chief of staff; *Condoleezza Rice,* National Security Adviser; *Karen Hughes,* special adviser to George W. Bush; Mary Matalin,

---

[16] *UN report slams US on rights 'Shut Guantanamo', D. Ravi Kanth, Deccan Herald, May 20, 2006, http://deccanherald.com/deccanherald/ may202006/foreign2254172006519.asp.*

[17] *Bolten to Replace Card As Chief of Staff, Terence Hunt, Associated Press, March 28, 2006, http://abcnews.go.com/Politics/wireStory?id=1777279.*

[18] Ibid.

special adviser to **Dick Cheney**; **Stephen Hadley**, Deputy National Security Adviser; Nicholas E. Calio, Assistant to the President for Legislative Affairs; and James R. Wilkinson, Deputy Director of Communications for Planning.[19]

> *"From a marketing point of view, you don't introduce new products in August."*
>
> *—Andrew Card, Iraq War product marketing manager,*
> *September 2002*

Some have claimed that Judith Miller, who resigned on November 9, 2005, from the *New York Times*, was also included. Whether or not that's true, her columns, at the time, were very supportive of the White House position on Iraq. Her testimony before the grand jury in the Valerie Plame Wilson leak case also indicates a certain degree of coziness with the group.

> *"They [WHIG] were funneling information to Judy Miller. Judy was a charter member."*
>
> *—Former intelligence officer (unnamed)[20]*

Whether there will be further indictments in the leak case and whether they will include Andrew Card remains to be seen. Whatever happens, it will probably be unaffected by his March 28, 2006, resignation.

CBN: Christian Broadcasting Network. *See* **Robertson, Pat.**

CCC: *See* **Council of Conservative Citizens.**

Celebrations for Children, Inc.: *See DeLay, Tom.*

chad: The artifact that has come to symbolize the drama of the 2000 presidential election. A chad is the small rectangle of card that is removed when a hole is punched in a punch

---

[19] *Kucinich Uses Resolution Of Inquiry To Demand Documents From White House Group That Developed Strategy To "Sell" War, October 20, 2005, http://afterdowningstreet.org/whig.*

[20] *Prez Iraq team fought to squelch war critics, James Gordon Meek and Kenneth R. Bazinet, New York Daily News, October 19, 2005, http://nydailynews.com/10-19-2005/news/wn_report/story/357082p-304302c.html.*

card. Although punch card voting machines were used all over the country during the 2000 election, the ones receiving the attention were in Florida.

The cards used for punch card voting have pre-scored chads that are pushed out with a stylus-like device, guided by a template (e.g., the notorious **butterfly ballot**). If the voter doesn't press hard enough with the stylus, the chad may not be fully removed. Its state may be referred to as "dimpled" (having a small depression), "pregnant"(having an obvious depression) or "hanging" (partially pushed out, but still attached by one, two or three corners).

During the limited manual recount of the 2000 election, the Bush campaign didn't want the vote corresponding to any chad that was still attached—least of all those that were merely dimpled—to be counted. The Gore campaign maintained that the spirit of Florida election law should prevail, with the recognizable intent of the voter being the standard. The Bush campaign claimed that scrutinizing the chads for intent was tantamount to mind reading (in their words, *"divining the intent of the voter"*). The Gore campaign pointed out the obvious—that, at the very least, pregnant and hanging chads indicated an intent to vote for the candidate corresponding to the chad's position on the card. Ultimately, the U.S. Supreme Court settled the matter by, unbelievably, stopping the recount (*see **Felonious Five***).

Chalabi, Ahmad (or Ahmed): Until May 2004, George Bush's favorite Iraqi. Prior to Operation Iraqi Freedom, Chalabi and his Iranian National Congress associates were the most prolific suppliers of "intelligence" on Saddam Hussein's intentions to George Bush, **Donald Rumsfeld**, and the CIA.[21] As neither he nor his associates had lived in Iraq for many years,[22] the information he was providing should have been viewed with suspicion. However, as it supported Bush's, **Cheney's** and Rumsfeld's rationale (at least, the publicly declared one) for going to war, it was received enthusiastically—so enthusiastically that the ad-

---

[21] Although it appears that the CIA never really trusted him.
[22] In Chalabi's own case, since 1958.

ministration was paying him and his associates $340,000 per month to continue what they were doing.

To the more or less objective observer, there was reason to suspect Chalabi's motives from the start. After all, he had been convicted in Jordan (in absentia) for fraud and the embezzlement of about $70 million. The sentence was 22 years, which he'll have to start serving if he ever sets foot in Jordan.[23] Jordan's foreign minister, Dr. Marwan Muashar, has also claimed that Chalabi was involved in "financial irregularities" in Switzerland and caused the collapse of two banks in Lebanon.[24]

After May 2004, Chalabi, who was made a member of the now disbanded Iraqi Governing Council, fell out of favor with the administration, mainly because of his dealings with Iran, where he appeared to have played both ends against the middle, including leaking sensitive information. Prior to Operation Iraqi Freedom, he maintained, at U.S. taxpayer expense, a $36,000 per month Iraqi National Congress office in Tehran.[25]

On August 8, 2004, it was revealed that the interim Iraqi government had issued a warrant for his arrest for counterfeiting. At the same time, they issued a warrant for his nephew, Salem Chalabi, on murder charges.[26] Neither warrant seems to have been served and, amazingly, by the Fall of 2005, Chalabi had managed to get himself elected to the Iraqi government, where he serves as Deputy Prime Minister. In November 2005, he once more raised suspicions about his Iranian connections when, just prior to a visit to the United States with other Iraqi government officials, he paid a visit to Tehran, where he met with Iran's new hardline president, Mahmoud Ahmadinejad.

---

[23] Under Jordanian law, he can go to Jordan and request a new trial.

[24] *Meet the Press, NBC, April 27, 2003.*

[25] *Intelligence: A Double Game. Has Chalabi given 'sensitive' information on U.S. interests to Iran? He denies it, but the White House is wary. Mark Hosenball, Newsweek, May 10, 2004, http://msnbc.msn.com/id/4881157.*

[26] *Iraq Issues Warrants for Chalabi, Nephew; Jamie Tarabay, Associated Press, August 9, 2004, http://story.news.yahoo.com/news?tmpl=story &u=/ap/20040808/ap_on_re_mi_ea/iraq_arrest_warrants.*

If we are to judge Bush, Cheney and Rumsfeld by the company they keep, Ahmad Chalabi, his survival instincts notwithstanding, gives them a lot to answer for. In the meantime, one outcome of the December 15, 2005, Iraq election could be that Chalabi will be given a significant role in the new Iraqi administration, although that administration was still in chaos as late as April 2006.

Chambliss, Saxby: Republican Senator from Georgia. In the 2002 mid-term election, Chambliss defeated incumbent Democratic Senator Max Cleland. The tide turned against Cleland (who lost two legs and one arm in Vietnam and was a recipient of the Bronze and Silver Stars and, obviously, the Purple Heart) after the Chambliss campaign, supported by George Bush, impugned Cleland's patriotism shortly before election day with a simplistic campaign ad claiming that Cleland had voted against the formation of the *Department of Homeland Security.*[27] What was particularly galling to Cleland was that Chambliss, who had supported the Vietnam War, had avoided actually serving in it (because of a "trick knee"). In February 2004, Democratic presidential hopeful John Kerry (not yet the candidate) wrote a letter to George Bush in which he referred to Chambliss' 2002 campaign as "one of the most despicable campaigns ever conducted."[28]

Although it cannot be proved, there was some suspicion that electronic voting machines (with no paper trail) might have been rigged to assure Chambliss' win. With respect to patriotism and support for the nation's security, Cleland was considered to be unassailable.

---

[27] Cleland had voted against several forms of or amendments to the bill, which is normal during the process by which the Senate reaches a compromise on which a majority can agree.

[28] The letter was triggered by a conference call, arranged by the Bush campaign, in which Saxby Chambliss said that Kerry had a "32-year history of voting to cut defense programs and cut defense systems." Kerry saw the tactic as a repeat of George Bush's tactics against Senator John McCain (another Vietnam war hero) in the 2000 Republican primaries and, on behalf of Saxby Chambliss, against Max Cleland in 2002. Source: *My Way News, Kerry Blasts Bush Over Attacks on Record, http://apnews. myway.com/article/20040222/D80S2RDO1.htm).*

Right wing spin on the contest was provided by Paul Weyrich, of the *Free Congress Foundation*, who credited single-issue pro-life voters with tipping the scales for Chambliss.[29] That may in fact have been a factor, but it may have taken Election Day irregularities to tip the scale.

Cheney, Dick: U.S. Vice President; former CEO of Halliburton.

The Electoral College vote count that made Cheney Vice President in his first term is tainted by the Florida voting irregularities and by his own brazen disregard for the 12th Amendment to the Constitution, which does not allow the candidates for President and Vice President to be residents of the same state. Cheney got around the 12th Amendment by way of a dubious technicality, flying back to Wyoming, just before his position on the ticket was announced, to register as a voter there. Based on the fact that his residence was still in Texas and that Wyoming does not allow people to assert residency overnight, three groups sued unsuccessfully[30] to have him disqualified as the candidate for Vice President. Even his choice as Bush's vice presidential running mate was somewhat dubious, as he had been given the task of finding a suitable person for that job, with no thought (at least in the public's mind) of him being the choice. His self selection was described by Robert Scheer as a forewarning of the Machiavellian arrogance he has displayed ever since.[31]

> *"Principle is okay up to a certain point, but principle doesn't do any good if you lose."*
> —*Dick Cheney, during Ford Administration*[32]

---

[29] *NewsMax.com, The Pro-Life Advantage at the Polls, Paul Weyrich, November 19, 2002, http://www.newsmax.com/archives/articles/2002/11/18/200423.shtml.*

[30] Obviously.

[31] *The Man Behind the Oval Office Curtain, Robert Scheer, thenation.com, October 26, 2004, http://www.thenation.com/doc/20041108/scheer1026.*

[32] As quoted by John Dean, in his book, *Worse Than Watergate: The Secret Presidency of George W. Bush, Little Brown and Company, April 2004,* ISBN 0-31600-023-X.

Cheney was a six-term congressman from Wyoming, which has only one congressional seat. He gave up his seat in 1989 to accept *George H.W. Bush's* invitation to become Defense Secretary, a position he held until the end of Bush's single term. Both Operation Just Cause (the invasion of Panama) and Operation Desert Storm (the first Gulf War) took place on his watch.

His congressional career was not his first involvement in politics. After obtaining a Masters degree in political science from the University of Wyoming, he had won a congressional fellowship and moved to Washington, in 1968, where he progressed fairly rapidly from the office of the Congressman from Wyoming, William Steiger, all the way to being the youngest ever White House chief of staff (at 34), under Gerald Ford. That last position was one for which his boss, **Donald Rumsfeld**, had recommended him, following Rumsfeld's own service in the same position.

In view of some of Cheney's subsequent activities as Vice President, initially as chairman of the **Energy Task Force**, his employment between the two Bush presidencies is particularly interesting. Although he had no business experience (or, indeed, any private sector experience), the giant oilfield services company, Halliburton, hired him as their Chief Executive Officer. His critics can perhaps be forgiven for viewing this transition with a certain amount of cynicism. The **revolving door** between government and big business is a well-known fact of life. However, this was, to use one of Cheney's own expressions, big time. His contacts from his former role as Secretary of Defense during the Gulf War put him in an incredibly strong position with respect to obtaining oilfield contracts in that region, in addition to government contracts elsewhere.

Cheney has earned a reputation as the most powerful Vice President in U.S. history, so much so that it has been said that, if Cheney were to die, George Bush would have to take over. Powerful does not, of course, equate to good. For one thing, his acquaintanceship with the truth seems to be a very distant one, especially with respect to his frequent misleading statements before and since the start of the Iraq War, even continuing into 2006.

Both Cheney and Bush have practiced what might be called lying by juxtaposition, of which the most common example is mentioning 9/11 and *Saddam Hussein* in adjacent sentences. That example is not surprising, as both of them had their eye on Saddam from before the start of Bush's first term. The events of 9/11 provided a convenient starting point for the mounting deception that led to the attack on Iraq

> *"[Secretary of State Colin Powell] detected a kind of fever in Cheney ... Cheney was beyond hellbent for action against Saddam. It was as if nothing else existed."*
>
> —*Bob Woodward, Plan of Attack, April 2004*[33]

One of Cheney's two best known and possibly most persistent lies concerns Mohammed Atta, the eleventh 9/11 highjacker, Cheney repeated a claim that Atta had a meeting in 2001, in Prague, with an Iraqi agent, long after the story had been totally discredited by U.S. and other intelligence agencies.

The second of the best-known Cheney lies concerns *Abu Musab al-Zarqawi*. In spite of CIA statements refuting his claim, Cheney has said again and again that Zarqawi entered Iraq with Saddam Hussein's permission. The fact is that Zarqawi entered Iraq using a false identity. Not only that, he set up his base of operations in the Kurdish north, well out of Saddam's reach.[34]

The fictional weapons of mass destruction have also received frequent Vice Presidential exposure, especially with his pre-war declaration, *"We know Saddam Hussein's been absolutely devoted to trying to acquire nuclear weapons, and we believe he has, in fact, reconstituted nuclear weapons."*[35]

---

[33] *Plan of Attack, Bob Woodward, Simon and Schuster, April 2004, ISBN 074325547X.*

[34] *The Man Behind the Oval Office Curtain, Robert Scheer, thenation.com, October 26, 2004, http://www.thenation.com/doc/20041108/scheer1026.*

[35] *The Nation, Blog, The Online Beat: Case Against Cheney, John Nichols, October 18, 2005, http://thenation.com/blogs/thebeat?bid=1&pid=29442.*

Cheney's aide until October 28, 2005, was *I. Lewis Libby*, who bears the unlikely nickname, *Scooter*. Libby's resignation on that date was because of with his indictment for perjury and obstruction of justice, following inquiries into his role in the "outing" of Valerie Plame Wilson as a covert CIA agent. It's possible that, as Libby's boss, Dick Cheney may also be at risk of indictment. It was Plame's husband, former Ambassador Joseph Wilson, who had revealed another of Cheney's frequent assertions to be a lie.

> *"And no one, repeat no one, in Washington is known to be more vindictive than Dick Cheney."*[36]
>
> —*John Nichols, The Nation, October 18, 2005*

Specifically, Wilson had reported that documents purporting to show the sale by Niger to Iraq of uranium "yellowcake" were crude forgeries. When his report was ignored, he went public on July 6, 2003, with an article in the *New York Times*.[37] More than anyone, Cheney had reason to want to punish Wilson for telling the truth.

Other than when making the occasional speech to carefully selected audiences, Cheney has spent much of his time out of the public eye, which inevitably distances him from the American people. In the week following Hurricane Katrina, Cheney was nowhere to be seen, while the director of FEMA and others were demonstrating their bumbling incompetence.[38] When he eventually showed up, it appeared to be mainly for photo ops.[39]

---

[36] *Ibid.*

[37] *What I Didn't Find in Africa, Joseph Wilson 4th, New York Times, July 3, 2003, http://www.commondreams.org/views03/0706-02.htm.*

[38] To be fair, former FEMA director Michael Brown has since been shown to have had moments of competence, as evidenced by the videotaped briefing in which he provided an apparently catatonic George Bush with a warning of the seriousness of the upcoming hurricane.

[39] George Bush's own appearances in the aftermath of Katrina were also little more than photo ops. It was during one such photo op that he told Michael Brown, Director of FEMA (until his resignation a couple of days later), "Brownie, you're doing a heck of a job."

With Cheney's record, one would expect reasonable people to become somewhat disenchanted with him. That is indeed what has happened, with his approval rating sinking, on March 1, 2006, to 18% in a CBS poll.

Cheney, Elizabeth (Liz): Principal Deputy Assistant Secretary of State for Near Eastern affairs and coordinator for broader Middle East and North Africa initiatives. Secretary of State *Condoleezza Rice* appointed her to the two positions on February 14, 2005. Ms. Cheney previously served as Deputy Assistant Secretary of State for Near Eastern affairs under former Secretary of State, *Colin Powell*. Prior to that, she held positions as Special Assistant to the Deputy Secretary of State for Assistance to the former Soviet Union, and as a USAID officer in US embassies in Budapest and Warsaw.

She is the older of Dick and **Lynne Cheney**'s two daughters. Could her succession of State Department appointments be nepotism? It's something that's hard to prove, but it is not beyond the bounds of probability.

Cheney, Lynne: Wife of Vice President Dick Cheney. She has a PhD in British Literature and a long record of conservative political activism (see, for example, *American Enterprise Institute*), with a strong loyalty (not surprisingly) to the *Republican Party*.

Prior to the 2000 Bush/Cheney election campaign, she was a fairly frequent participant on CNN's Crossfire program, sitting on the right (obviously). Along with her two daughters, she was very much involved in the 2004 election campaign and was a speaker at the Republican Convention in New York.

Cheney, Mary: Dick and Lynne Cheney's younger daughter. Mary Cheney is openly lesbian and her parents say they are supportive of her, although she was conspicuously absent from family photographs taken during the 2004 Republican Convention. This was in spite of the fact that she participated in her father's campaign for his and George Bush's reelection and was present at the Convention. What was more surprising was that she was willing to campaign for her father on a ticket that included George Bush, who has called for a constitutional amendment banning gay marriage.

Chertoff, Michael: Secretary of Homeland Security. The Senate confirmed Chertoff on February 15, 2005, by a 96 to 0 vote. He was George Bush's second nominee for the position. Bush's first was **Bernard Kerik,** who turned out to be a disastrous choice. According to some commentators, Chertoff's track record as an obvious opponent of civil liberties made him an equally bad (or worse) choice.

In the view of *The Progressive*[40] and of the American Civil Liberties Union,[41] Chertoff did not deserve to be confirmed as Secretary of Homeland Security. He was after all the author, with Viet D. Dinh,[42] of the **USA PATRIOT Act.**

> *"[Michael Chertoff] ... has been an active and uncompromising proponent, even before 9/11, of national security policies that push, or breach, the outer limits of what is permissible under the Bill of Rights."* [43]
>
> —*ACLU Memo, January 28, 2005*[44]

It was Chertoff who engineered the roundup of about eleven hundred Muslims following 9/11, putting them in federal prison without access to legal counsel. None was convicted of a crime and, as it turned out, none had any connection with terrorism.[45]

---

[40] *Dems lie down for Chertoff, February 16, 2005, http://progressive.org/ webex05/wx021605.php.*

[41] *ACLU's Memo to Interested Persons on the Civil Liberties Record of Designate Michael Chertoff, January 28, 2005, http://aclu.org/SafeandFree/ SafeandFree.cfm?ID=17378&c=206.*

[42] Viet Dinh, the chief architect of the PATRIOT Act, was Assistant Attorney General, under John Ashcroft, at the time.

[43] *ACLU's Memo to Interested Persons on the Civil Liberties Record of Designate Michael Chertoff, January 28, 2005, http://aclu.org/SafeandFree/ SafeandFree.cfm?ID=17378&c=206.*

[44] The memo also acknowledged Chertoff's *"accomplished record as a jurist and attorney."*

[45] *Chertoff's Preemptive Crackdown, Mike Whitney, Counterpunch, August 2, 2005, http://counterpunch.org/whitney08022005.html.*

> *'"Failing upwards" is a long-standing tradition in the Bush White House and Chertoff has become the resident poster child."*[46]
>
> —*Mike Whitney, Counterpunch, August 2, 2005*

Since his appointment, Chertoff has done very little to allay the fears of the ACLU and other progressive organizations.

Only five months into his tenure, in July 2005, under the banner of *Operation Community Shield,* he organized the arrest of over 600 gang members all over the country. Then he went on TV and said that over half of them had "prior criminal histories." He failed to mention that, as clearly implied by the word "prior," they had already served their time for the crimes. When it was all over, only 76 of the 600 were charged with a crime.[47] In trying to present himself as tough on crime, he had neglected the requirement to establish probable cause before arresting someone—an oversight one does not expect from a former Federal Appeals Court judge.

Doubts about Chertoff's suitability for his job really came to a head in August and September 2005, in the aftermath of Hurricane Katrina (*see* **Brown, Michael D.**), and again in testimony at a Senate hearing on February 15, 2006.

On September 3, 2005, Chertoff told reporters that government planners did not predict that a disaster on the scale of Hurricane Katrina would occur.[48]

> *"That 'perfect storm' of a combination of catastrophes exceeded the foresight of the planners, and maybe anybody's foresight."*[49]
>
> —*Michael Chertoff, September 3, 2005*

At least two things contradict Chertoff's assertions. One is that, after 1965's Hurricane Betsy, which was a Category 2

---

[46] Ibid.

[47] Ibid.

[48] *Chertoff: Katrina scenario did not exist, CNN.com, September 5, 2005, http://www.cnn.com/2005/US/09/03/katrina.chertoff.*

[49] Ibid.

storm, the levees around New Orleans were reinforced to as to be able to withstand a Category 3 storm. However, Katrina was forecast, well before it hit, to be at least Category 4, making breaches of levees a virtual certainty. The other was Hurricane Pam. Pam was not a real hurricane, but a massive simulation, conducted in 2002, in which over forty state local and volunteer organizations participated. According to Reuters news agency, they had to deal with the hypothetical destruction of over half a million buildings in New Orleans and with the forced evacuation of a million residents.[50]

Also in 2002, the *New Orleans Times-Picayune* ran a massive five-part special report[51] that opened with the statement:

> *"It's only a matter of time before South Louisiana takes a direct hit from a major hurricane. Billions have been spent to protect us, but we grow more vulnerable every day."*

The five parts took readers through the first five days of a hurricane and its probable aftermath. Although it contained no reference to the "Hurricane Pam" scenario, part 4 of the report did deal with the use of computers to simulate the effects of hurricanes, including a simulation of Hurricane Betsy, based on the contemporary New Orleans landscape, rather than that of 1965, when the real Betsy occurred.

> *"One year to the day after he won unanimous Senate confirmation as secretary of Homeland Security, Chertoff faced not only hostile questioning from senators[52] but also the release of a House committee report that accuses his agency of being too passive in its response to the hurricane, delaying desperately needed help to stranded storm victims."*[53]
>
> —*Bruce Alpert, The Times-Picayune, February 16, 2006*

---

[50] Ibid.

[51] *Washing away, Times-Picayune, republication of series published from June 23-27, 2002, http://www.nola.com/hurricane/?/washingaway.*

[52] Including Republican senators.

[53] *Chertoff: Katrina response a failure, Bruce Alpert, The Times Picayune, February 16, 2006, http://www.nola.com/news/t-p/frontpage/index.ssf?/base/news-5/1140076569113660.xml.*

Between September 2005 and February 2006, Chertoff apparently developed a little humility. The *Times-Picayune* described him as being quite contrite as he gave his testimony before the Senate. It remains to be seen whether George Bush will do the right thing and find a qualified and competent replacement to head Homeland Security.

civil unions: *See gay marriage and civil unions.*

Children's Environmental Health Network (CEHN): In their own words, they are *"a national multi-disciplinary organization whose mission is to protect the fetus and the child from environmental health hazards and promote a healthy environment."*

During the 2000 presidential campaign, they submitted a five-question survey to the candidates, asking what they would be doing in certain areas to protect children's environmental health. The Bush campaign provided, in George Bush's name, a written response, containing a number of assurances, including the following (emphasis added):

> *"I strongly support the goals of the April 1997 Executive Order*[54] *on children's environmental health. I believe, however, that the key issue is not just whether to assess environmental risks confronting children in their homes, schools, and communities, but how to do the harder work of actually safeguarding children's health. Scientific research has not explored nearly enough the nature of children's particular exposures and susceptibilities to various compounds, and as a result, we don't know enough on how best to protect children's health. The bipartisan Commission on Risk Assessment and Risk Management has developed a sound blueprint for determining the effectiveness of actions taken to protect people from environmental health hazards. As President, I will utilize this blueprint and **work cooperatively with** states, local communities and **the private sector** to target our efforts where they are most needed to*

---

[54] *Executive Order: Protection of children from environmental health risks and safety risks, signed by Bill Clinton on April 21, 1997, http://yosemite.epa.gov/ ochp/ochpweb.nsf/content/whatwe_executiv.htm.*

> *protect children and ensure their healthy development,*
> *from the womb to adulthood."*

Evidently, Bush's cooperative work, if any, was with the private sector, as CEHN gave him a failing report card[55] for the period, 2001-2004, stating that *"this Administration's track record is toxic to our children, lessening protections for children and missing opportunities to keep toxicants out of our children's environment."* They gave him an F in eleven of sixteen categories. He managed only a C in the remaining five. In every category, the situation had worsened since he took office.

Christian Broadcasting Network (CBN): *See Robertson, Pat.*

Christian Nation: There is a popular misconception among Christian fundamentalists, evangelicals and others that the United States is a "Christian Nation." *George Bush* and many of those around him, including former Attorney General *John Ashcroft*, seem to share that misconception.[56]

The fact is that the *U.S. Constitution* scrupulously avoids mention of religion, except to say that there shall be no religious test for public office and, in the First Amendment, that *"Congress shall make no law respecting an establishment of religion, or prohibiting the free exercise thereof."*[57]

> *"The United States of America is not a Christian nation—in law or in fact."*
>
> *—J. Brent Walker, Executive Director,*
> *Baptist Joint Committee on Religious Liberty,*
> *April 10, 2006*

---

[55] *Children's Environmental Health Bush Administration Report Card, 2001-2004, http://www.cehn.org/cehn/reportcard2004.html.*

[56] The Attorney General, especially, should have a thorough understanding of the U.S. Constitution and should be familiar with U.S. Supreme Court precedent in its interpretation. That George Bush appears to have no more than a passing acquaintanceship (if that) with the document is very disturbing.

[57] A full discussion of the Christian Nation issue, *Is America A 'Christian Nation'? Religion, Government And Individual Freedom,* can be downloaded from *http://au.org/site/DocServer/Is_the_United_States_a_Christian_nation.pdf.*

The Christian Nation (CN) proponents argue that many involved in the Constitutional Debates argued for the incorporation of God into the Constitution. However, they neglect to mention that they were the ones who lost the debate. They also point to the three theistic-sounding references in the Declaration of Independence (*"endowed by their Creator," "Nature's God,"* and *"Divine Providence"*). All of these are quite abstract, include no definition of those terms, and make no mention of the God of Christianity. The CN proponents will further argue that the capitalization of "Creator" must mean something. They are wrong again, in that it was common in public documents to follow the German practice of capitalizing all nouns. Finally, of course, the Declaration of Independence, although important historically, is not a legal document. The opening and closing remarks follow the customary flowery style, with the important core of the document more or less telling King George to take a flying leap.[58]

See, also, **Bill of Rights: Article I (Freedoms): Religion and Religious Freedom** *and* **church/state separation.**

church/state separation: This is one of the guarantees implicit in the First Amendment (*see* **Bill of Rights**). George Bush (who is no constitutional scholar) is, his rhetoric notwithstanding, no friend of the First Amendment. IRS regulations reward churches by giving them a tax exemption if they stay out of politics. In return (although it's not an explicit quid pro quo), the Government is supposed to stay out of religion. Clearly, financing, at taxpayer expense, religious charities that proselytize to their beneficiaries or use religious discrimination in their hiring practices or provide benefits only to the faithful violates the principle of church/state separation. Nonetheless, this is what George Bush has done, not through legislation via Congress (which has received insufficient votes to pass), but by way of ex-

---

[58] Large numbers of people seem to be telling the American King George to do the same thing. Many of them regret not having done so in the 2004 election.

ecutive orders. For a fuller discussion of this, see *Towey, Jim.*

class warfare: Term used by Republicans to characterize the actions or positions of the Democratic Party when members of the latter object to moves (e.g., massive income tax cuts for the wealthy) that increase the economic differences between the haves and the have-nots. This is disingenuous for two reasons: 1. The fight is not between the have-nots and the haves, but between those who speak for the have-nots and those who enact legislation disproportionately benefiting the haves; 2. The conflict, if any, was caused by the legislative actions of the Republicans (with some Democrat complicity, to be sure). It's somewhat like the bully complaining when the little guy fights back.

Webster's definition of class warfare is as a variant of class struggle or class conflict. The particular term, *class warfare,* is associated with Karl Marx—which is probably the reason Republicans prefer it as something to associate with those "terrible liberals."

Clear Skies Initiative: Doublespeak for a policy that is, in fact, permissive with respect to air pollution. The Bush administration's claim is that the Clear Skies Initiative will reduce pollution faster than the existing Clean Air Act. It will not. It relies on the manipulation of science, mathematical sleight of hand, and the omission of essential facts to make its case. It delays some of the goals of the Clean Air Act and sets much less ambitious goals for the reduction of pollutants. For example, the Clean Air Act aimed to reduce oxides of nitrogen (NOx) to (not by) 1.25 million tons by 2010. Without mentioning the goal set in the Clean Air Act, the Clear Skies Initiative sets a goal of 4.5 million tons—3.6 times as much. For sulfur dioxide (SO_2), the comparison is almost as bad, with the Clean Air Act aiming for a reduction to 2 million tons by 2010 and the Clear Skies Initiative providing a reduction to 4.5 million tons.

The Clean Air Act allows the states to set stricter standards than those mandated by the EPA. Incredibly, the Clear Skies

Initiative does not. It also loosens standards with respect to the emission of particulate matter, which is known to be a major cause of premature death.[59]

See also **Leavitt, Michael O.**

coalition of the willing: The countries that signed on as U.S. allies in Operation Iraqi Freedom.

George Bush, **Donald Rumsfeld, Colin Powell** and others were fond of citing the number of countries in this so-called coalition. In his January 2004 State of the Union speech, George Bush even listed what apparently purport to be the principal members, namely Britain, Australia, Japan, South Korea, the Philippines, Thailand, Italy, Spain, Poland, Denmark, Hungary, Bulgaria, Ukraine, Romania, the Netherlands, Norway and El Salvador. The remainder, he lumped together as *"17 others."* Including the United States itself, that comes to a total of 36. In a February 2004 article[60] on the White House website, then National Security Advisor Condoleezza Rice characterized the number as *"nearly 50 nations."* Possibly she was including some of the *"15 other nations"* to which Colin Powell once alluded.

Paul Gillfeather, in an article[61] in the March 22, 2003 edition of the *Mirror* (UK), referred to the coalition as *"The Coalition of the Bribed, Bullied and Blind."* In the article, he enumerated which ones fall into each of those three categories.

---

[59] There are many detailed articles on the Clear Skies Initiative and its deficiencies on the Internet. They can be easily found with a Google (or other search engine) search on *clear skies initiative*.

[60] Strangely, and it may not mean anything, although the article is said to be "For immediate release, February 4, 2004," the name of the page on which it appears includes the date 20030326 (i.e., March 26, 2003). The page can be found at *http://www.whitehouse.gov/infocus/iraq/news/20030326.html*.

[61] A copy of the article is available at *http://www.commondreams.org/views03/0323-07.htm*. **Warning:** It appears that the text in the original article (on the *www.mirror.co.uk* website) may have been in tabular format, resulting in the copy (which is not tabular) on the Common Dreams website being out of sequence and, therefore, somewhat confusing.

In another, article, *"Bush's Coalition of the Willing?"*,[62] which was posted on the Internet on March 20, 2003, Dr. Leslie Jermyn cited a total of eight categories, plus another coalition, namely, *"The coalition of those opposed to the young emperor for one reason or another."* Although not really a coalition, it consists of the 160 nations who didn't go along (as compared to the few who did) with the plans of Bush, Cheney, Rumsfeld and the neoconservatives. Dr. Jermyn also points out that that the "willing" (his first category) consisted, not of nations, but of three people — **Tony Blair, José Maria Aznar** and **Silvio Berlusconi** — whose governments joined the coalition, contrary to the will of the majority of the people in Britain, Spain and Italy.[63]

Dr. Jermyn's other seven "coalitions" are:

- **The bribed or really wanting to be bribed**, consisting of Albania, Azerbaijan, Bulgaria, the Czech Republic, El Salvador, Estonia, Georgia, Hungary, Latvia, Lithuania, Macedonia, Nicaragua, Poland, Romania, Slovakia and Uzbekistan.

- **Those who need help squashing resistance in their own countries**, specifically Colombia, the Philippines and Turkey.

- **The coalition of instrumental friendship** (hoping for benign intervention in their border dispute). They are Eritrea and Ethiopia.

- **Those who benefited from the last regime change crusade and therefore don't have any choice**. This isn't really a coalition, but a single nation — Afghanistan.

---

[62] *http://www.globalaware.org/Artlicles_eng/willing.html.*

[63] It's interesting to note that, at the time, Aznar enjoyed the support of only 14% of his people. Berlusconi's support, at 34%, was not much better. Tony Blair seems to have weathered the storm. His leadership of the Labour Party, which was initially thought to be in jeopardy, was still intact at the close of the 2004 Labour Party Conference.

- **Those hoping to look really good fixing up the mess**. Dr. Jermyn speculates that the three members of this group, Denmark, Japan and the Netherlands,[64] may have been hoping for some special deals on oil. They are probably in for a long wait.

- **We like Americans**. This is Australia, but not all Australians.

- **We hate Americans but are virtually an American-occupied territory:** South Korea.

At least one of the above countries is a dictatorship. Politics and the invasion of other countries make strange bedfellows.

Not surprisingly, the "coalition" has not held up. As of mid-May, 2004, a number of its members had pulled back either somewhat or completely. Spain, Honduras, the Dominican Republic, Nicaragua and Kazakhstan announced that they were withdrawing their troops, with Spain withdrawing their 1300 in April 2005 and Honduras removing their 370 in the same month; South Korean and Bulgarian troops returned to their bases; and New Zealand started withdrawing its engineers. To save the life of a hostage, the Philippines withdrew its 51 troops in mid 2004. Ukraine started a phased withdrawal of its 1650 troops in the spring of 2005, with completion scheduled for year-end. Even Poland, which canceled a planned withdrawal following the Iraqi elections and after some persuasion by U.S. Secretary of State Condoleezza Rice, announced that it would be fielding 200 fewer troops on its first rotation of the second half of 2005.[65] Finally, on July 8, 2005,[66] Italy's Prime Minister, Silvio Berlusconi, announced the phased withdrawal, to be completed by the end of 2006, of the 3000 Italian troops,

---

[64] On January 14, 2005, the foreign minister of the Netherlands, Ben Bot, announced that all Dutch troops would be withdrawn in March 2005. Source: *Agence France-Presse, as reported at DefenseNews.com, http://www.defensenews.com/story.php?F=600301&C=mideast.*

[65] *Bush's Iraq Speech: Long On Assertion, Short On Facts, FactCheck.org, June 30, 2005, http://factcheck.org/article334.html.*

[66] On the closing day of the G8 Conference, in Gleneagles, Scotland.

starting with an initial 300 in September. Initially, Italy's contingent was the fourth largest, after the United States, the United Kingdom and South Korea.

Coleman, Norman: Former Mayor of St. Paul, MN, and now Republican junior Senator from Minnesota, elected in the wake of the death of Senator Paul Wellstone during his 2002 reelection campaign. Coleman's opponent was former Vice President, Walter "Fritz" Mondale, who had been persuaded to take over Wellstone's candidacy. Prior to Wellstone's death, Coleman had come very close to accusing him of being an agent of Al Qaeda. After Wellstone's death, he feigned grief and claimed Wellstone's mantle, ostensibly to carry on his *"passion and commitment."* In a Salon.com opinion piece in November 2002,[67] Garrison Keillor[68] referred to Coleman as *"a cheap fraud."* Coleman, of course, considers himself to be a very fine fellow, even going as far as to say to Roll Call, in April 2003, *"I am a 99% improvement over Paul Wellstone."* In the face of very strong protest, including a gathering of one hundred protesters outside his office, he eventually apologized for the statement.

Coleman, who switched from the Democratic Farm-Labor Party to the Republican Party, in January 1997, during his first term as mayor of St. Paul, is such an ardent supporter of George W. Bush that a website called BushBoy[69] has been set up just to track, sometimes satirically, his ongoing legislative activities in the U.S. Senate and his contributions from corporations seeking favorable legislation. According to the site, his priorities are being George Bush's lapdog and catering to the wishes of large corporations, rather than to the needs of Minnesotans.

---

[67] *http://salon.com/politics/feature/2002/11/13/coleman/index_np.html.*

[68] In addition to being the creator and host of *A Prairie Home Companion*, on PBS, Garrison Keillor is also a passionately committed Democrat and was a strong supporter of Paul Wellstone, someone he regarded as one of the few really honest politicians.

[69] *http://bushboy.com.*

At the time of his change of allegiance, Coleman described himself as a *"Jack Kemp Republican."*

Commission on Federal Election Reform: A private, bipartisan commission, co-chaired by *James A. Baker III* and former President Jimmy Carter. Its membership included former Senate Minority Leader Tom Daschle (D), former House Minority Leader Bob Michel (R), former U.S. Representatives Lee Hamilton (D) and Susan Molinari (R), university presidents, scholars and community leaders. The Commission's formation was announced on March 24, 2005, its work was organized by the Center for Democracy and Election Management (CDEM) at American University, and it released its report[70] in mid-September, 2005.

The report received mixed reviews. One of its recommendations was universal voter registration, which is the practice in most western democracies. However, it had no recommendation on how the government might go about implementing such registration or how it might ensure its completeness. If successful, though, it would eliminate the current practice of registration through political party organizations, which is open to abuse and, moreover, involves an implicit declaration of the voter's party affiliation or loyalty.

A very good recommendation was that electronic voting machines provide a document assuring the voter that his or her vote was recorded as intended (i.e., a paper trail). After being deposited in a secure container, the document would then be available in case of a manual recount.

The most criticized aspect of the report was the requirement for a national voter identification card, despite a call from many civil and voting rights organizations,[71] shortly after the Commission's formation, to reject such an idea.

---

[70] *Commission on Federal Election Reform, Final Commission Report: Building Confidence in U.S. Elections, http://american.edu/ia/cfer.*

[71] *Voting Rights Groups Urge Carter-Baker Election Commission to Oppose National Voter Identification Card, Demos, June 29, 2005, http://www.demos-usa.org/page338.cfm.*

Caroline Frederickson, Director of the ACLU Washington Legal Office had the following to say about the identification requirement (which would take the form of a standardized driver's license or, for non-drivers, an equivalent ID card):

"[T]he commission recommends requiring photo identification in order for citizens to vote, which will disproportionately impact the poor and the elderly, who may not have drivers' licenses or access to a location where they can obtain IDs. Additionally, the proposed database in which states can share voter identification information raises serious concerns about protecting Americans' private information."[72]

Others have commented that the voter identification card attempts to solve a problem that is almost non-existent, namely voter fraud. The problems associated with the 2000, 2002 and 2004 elections overwhelmingly involved fraud and/or incompetence by election officials.

Frederickson also criticizes the Commission for failing to follow a truly democratic process. For example, they held only two hearings and did not give the public the opportunity to comment. Open meetings would have allowed the civil rights concerns raised by the voter identification recommendation to be addressed, rather than discounted.[73]

Frederickson called on Congress to not only guarantee the right to vote, but also the right to privacy.

Additional recommendations (of a total of 87) by the Commission include putting control of voter registration lists in state, rather than local, hands, setting up uniform standards for counting provisional ballots, and moving towards the non-partisan administration of elections.[74] "Moving towards" could, of course, be a very slow process. Mandating non-

---

[72] *ACLU Questions Carter-Baker Voting Commission's Recommendations, September 19, 2005, http://aclu.org/VotingRights/VotingRights.cfm?ID=19100&c=32.*

[73] Ibid.

[74] *Online News Hour, Conversation: Carter and Baker, Margaret Warner, September 19, 2005, http://www.pbs.org/newshour/bb/politics/july-dec05/reform_9-19.html.*

partisan administration (as practiced in other western democracies) as soon as possible would be more appropriate.

It remains to be seen whether Congress will, in fact, act on any of the Commission's recommendations. Given the current dominance, in Congress, of those opposed to meaningful election reforms, it seems somewhat unlikely, thus possibly rendering the recommendations moot.

compassionate conservative: A Bush 2000 campaign slogan, claiming to be descriptive of Bush himself (as in *"I'm a compassionate conservative."*), that is both oxymoronic and untrue (although, as it's oxymoronic, it's untrue by definition). Bush has shown himself to be anything but compassionate (*see* **unfunded mandate**) and, in the traditional sense, not conservative. *See, also* **Barbour, Haley**.

George Bush revived the use of the term in the closing days of the 2004 presidential campaign.

compassionate conservativism: Notwithstanding the foregoing assertion of the oxymoronic qualities of *compassionate conservative,* the attempt to define compassionate conservatism in a *New York Times* editorial of December 28, 2003[75] is instructive:

> *"This, it appears, is what compassionate conservatism really means. The conservative part is a stern and sometimes intrusive government to regulate the citizenry, but with a hands-off attitude toward business. The compassionate end involves some large federal programs combined with unending sympathy for the demands of special interests. If only it all added up."*

Concerned Women for America (CWA): Organization founded by Beverly LaHaye, whose husband, Pastor Tim LaHaye, is the author of the *Left Behind* books, which are novels based on the fundamentalist "end times" doctrine. CWA's mission is *"to protect and promote Biblical values among all citizens — first through prayer, then education, and finally by influencing*

---

[75] *http://nytimes.com/2003/12/28/opinion/28SUN1.htm.*

our society—thereby reversing the decline in moral values in our nation." They have several core issues, of which the first is their definition of the family—*"one man and one woman, joined in marriage, along with any children they may have."* They seek to protect *"traditional values that support the Biblical design of the family."* Their position on marriage does not appear to respect diversity or any "traditional" marriages[76] that are not based on their view of the Christian bible, including those of other religions and cultures and of the non-religious. Their positions on reproductive choice, embryonic stem cell research, same-sex marriage (and homosexuality in general), and similar issues are of course very similar, if not identical, to those of other right wing organizations.

CWA has a legislative action committee and, on their website,[77] they maintain a "Vote Scorecard"[78] on both the Senate and the House of Representatives. As of mid-September, 2005, the individual results for nine Senate votes[79] and eight House votes[80] were tabulated. CWA awards a plus sign to those who vote as they recommend and a minus sign to those who vote the other way. For each member, the table shows the total number of pluses, the total number of minuses, and the pluses as a percentage of the total number of votes. Not surprisingly, almost all Republicans have a 100% score, with the majority of Democrats receiving a 0% score. The two independents from Vermont, Senator Jim Jeffords and Congressman Bernie Sanders,[81] also received a 0% score.

---

[76] An article by Nancy Haught on *Newhouse News Service* deals with the myth of the "traditional" marriage—*Experts: U.S. Marriage Model is Not Universal Norm, http://newhousenews.com/archive/haught050304.html.*

[77] *http://cwfa.org/main.*

[78] As do many organizations, both progressive and conservative. However, the CWA scorecard tabulates votes only on matters relating to CWA's core issues.

[79] *http://congress.cwfa.org/cwfa/scorecard/?chamber=S&session=109.*

[80] *http://congress.cwfa.org/cwfa/scorecard/?chamber=H&session=109.*

[81] Sanders will be a candidate for the Senate in 2006, hoping to replace the retiring Jim Jeffords.

conservative: Along with liberal, this is a term that has been distorted, for political purposes, by the right. Webster's defines the adjective as meaning disposed to preserve existing conditions, institutions, etc., and to agree with gradual rather than abrupt change. As a noun, it describes someone who is conservative in principle, actions, habits, etc.

In its distorted form, it has become a "respectable" code word for those who proudly and rigidly favor the pro-life (anti-choice) position, the death penalty (which would appear to contradict pro-life), militarism, mandatory school prayer, private/religious schools (or home schooling), the drug war, mandatory minimum sentencing laws, incarceration of drug addicts, etc., and who are intolerant of views that differ from their own. At least one person (*Ann Coulter*) who dons the conservative mantle regards those who disagree with those views as traitors.

Constitution: *See **U.S. Constitution**.*

contracts, no-bid: *See **no-bid contracts**.*

Cooney, Philip: Until his resignation on June 9, 2005, chief of staff for the White House Council on Environmental Quality, which is the office that devises and promotes Bush administration environmental policies.

Prior to his appointment in 2001, Cooney was a lawyer for the American Petroleum Institute, the oil industry's main lobby, where he fought restrictions on greenhouse gases. So his White House job was truly a case of the *fox guarding the hen house.*

Cooney had no scientific training. Nonetheless, he had been editing government climate reports in such a way as to cast doubt on the link between greenhouse gas emissions and global warming. A White House deputy press secretary, Dana Perino, claimed that his resignation was motivated by wanting to spend time with his family. If so, his timing was very odd.

Unfortunately, Cooney is only one of many people in the Bush administration who are cooking the books to favor various industries, at the expense of environmental quality and, thus, the health of many people.

Coulter, Ann: Possibly the most raving and virulent anti-liberal writer and commentator to ever emerge from the remote recesses of the far right. As a beneficiary of the largesse of the very right-wing **Richard Mellon Scaife**,[82] Coulter used to be referred to as a **Scaifette**. Some have alleged that the sales of her books owe much to massive block purchases by Scaife's organization.

> *Finally, we've decided that syndicated columnist Ann Coulter has worn out her welcome. Many readers find her shrill, bombastic and mean-spirited. And those are the words used by readers who identified themselves as conservatives.*
>
> *—David Stoeffler, Arizona Daily Star, August 28, 2005*[83]

Coulter's books include *Treason: Liberal Treachery from the Cold War to the War on Terrorism, Slander: Liberal Lies About the American Right*, and *How to Talk to a Liberal (If You Must): The World According to Ann Coulter.*

coulterisms: Outrageous statements by Ann Coulter. They include the following:

> *"Even Islamic terrorists don't hate America like* (sic) *Liberals do. They don't have the energy. If they had that much energy, they'd have indoor plumbing by now."*

> *"The good part of being a Democrat is that you can commit crimes, sell out your base, bomb foreigners, and rape women, and the Democratic faithful will still think you're the greatest."*

There is even an Ann Coulter Talking Action Figure,[84] which repeats one of seventeen coulterisms at each touch of a button.

---

[82] This may or may not still be true.

[83] *http://dailystar.com/dailystar/opinion/90500.php.*

[84] Available for $29.99 from *TalkingPresidents.com*. The Ann Coulter doll is one of two non-presidential dolls in their lineup; a Dennis Miller doll is the other.

Council for National Policy: Marc J. Ambinder, of ABC News, calls this group *"the most powerful conservative group you've never heard of."* They are very secretive and operate as a conservative version of the Council on Foreign Relations. They see themselves, according to a prominent member, as a self-selected counterweight against "liberal domination of the American agenda."[85]

Its members include (or have, in the past, included) *John Ashcroft* (former Attorney General), Tommy Thompson (former Health and Human Services Secretary), two end-of-the-world Christian theologists (John Ankerberg and Dave Breese), televangelist *Pat Robertson,* Don Wildmon (American Family Association), the late Christian reconstructionist,[86] Rousas J. Rushdoony, creationist Henry Morris, Phyllis Schlafly (of the Eagle Forum) and *Oliver North* (notorious for his role in the Iran-Contra scandal, and currently a talk show host).

Council of Conservative Citizens (CCC[87]): According to their own website,[88] *"The C of CC was founded as a non-profit organization to work for the rights and collective interests of true conservatives."*[89] Based on their record and most of their material, "true conservative" would appear to be code words for racist. Part of that material is the Confederate flag on their home page. Another part is an article on Martin Lu-

---

[85] *Vast, Right-Wing Cabal? Meet the Most Powerful Conservative Group You've Never Heard Of, Marc J. Ambinder, ABC News, http://abcnews.go.com/sections/politics/DailyNews/council_020501.html.*

[86] Christian Reconstructionists believe, among other things, that U.S. law should conform to Old Testament law and that homosexuals should be executed.

[87] Ironically, CCC also stands for Center for Community Change (*http://communitychange.org*), a progressive organization that, in its own words, *"is a non profit, nonpartisan social and economic justice organization helping low income and minority communities build powerful effective organizations through which they can change their communities and public policies for the better."*

[88] *http://cofcc.org.*

[89] Although, within the organization, they use the abbreviation "C of CC," many others usually refer them to them as "CCC." The similarity of the latter style to "KKK" is probably intentional.

ther King, Jr., which claims that the KGB financed him and that his speeches were written by a KGB agent. Yet another is their reference to homosexuals as queers,[90] which, while not actually racist, is an attitude that is certainly the philosophical sibling of racism.

In 1992, former Senate Majority Leader **Trent Lott** (R-MS) told CCC's members that they stood *"for the right principles and the right philosophy."* Six years later, he claimed to have no "personal knowledge" of the organization and repudiated their views.[91]

Others whose names, views and activities have been associated with the CCC include **Haley Barbour,** now the Republican Governor of Mississippi and former Republican Congressman Bob Barr.[92]

Cox, Christopher: Chairman of the Securities and Exchange Commission (SEC), replacing William Donaldson. He was nominated on June 2, 2005, one day after Donaldson announced his resignation. The Senate confirmed his appointment, unanimously, on August 3. Prior to his appointment, he was the Republican congressman from California's 48th District.

Cox's appointment is consistent with Bush's inclination to nominate those who support his corporate allies, often at the expense, in this case, of ordinary investors. It is seen by many as a victory for corporate lobbyists and the U.S. Chamber of Commerce, who were less than happy with

---

[90] It should be noted that, although many homosexuals and homosexual activist groups (e.g., Queer Nation) refer to themselves proudly and openly as queer, the term is used by homophobes as one of derision and condemnation.

[91] *Lott Renounces White 'Racialist' Group He Praised in 1992, Thomas B. Edsall, Washington Post, December 16, 1998, http://www.washingtonpost.com/wp-srv/ politics/daily/dec98/lott16.htm.*

[92] To his credit, since retiring from Congress, Bob Barr has been involved, as a consultant, in the American Civil Liberties Union's opposition to the **USA PATRIOT Act**. He gave a very moving speech on the subject to the 2004 ACLU Conference in San Francisco.

Donaldson's strict, by-the-rules treatment of corporate wrongdoers.[93]

Cruella de Vil: 1. Evil character in Disney's "101 Dalmatians." 2. *See* **Harris, Katherine.**

Cunningham, Randy "Duke": Former Republican congressman from California's 50th District[94] and the new poster child for political corruption, at least temporarily replacing his fellow Republican, *Tom DeLay*, who has yet to be tried, let alone convicted.

Cunningham resigned on November 28, 2005, after pleading guilty to receiving about $2.4 million in gifts (also known as bribes) from military contractors.

> *"Duke Cunningham is a hero. He is an honorable man of high integrity."*
>
> *— Tom Delay, June 14, 2005*

In calling Randy Cunningham a hero, Tom Delay was technically right. Whatever one's views about war in general and the Vietnam War in particular, there seems little doubt that Cunningham was one of the most skilled, fearless and successful naval fighter pilots, as recognized by the numerous medals he received during that conflict. Subsequently, he was an instructor at the famous *Top Gun* training school for fighter pilots and, according to some claims (including, especially, his own), the inspiration for Tom Cruise's character in the movie of the same name.[95]

---

[93] The issues surrounding criticism of Cox's appointment are quite complex and beyond the scope of this book. However, *Stock Split,* by Noam Scheiber, in the June 27 issue of The New Republic, does a very good job of explaining it. It is available online at *http://www.tnr.com/doc.mhtml?i=20050627&s=scheiber062705.* (A subscription may be required to view the article.)

[94] The 50th District is in Southern California. Cunningham's district office was in Escondido.

[95] This claim is denied by Jack Epps, Jr., who co-wrote the screenplay for Top Gun. He says, "Cruise's character wasn't based on any one real-life aviator." He says that neither he nor his co-writer even spoke to Cunningham during their research. Source: *Shooting Down Cunningham's Legend, Alex Roth, San*

In calling him an honorable man of high integrity, DeLay was well off the mark. For one thing, Cunningham was involved in the 1991 Tailhook scandal,[96] where over eighty women were stripped and/or required to run a gauntlet of leering, groping naval pilots—an exercise blamed by one investigator on the "Top Gun mentality" of the men involved.[97] Although his experience in the scandal and its aftermath should have been a wake-up call for Cunningham, regarding the roles and rights of women in the military, he tried, once he was in Congress, to block efforts to curb sexual harassment of military women.[98]

> *"Cunningham is a clumsy speaker burdened with a boorish personality. The Duke got by on implacable loyalty to his party and, more decisively, on blind obedience to his political patrons."*[99]
>
> —*Jeffrey St. Clair*

Cunningham was in his eighth term in Congress and was on the Defense Appropriations Committee, where he was in a position to do the bidding of those defense contractors who had bribed him. Two of them obtained contracts totaling over $240 million. His guilty plea, which was based on a plea bargain, finally netted him, on March 3, 2006, an eight year and four month sentence, with the possibility of a fifteen-month reduction for good behavior. This is the longest sentence ever imposed on an errant member of Congress. His conviction is almost certainly not the last, and may very well be just the first in a series. Some of his

---

Diego Union Tribune, January 15, 2006, http://www.signonsandiego.com/ uniontrib/20060115/news_lz1n15legend.html.

[96] The actual event was somewhat inappropriately named the "Tailhook Symposium."

[97] *Randy Cunningham's Crash Landing: The Duke and the Enterprise, Jeffrey St. Clair, Counterpunch, http://counterpunch.org/stclair11292005.html. (Excerpted from the first chapter of St. Clair's book, Grand Theft Pentagon, Common Courage Press.)*

[98] Ibid.

[99] Ibid.

former fellow members of Congress are either under investigation or under indictment (e.g., Tom Delay).

*See, also, **flag desecration amendment.***

Curveball: Codename for an Iraqi refugee in Germany, who was the chief source of U.S. intelligence, prior to the Iraq War, on Iraqi biological weapons. According to the former deputy director of operations and head of the clandestine service of the CIA, James L. Pavitt,[100] Curveball was unreliable.[101]

> *"My people were saying: 'we think he's a stinker.'"*
>
> —*James L. Pavitt, former CIA Deputy Director*

Despite Pavitt's view and the fact that the former chief of the CIA's European Division, Tyler Drumheller,[102] had issued repeated warnings about the credibility of Curveball's claims, Secretary of State Colin Powell vouched for those claims—that Saddam Hussein had secretly built lethal germ factories on trains and trucks—in his crucial address to the United Nations. Pavitt and Drumheller both claim to have warned both CIA Director George Tenet and his deputy, John McLaughlin, about Curveball's unreliability.[103] Tenet, who did not pass the warnings on to Powell, has denied that he was ever informed. The fact remains that Curveball was a single uncorroborated source.

CWA: *See **Concerned Women for America.***

---

[100] Pavitt retired in the Summer of 2004.

[101] *'Curveball' Debacle Reignites CIA Feud, Bob Drogin and Greg Miller, Common Dreams, http://commondreams.org/headlines05/0402-01.htm.*

[102] Drumheller retired in November 2004, after 25 years with the CIA.

[103] And, apparently, have a fair amount of documentation to back their claim.

D

D is for Difference, as in *"I am mindful of the difference between the executive branch and the legislative branch. I assured all four of these leaders that I know the difference, and that difference is they pass the laws and I execute them."*
—George Bush, Washington, DC, December 18, 2000
(Gubernatorial habits die hard.)

Defense Policy Board: This is a committee that was established to provide the Secretary of Defense and his Deputy Secretary and Under Secretary for Policy with independent, informed advice and opinion on major matters of defense policy. Membership consists of people from both the public and private sectors. Unfortunately, quite of few of the private sector members represent defense industry contractors, which inevitably skews the advice of those members in a manner that favors those contractors. *Richard Perle,* the former chairman and a *neoconservative,* resigned from that position in 2003, owing to a clear conflict of interest. In February of 2004, he resigned from the board altogether.[1]

Each of the following members represents companies whose defense contracts, in 2002 alone, totaled over $1 billion (per member).[2]

> **Ronald R. Fogleman**: Board member of eight companies, with 2002 defense contracts totaling just under $1.6 billion.

---

[1] According to his attorney, Samuel Abeday, Perle quit because he wanted to sue the news organizations that *"falsely accused him of conflicts of interest."* Source: *Perle Resigns, ABC News, http://abcnews.go.com/sections/wnt/Investigation/perle_resignation_04 0225.html.*

[2] *Corporate Affiliations of Defense Policy Board Members, The Center for Public Integrity, http://www.public-i.org/dtaweb/report.asp?ReportID=515.*

David Jeremiah: Chairman of Wackenhut Services and a board member, advisory board member or trustee of six other contractors, with total 2002 defense contracts of over $10 billion. Northrop Grumman, where Jeremiah serves on the advisory board, accounts for nearly $9 billion of that total.

Jack Sheehan: Senior Vice President, Bechtel, whose 2002 contracts totaled a little over $1 billion.

Chris Williams: Lobbyist for Boeing, Northrop Grumman and TRW, whose contracts were just over $17 billion, just under $9 billion and just over $2 billion, respectively.

Obviously, defense contractors are expected to do business with the Department of Defense. Taxpayers are justified in expecting them to secure that business purely on merit. Representing, lobbying or working for those contractors while serving on the Defense Policy Board is clearly a conflict of interest that makes it very difficult to provide dispassionate, unbiased advice.

The full name of the Defense Policy Board is Defense Policy Board Advisory Committee. It is sometimes shortened to Defense Advisory Board.

death tax: *See estate tax.*

DeLay, Tom: Former Republican Majority Leader in the House of Representatives and, before that, Majority Whip.

> *House Majority Leader Tom DeLay is hands-down one of the most corrupt politicians in the United States.*
>
> *— Katrina vanden Heuvel, Editor, Nation Magazine*

Delay, a former bug exterminator, is (or possibly was) the darling of the religious right, seeing himself as being *"on a mission from God to promote a 'biblical worldview' in American politics."* On March 8, 2004, according to that day's *Washington Times,* he was *"about to announce his own legislative agenda."*

In a party with an abundance of extremists, DeLay is the most extreme of all. An example of his extremism is his desire to bar the U.S. Supreme Court from reviewing acts of Congress.

On June 15, 2004, Congressman Chris Bell (D-TX) filed a 187-page complaint against DeLay with the House Committee on Standards of Official Conduct (usually known as the House Ethics Committee), alleging that in the preceding few months DeLay had violated the rules of the U.S. House of Representatives, the Federal bribery statute, and the campaign finance laws of Texas to advance his political interests in the state of Texas.[3] The Ethics Committee accepted the complaint for the customary 45-day review period and extended that period by another 45 days on July 23. In the end, it took until October for the Ethics Committee to make a decision and two announcements in a two-week period — admonishing him, first, on one of the counts in Chris Bell's complaint, then on two others. They deferred action on a further count that alleged fund-raising irregularities in DeLay's political action committee, because of an ongoing criminal investigation in Texas.

Congressman Bell lost his seat in Texas after DeLay pushed through a very undemocratic *redistricting* plan designed to ensure the election of Republicans. On a map, many of the new districts can be seen to be very long and narrow, which shows just how far DeLay was willing to go to ensure that each district would have a comfortable Republican majority.[4] Prior to Bell's complaint, Citizens for Responsibility and Ethics (CREW), a non-partisan group, filed a succession of complaints against DeLay.[5]

In 2003, through surrogates who included his daughter, DeLay set up an tax-exempt non-profit group called Cele-

---

[3] A summary of the complaint may be retrieved at *http://citizensforethics.org/ filelibrary/summary_delay2.pdf*.

[4] The ability to gerrymander districts this way provides a very strong argument for the elimination of the system in which voters are registered by party affiliation.

[5] *Tom DeLay's Amoral Code*, Katrina Vanden Heuvel, *The Nation*, June 29, 2004, *http://alternet.org/story/19080/*.

brations for Children, Inc. Large donors, whose names would not appear on the group's books, were promised access to DeLay, at parties, dinners and cruises, during the 2004 Republican Convention in New York. 75% of each donation would, indeed, go to charity. However, a whopping 25% was earmarked for the Convention events. DeLay's plans were foiled after a public outcry by New York Mayor, Michael Bloomberg, because DeLay wanted to house members of Congress, lobbyists and others on a luxury cruise ship, something Bloomberg said would draw more than $3 million away from New York businesses, especially hotels. Even before Bloomberg's decision, two watchdog groups, *Democracy 21* and the *Campaign Legal Center,* filed a complaint with the IRS, asking for Celebrations for Children, Inc.'s tax-exempt status to be disallowed on the grounds that DeLay was using it to raise prohibited soft money.[6]

On August 20, 2004, the Democratic Party chairmen in Texas (Charles Soechting) and California (Art Torres) called for the appointment by the House Ethics Committee of an independent counsel to investigate charges of criminal corruption against DeLay. Why an independent counsel? Fourteen of the fifteen Republican members of the Ethics Committee had taken money from Tom DeLay (raised by Tom DeLay's own PAC). Of the fourteen, the leading beneficiaries were Congressmen Kevin Brady and Sam Johnson of Texas (combined total of $10,545), and John Doolittle of California ($4,375).[7] Given their involvement with DeLay, the probability of their conducting an impartial and dispassionate examination of his transgressions was probably nil.

In May 2005, a Texas state judge ruled that the treasurer of TRMPAC (Texans for a Republican Majority Political Action Committee), which was founded by DeLay, violated Texas

---

[6] *Combustible DeLay May Be Low Key at RNC, Associated Press/ABC News,* http://abcnews.go.com/wire/Politics/ap20040829_1663.html.

[7] *Texas, California Leaders Call For Independent Counsel in House Ethics Committee Review of Corruption Charges Against Tom DeLay, Texas Democratic Party Press Release, August 20, 2004,* http://txdemocrats.org/news/detail/?id=226.

election law by failing to report nearly $700,000 in donations in 2002.[8] DeLay was not mentioned in the ruling and, when asked, he said that it had no implications for him, as he was not "part of it." Given that, along with some advisers, he was the founder of TRMPAC and had been involved in raising funds from TRMPAC donors, his optimism turns out to have been misplaced. Five defeated state Democratic candidates, who had brought the lawsuit on which the judge ruled, were awarded a total of almost $200,000 in damages. A separate criminal case came to a head on September 28, 2005, when DeLay was indicted on one count of criminal conspiracy in a case of alleged campaign money laundering.[9] Specifically, it appears that a total of $190,000 in corporate contributions was made to TRMPAC. Subsequently TRMPAC made a number of contributions to the Texas arm of the Republican National Committee (RNC-TX). In turn, TRMPAC made contributions totaling $190,000 to the campaigns of five Republican candidates for the Texas legislature. Through this scheme, the candidates' campaigns were beneficiaries of corporate contributions, which is illegal under Texas law. Their successful campaigns gave Republicans a majority in the Texas house following the 2002 state elections, enabling them to push through DeLay's redistricting plans for Texas, which eventually increased the Republican majority in the U.S. House of Representatives in the 2004 federal elections.

Because of the indictment, DeLay was forced to step down as House Majority Leader, a position filled on an acting basis by another arch-conservative, Missouri Congressman and Majority Whip Roy Blunt (R-MO), then by *John Boehner* (R-OH), who was chosen by his House colleagues over Roy Blunt on February 2, 2006.

---

[8] *Treasurer of DeLay Group Broke Texas Election Law, Sylvia Moreno and R. Jeffrey Smith, Washington Post, May 27, 2005, http://www.washingtonpost.com/wp-dyn/content/article/2005/05/26/ AR2005052600875.html.*

[9] Followed, one week later, by another indictment by second grand jury. A judge ruled against the criminal conspiracy indictment, but the more serious money laundering indictments remained.

DeLay's problems didn't end there, given that one of his "closest and dearest friends" (DeLay's own words), lobbyist *Jack Abramoff*, was indicted on several counts, on three of which he pleaded guilty, resulting in a prison sentence of five years and ten months. Having made a deal with the prosecutors, he has been spilling the beans regarding everyone in Congress, including Tom Delay, with whom he was involved.

On April 4, 2006, DeLay finally did the right thing, announcing that he was withdrawing his name from the ballot for the November mid-term election. As Texas law doesn't allow his name to be removed from the ballot unless he dies, is convicted of a felony, or leaves the state, and as the first is unlikely and the second probably won't happen before November, he decided to use his Virginia address as his official residence. He also announced his plans to resign in June 2006.

See, also, **Marc Racicot**.

DeMint, James: Republican U.S. Senator from South Carolina. He was elected in 2004, replacing the retiring Democratic Senator, Fritz Hollings. He is a supporter of regressive taxation, believing that the IRS (and, therefore, federal income tax) should be eliminated and replaced with a 23% national sales tax (on **all** goods and services).[10] It doesn't take a genius to see that this would be an enormous benefit to the wealthy and the upper middle class, and an equally enormous burden for the poor and the rest of the middle class. His views on other social issues are equally regressive. He believes that neither gays nor single mothers living with their boyfriends should be allowed to teach in public schools, although he has defensively claimed that that is only a personal position, rather than issues he could or would deal with in Congress. He is in favor of banning all abortions, with no exceptions for rape, incest, health, or threat to the pregnant woman's life. It should come as no surprise that he believes that same sex marriage is a threat

---

[10] *Studio QB: Famous Quotations by Jim DeMint, http://www.studioqb .com/quotes/author/Jim-DeMint.html.*

to traditional marriage. Unfortunately for equal rights, neither he nor other Republicans are alone in that view. Some Democrats in Congress are apparently afraid any other position will lose them votes in the next election.

Department of Homeland Security (DHS): A cabinet-level agency consolidating 22 existing agencies whose existing functions related to various aspects of the nation's security. It was established in November 2002, following the passage of the Homeland Security Act, and activated on January 24, 2003. Initially, the Secretary of DHS was former Pennsylvania Governor Tom Ridge, whose performance turned out to be somewhat less than spectacular. Ridge resigned at the end of George Bush's first term and was replaced by *Michael Chertoff*, formerly a Bush-appointed circuit court judge.[11]

In late 2003, under Tom Ridge's leadership, immigration officers were, without notification to foreign media outlets of any new requirements, detaining and deporting journalists who arrived in the U.S. without special visas. They did so, even for those journalists from countries whose citizens can stay in the U.S. for up to 90 days when arriving either as tourists or on business. As if that were not outrageous enough, they were treated like criminals and were marched through airports in handcuffs, photographed and fingerprinted, and required to provide a DNA sample.[12,13] Apparently, journalists have required visas for a long time; however, owing to the absence of any enforcement (before 9/11), it's a fair assumption that many journalists were not even aware of the requirement.[14]

---

[11] Third Circuit Court of Appeals, Philadelphia, PA.

[12] *A repressive embarrassment, Toledo Blade editorial, December 13, 2003,* http://toledoblade.com/apps/pbcs.dll/artikkel?SearchID=73156767336 87&Avis=TO&Dato=20031213&Kategori=OPINION02&Lopenr=11213015 9&Ref=AR.

[13] *Coffee, Tea or Handcuffs? An Australian journalist gets a taste of Department of Homeland Security hospitality, Steve Mikulan, LA Weekly, December 19-25, 2003,* http://laweekly.com/ink/04/04/open-mikulan.php.

[14] The U.S. Statement Department specifies the requirements at http://travel.state.gov/visa/temp/types/types_1276.html.

DHS inherited, from John Ashcroft's Justice Department, the much parodied and often abused color-coded terror threat alerts. Correlation is not necessarily causation, but the timing of alerts was, from the start, very suspicious, and didn't become less so when DHS took them over. An elevation in the national threat level from yellow to orange (the second highest level) seemed to coincide with news that either depressed or threatened to depress Bush's poll ratings, which would then recover somewhat in the days following the level change. The five levels, with their redundant comments (in three cases) are:

5. Red: SEVERE—Severe risk

4. Orange: HIGH—High risk

3. Yellow: ELEVATED—Significant risk

2. Blue: GUARDED—General risk

1. Green: LOW—Low risk

The numbers have been added. For some reason (or possibly no reason), DHS does not assign a number to each level.

The fact that there have never been guidelines for determining the relationship between a threat and the alert level to be declared led even Tom Ridge to question its usefulness. It is now used very little, and then only for regional threats, which avoid alarming the entire U.S. population. However, the approach of the 2006 mid-term elections means that politically motivated threat-level changes are not entirely unlikely.

In the meantime, the list of ways in which DHS is failing to protect the nation is a long one. For example, only a small fraction of cargo containers arriving in U.S. ports are checked for explosives and other dangerous contraband (e.g., chemical or biological weapons). DHS says that it screens all cargo containers and inspects those that are "high risk." However, it does not say what criteria are used to determine what is and what is not high risk. They claim that they use intelligence and a risk-based strategy to screen information on all cargo before it is loaded. Screening information on cargo (which is not the same as screening the actual cargo) is susceptible to fraud and to honest error. The usual asymmetry applies, in that terrorists only need to be successful now and then. In the ideal situation, DHS has to be 100% successful. The DHS budget for port security in 2005 was $1.6 billion. That seems like a great deal of money. However, it is only $4.4 million per day. Given the number of U.S. ports and the amount of cargo flowing through them, it seems hopelessly inadequate. Transferring a tiny fraction of the military budget[15] to DHS could make an enormous difference.

To continue with the list, airline passenger luggage is examined while air cargo is mostly unchecked; nuclear power stations and chemical plants have no protection; the border patrol is woefully understaffed;[16] airport security is constantly breached by those assigned to test its effectiveness; and on and on. Despite his many apparent shortcomings, neither the current DHS Secretary, Michael Chertoff, nor his predecessor, Tom Ridge, can be held wholly responsible for the situation. Bush and Congress, while having allocated close to $300 billion to Iraq, have underfunded DHS.

Two of DHS's most controversial agencies are the Transportation Security Administration (TSA) and the Federal Emergency Management Agency (*see* **FEMA**). Travelers showing up at airline check-in counters are often surprised to find that they are on the TSA's "no-fly" list. They don't know how they got there and they don't know how to have their names removed. More than likely, they have the same name as someone regarded as suspicious by TSA. Those on the list are subjected to questions by security personnel before

---

[15] Much of the military budget (which is equal to that of all other countries combined) is wasted on weapons (e.g., missiles with nuclear warheads, certain types of aircraft, etc.) designed for an unthinkable all-out war between superpowers (the Cold War "balance of terror"). Much of it also appears to be wasted on excessive prices charged by defense contractors.

[16] Those crossing the Mexico/US border for economic reasons pose no security threat, but there is no way to tell how many who cross the border have merely passed through Mexico in order to enter the United States to commit terrorist acts.

they are allowed to get a boarding pass. Those on a second "selectee" list have their boarding passes stamped with an S, and are subjected to further questioning when they arrive at the departure gate. Some from either category can be denied boarding. Under the Freedom of Information Act (FOIA), the Electronic Privacy Information Center (EPIC) has, since 2002, been demanding (and receiving, albeit in redacted form) information on how watch lists are put together and how names are selected for those lists.[17] For example, does membership in activist groups (including peace groups) put one in a suspect category? What about critics of government policy? Very little of the information EPIC has received provides real answers, so they have drawn up a new list of questions, namely:

- How many people are on the "no fly" and "selectee" lists? How many are American citizens or legal permanent residents?
- Who is responsible for oversight of the list? Who verifies that the names are selected appropriately and whether the information is accurate?
- How does the operation of the watch lists comply with the Privacy Act of 1974?
- How effective have the watch lists been?
- How can those who have been misidentified as watch list matches clear their names?
- Why is there a need for a new passenger prescreening program if intelligence agencies are already coordinating to ensure that certain high risk individuals on government watch lists do not board planes?
- How will Secure Flight[18] respect people's due process rights?

---

[17] *Documents Show Errors in TSA's "No Fly" and "Selectee" Watch Lists, Electronic Privacy Information Center, http://epic.org/privacy/airtravel/ foia/watchlist_foia_analysis.html.*

[18] "Secure Flight" is the proposed prescreening program.

disassemble: Take apart, as in "He disassembled the entire mechanism." However, in Bush's vocabulary, disassemble appears to have an entirely different meaning.

> *"It seemed like to me they based some of their decisions on the word of—and the allegations—by people who were held in detention, people who hate America, people that had been trained in some instances to disassemble—that means not tell the truth."*
>
> *—George W. Bush, May 31, 2005 Press Conference*

His meaning may, of course, be applicable to him.

distortion: This is the stock in trade of the Bush administration. Highlighting many of the administration's distortions is a report,[19] issued by the Union of Concerned Scientists on February 18, 2004. It was put together by a group of about 60 influential scientists, including 20 Nobel laureates and a number of National Medal of Science recipients. In it, they say that the Bush administration has deliberately and systematically distorted scientific fact in the service of policy goals on the environment, health, biomedical research and nuclear weaponry at home and abroad. They specifically accuse the administration of repeatedly censoring and suppressing its own scientists' reports, stacking advisory committees with unqualified political appointees, rather than experts, disbanding government panels that have provided unwanted advice (i.e., advice not congruent with the administration's political or contributor-rewarding objectives), and in some cases, refusing to seek independent scientific advice. They note that, although other administrations have sometimes engaged in such practices, none has done so in such a systematic and wide-ranging manner. Scott McClellan, the White House spokesman, provided an assurance that *"... this is an administration that makes decisions based on the best available science."*

---

[19] *Scientific Integrity in Policymaking: An Investigation into the Bush administration's Misuse of Science.*

Whom do we believe? George Bush's mouthpiece or sixty or so highly reputable scientists? The report took about a year to prepare and was released as soon as it was ready. Any claims, therefore, that it was put together to coincide with the Democratic Primaries would not be credible.

A summary of the report can be found on the website of the Union of Concerned Scientists.[20] The full 46-page report can be downloaded from the same site.[21]

Specific distortions by the Bush administration include the *Clear Skies Initiative,* which allows polluters to regulate themselves (with the inevitable result that the skies become less clear) and the *Healthy Forests Initiative,* which apparently seeks to improve the health of forests by allowing the logging industry to cut them down without restriction.

See, also, **lies.**

dittohead: One who unquestioningly accepts the word of *Rush Limbaugh* as incontrovertible fact.

Dobson, James: Founder and leader of Focus on the Family. Dobson was also the founder of the *Family Research Council.* As one might expect, as a leader of a religious right organization, he espouses all the extreme positions of the religious right and is, therefore, dedicated to undermining the Establishment Clause of the First Amendment (*see Bill of Rights*). Although he's often referred to as Dr. Dobson (and does, indeed, have a doctorate), he is not a minister. In spite of this, people sometimes mistakenly address him as Reverend Dobson.

> *Dobson has warned politicians of all stripes that their jobs will be in jeopardy if they fail to submit to his demands.*
>
> *—Jeremy Leaming, Americans United, February 2005*[22]

---

[20] *http://www.ucsusa.org/global_environment/rsi/page.cfm?pageID=1322.*

[21] *http://www.ucsusa.org/documents/RSI_final_fullreport.pdf*

[22] *James Dobson: The Religious Right's 800-Pound Gorilla, Jeremy Leaming, Americans United for Separation of Church and State, February 2005, http://www.au.org/site/News2?page=NewsArticle&id=7195.*

Richard Viguerie, the Republican direct-mail guru, credited Dobson with getting large numbers of evangelicals to the polls in the 2004 election.[23] At the same time as he was getting out the evangelical vote, Dobson was warning (and still warns, in anticipation of the 2006 mid-term elections) George Bush to appoint only "strict constructionist" judges to the judiciary and promised "a battle of enormous proportions" if Bush fails to do so or if Democrats filibuster against such nominees.

Dobson is clearly a danger to the First Amendment and, thus, to democracy and secular government. Unsurprisingly, Bush considers him a valuable ally.

door, revolving: *See revolving door.*

Dover, Delaware: This is where the flag-draped coffins arrive, containing the bodies of American servicemen and women killed in Afghanistan and Iraq (and elsewhere). It has been the focus of many complaints, especially by next of kin, because the Bush administration will not allow the news media to photograph or videotape the incoming coffins. The excuse they have provided, that to do so would violate privacy, rings hollow, for the very simple reason that flag-draped coffins provide complete anonymity. The argument in favor of letting the public see the coffins (as they have during past conflicts) is that they will have a frequent reminder of the cost, in lives, of the invasion and occupation of Iraq.

Downing Street Memo: The "Memo" is the minutes a meeting held, on July 23, 2002, by British Prime Minister *Tony Blair*. It, and other documents subsequently leaked, provide hard evidence of the truth behind the Iraq War. That truth is not favorable to any of the key figures, including Blair himself, George Bush, *Donald Rumsfeld* and others.

---

[23] Ibid.

> *"C reported on his recent talks in Washington. There was a perceptible shift in attitude. Military action was now seen as inevitable. Bush wanted to remove Saddam, through military action, justified by the conjunction of terrorism and WMD.* **But the intelligence and facts were being fixed around the policy.** *The NSC had no patience with the UN route, and no enthusiasm for publishing material on the Iraqi regime's record. There was little discussion in Washington of the aftermath after military action."*
>
> *—From the Downing Street Memo,*
> *Matthew Rycroft,[24] July 23, 2002[25]*

Many progressives had pointed out (mostly on the Internet) that the fix was in with respect to the intelligence, especially with its very selective use. Their position was more than vindicated by the memo and subsequently released (or leaked) documents.

Dubya: One of the less insulting of George W. Bush's nicknames, based on the Texas pronunciation of his middle initial. *See also* **Smirking Chimp** *and* **Village Idiot.**

dubyanomics: Economics, Bush style, in which massive tax cuts for the very wealthy supposedly benefit everyone through the creation of new jobs. In the Reagan era, this was known as trickle-down economics. In the 1980 presidential primaries, Bush's father referred to such theories as *voodoo economics,* a position he abandoned when, having lost the primaries to Reagan, he agreed to be Reagan's running mate.

Bush claims that his tax cuts help the small businessman. Unfortunately, the small businessman who is materially helped is a very wealthy person with a small business on the side (or any wealthy person who is required to submit Schedule C in his or her federal income tax filing).

---

[24] Private Secretary to Tony Blair; subsequently appointed as UK Ambassador to Bosnia-Herzegovina.

[25] *The secret Downing Street memo, Secret And Strictly Personal—UK Eyes Only, David Manning, Times Online, May 1, 2005, http://www.timesonline.co.uk/ article/0,,2087-1593607,00.html.*

E

E is for Enduring, as in *"For a century and a half now, America and Japan have formed one of the great and enduring alliances of modern times."*
—George Bush, Tokyo, Japan, February 18, 2002
(Apart from a minor disagreement in the 1940s.)

Earl, Robert: Chief of staff of acting Deputy Defense Secretary, Gordon England. Given Earl's background in government service, this is an appalling appointment.

In November 1986, Earl worked for Lt. Col. *Oliver North*, at which time he destroyed and stole national security documents relating to the Arms for Hostages and Iran-Contra scandals. Earl was granted immunity for his testimony when North and others were tried for their role in the scandals. North was convicted, although the conviction was overturned on the basis of immunity that had been granted when he testified before Congress.[1]

"… this is a job that should be filled by someone who is beyond reproach."
—*Mary Boyle, Common Cause*[2]

The problem with Earl's appointment is that he is, once more, overseeing classified national security documents, this time in a senior position.

economics, voodoo: *See voodoo economics.*

enemy combatant (also unlawful combatant): An arbitrary classification that, at the time of its first use, had no recognized legal definition. George Bush and former Attorney General John Ashcroft used it to hold people indefinitely,

---

[1] *Pentagon confirms Iran Contra figure in senior job, Reuters, July 11, 2005, http://news.yahoo.com/s/nm/20050711/pl_nm/arms_irancontra_dc.*
[2] Ibid.

with no access to a lawyer and no formal charge against them. By this means, they made an end run around the justice system and normal due process—in apparent violation of the U.S. Constitution and, in the case of those apprehended elsewhere and brought to the U.S., of international law.

Kenneth Roth, Executive Director of Human Rights Watch, has said, *"There should be a strong presumption that anyone arrested in the United States, far from any battlefield, be granted the full legal protections of the criminal justice system—including the right to counsel and not to be held without charges. Simply accusing someone of working with Al Qaeda does not justify throwing him into a navy brig."* He was talking about the case of Abdullah al Mujahir, formerly (and better) known as José Padilla, who is a U.S. citizen. Human Rights Watch has contrasted the Padilla case, in which the detainee is a material witness (or was so considered at the time of his arrest), with that of Zacarias Moussaoui, the presumed "twentieth highjacker," who was prosecuted in Federal court on criminal charges.[3] In April 2005, a South Carolina trial judge ruled that Bush had overstepped his bounds by detaining Padilla for over three years. Unfortunately for Padilla, on September 9, 2005, a three-judge panel of the Fourth Circuit U.S. Court of Appeals unanimously overturned the lower court's decision, on the grounds that, after September 11, 2001, Congress had given Bush such powers. Padilla will still be entitled to a hearing, but the nature of that hearing will almost certainly be the subject of litigation.[4] Padilla's lawyer announced that he would appeal the circuit court's ruling. In the meantime (since September 9, 2005), the Justice Department brought new charges against Padilla, completely unrelated to the original reason for his

---

[3] Source: *Human Rights News (Human Rights Watch): U.S. Circumvents Courts With Enemy Combatant Tag, June 12, 2002, http://www.hrw.org/ press/2002/06/us0612.htm.*

[4] *Court Gives Bush Right to Detain U.S. Combatant, Neil A. Lewis, New York Times, September 10, 2005, http://nytimes.com/2005/09/10/politics/ 10padilla.html.*

arrest. A Florida grand jury indicted him in November 2005. The Bush administration then made a request to transfer him to civilian custody. The Fourth U.S. Circuit Court of Appeals denied that request, on the grounds that the administration had used one set of facts to hold Padilla without charges for over three years and another to convince the grand jury to indict him. Judge J. Michael Luttig, who wrote the court's opinion, said that the administration had risked its credibility, as it appeared to be trying to avoid having the U.S. Supreme Court review the extent of Bush's power to hold enemy combatants without charge.[5]

> *"These impressions have been left, we fear, at what may ultimately prove to be a substantial cost to the government's credibility before the courts, to whom it will one day need to argue again in support of a principle of assertedly like importance and necessity to the one that it seems to abandon today. While there could be an objective that could command such a price as all of this, it is difficult to imagine what that objective would be."*
>
> *—Judge J. Michael Luttig,*
> *Fourth U.S. Circuit Court of Appeals*

People continue to be held as presumed enemy combatants, especially at **Camp Delta**. How one can fairly determine, without a proper hearing, that someone is, in fact, an enemy combatant (as opposed to simply being someone who was in the wrong place at the wrong time) has never been satisfactorily answered.

In the 2004 offensive against the Iraqi city of Falluja, those remaining in the city at the time of the attack were deemed to be enemy combatants. In that attack, U.S. troops used white phosphorus, which burns on contact with the air and continues to do so until deprived of oxygen or until it has burned completely. When used against people, it can cause horrifying burns that go all the way to the bone. Lt. Col.

---

[5] *Appeals Court Refuses to Transfer Padilla*, Tony Locy, Associated Press, http://www.forbes.com/work/feeds/ap/2005/12/21/ap2409041.html.

Barry Venable, U.S. Army, told the BBC that the phosphorus was used against enemy combatants, though not against civilians, which is a distinction without a difference, given that the enemy combatant designation is completely arbitrary and can be applied to anyone, including civilians. There is an international treaty, to which the U.S. is regrettably not a signatory, restricting the use of white phosphorus against civilians.[6] Col. Venable made another distinction without much of a difference, claiming that white phosphorus was not a banned chemical weapon. It may not be banned, but it is a chemical and is usable as a weapon.[7] Another appalling aspect is that the official line was initially that the white phosphorus had only been used for illumination, which is indeed one of its common uses. It was only when the facts were revealed in the Italian media that its use against people was admitted.

energy policy: *See Energy Task Force.*

Energy Task Force: Very soon after his inauguration, George Bush established his Energy Task Force,[8] with Vice President *Dick Cheney* as its chairman. One can argue that there is nothing improper in assigning such a role to the Vice President. However, one can equally well argue that any task force chairman, whether or not he is Vice President of the United States, is obliged to follow all the rules applicable to Federal Government task forces. The rules, enumerated in the Federal Advisory Committee Act (FACA), require the observance of two fundamental standards: balanced membership and open meetings.

The Energy Task Force was an *ad hoc* one, rather than a continuing one. However, FACA states that, whether a task force is *ad hoc* or continuing, the President must include, in a report to be submitted to Congress by December 31 of

---

[6] *US used white phosphorus in Iraq, BBC News World Edition, November 16, 2005, http://news.bbc.co.uk/2/hi/middle_east/4440664.stm.*

[7] Its primary tactical purpose is usually to provide illumination or create a smoke screen.

[8] Correctly known as the *"National Energy Policy Development Group."*

each year, *"… the dates of its meetings, the names and occupations of its current members …"* The only exception is, not surprisingly, for national security, but even then, the report must contain a statement that such information is excluded.

Section 6 of the Act requires that *"agencies and advisory committees shall make available to any person, at actual cost of duplication, copies of transcripts of agency proceedings or advisory committee meetings."* Presumably, such transcripts would be expected to include the names of all who were in attendance (or, at the very least, those who had anything to say at a meeting), i.e., not just the regular task force members. The Act makes an exception for committees formed prior to its passage, where they may be subject to existing contractual agreements. As the Act was passed in 1972, the Energy Task Force hardly qualifies. Interestingly, no exception is made for task forces or committees consisting solely of government employees or other public servants, notwithstanding Dick Cheney's *ex post facto* claim to the contrary.

Apart from a commonsense exemption for local and civic groups, FACA exempts only two organizations from its rules: the CIA and the Federal Reserve System.

With respect to bias, FACA requires *"appropriate provisions to assure that the advice and recommendations of the advisory committee will not be inappropriately influenced by the appointing authority or by any special interest."*

Finally, no exceptions are made for the Executive Branch. The Act points out that its guidelines *"shall be followed by the President, agency heads, or other Federal officials in creating an advisory committee."*

To summarize, Federal Advisory Committees and task forces must:

- Have balanced membership
- Have open meetings and provide adequate notice of those meetings

- Make meeting transcripts available to anyone who asks (meaning that they must keep minutes)

- Avoid inappropriate influence

As is now well known, the Energy Task Force failed to meet those standards. As is also well known, Dick Cheney has successfully stonewalled all attempts aimed at getting the task force documents released. Finally, an energy bill that was passed in 2005 (minus some of the task force's recommendations), in addition to having massive amounts of pork associated with it, provides massive subsidies to oil and coal companies, despite the fact that one oil company CEO has been honest enough to say that they have such enormous profits, they don't know what to do with them.[9]

On the subject of oil company CEOs, five of them[10] answered questions before a joint meeting of the Senate Energy and Commerce committees on November 9, 2005. The very crusty Senator Ted Stevens (R-AK), who refused to hear a motion for the executives to answer questions under oath, chaired the meeting. When asked if their companies had participated in the energy task force, every one of the five said either that they had not or that they had no knowledge of such participation.

A week later, Senator Frank Lautenberg (D-NJ) called on the Justice Department to investigate whether the five provided false testimony. He and seven other Democratic Senators asked the Republican leaders to bring the executives back for another hearing.[11] The justification was a White House document obtained since the meeting, by the *Washington Post,* that shows that officials from four of the oil

---

[9] For information on oil company profits for 2004, see *http://democrats.org/a/2005/05/record_prices_r.php.*

[10] From BP America, Chevron, ConocoPhillips, Exxon-Mobil and Shell.

[11] *Democrats Want Oil Officials Back, Richard Simon, LA Times, November 17, 2005, http://www.latimes.com/news/nationworld/nation/la-na-oil17nov17,1,3455344. story?coll=la-headlines-nation.*

companies represented there did indeed meet with Cheney aides who were developing the national energy policy. Separately, the Government Accountability Office has said that the fifth oil company, Chevron, also gave "detailed energy recommendations" to the task force.

Perhaps the backroom shenanigans will finally be exposed. On the other hand, though, the very powerful Ted Stevens is unwilling to call the executives back to testify under oath. It would seem to be time for the Justice Department to step up to the plate.

Establishment Clause: *See* ***Bill of Rights*** *and* ***church/state separation.***

estate tax: The tax levied on estates whose value exceeds $2 million ($1.5 million prior to 2006). George Bush, with the support of most Republicans in the House and Senate, has called for its elimination.

The arguments for elimination, which start by disingenuously referring to it as the "death tax,"[12] are loaded with misinformation, not the least of which is the claim that the tax has led to the loss of family businesses, including farms. This is complete nonsense, as there is no record of a family business being lost as a result of such a tax payment. Most such families are not even subject to the tax. Those who are pay tax only on the excess over the exemption, and do so at an average rate ranging, typically, from 1.6% to 7.5%, with 40% of them at the low end of that range.[13] The revised exemption, in 2006, reduces this and, for some, eliminates the tax altogether. For those who continue to operate their businesses for at least ten years, the taxable amount of the estate can be reduced by anything from 40% to 70%.[14] Moreover, if the value of the business is at least 35% of the

---

[12] Just one more Republican talking point, regurgitated on cue by the more conservative talking heads (e.g., Kate O'Beirne) on TV.

[13] *Estate Tax Malarkey: Misleading ads exaggerate what the tax costs farmers, small businesses and "your family,"* FactCheck.org, *http://factcheck.org/article328m.html.*

[14] Ibid.

total estate, tax payments can be spread over fourteen years.[15]

Another argument is that the tax is an example of double taxation. Although this is true in some cases, in most cases the tax is on thus-far unrealized capital gains (which would be taxed when sold, anyway).[16]

The real reason for repeal of both the estate tax and dividend taxes would appear to be that the primary constituency of George Bush and his Republican colleagues consists of the very wealthy, who are, of course, big contributors. Although the wealthiest of them might be subject to some tens of millions of dollars in estate taxes, their after-tax wealth would still be in the hundreds of millions—hardly a needy or disadvantaged segment of the population. However, repeal of the estate tax would represent a fantastic return on investment for their campaign contributions.

Evans, Donald: Secretary of Commerce during Bush's first term of office.

extraordinary rendition: Put very bluntly, this is the outsourcing of torture. On the slightest suspicion of even the most tenuous association with terrorism or terrorists (often in the total absence of actual evidence), the U.S. government has been shipping ("rendering") people, for interrogation, to countries that are known to practice torture.[17]

> *"They are outsourcing torture because they know it's illegal. Why, if they have suspicions, don't they question people within the boundary of the law?"*
>
> *—Maher Arar, Canadian*

On September 26, 2002, then 34-year-old Maher Arar, who is a Canadian, an engineer, and a graduate of Montreal's McGill University, was returning to Canada, with a change of plane at New York's JFK Airport, from Tunisia, where he

---

[15] Ibid.

[16] Ibid.

[17] Syria, Egypt, Morocco, Jordan, Uzbekistan, and others.

had been visiting relatives.[18] To his surprise, he was told that he was on the U.S. Watch List of suspected terrorists and was arrested on the spot. After thirteen days, during which he was questioned about possible links to someone else on the list,[19] he was, with no formal charges, shackled and taken aboard an executive jet on which he was transported via a circuitous route to Amman, Jordan. From there he was taken by car to Syria, where he was put in a windowless underground cell and repeatedly tortured. Eventually, just to end the pain, he told his torturers what they wanted to hear.[20] His nightmare ended in October 2003. The Canadian government had taken up his cause, as a result of which the Syrian Ambassador to the U.S. said that his country had found no links between Arar and terrorism. The motivation of the Canadian government may be somewhat suspect (or at least inconsistent) because, prior to Arar's "rendition," they were informed of the plan to send him to Syria; they approved that plan.[21]

On January 22, 2004, Arar filed a lawsuit against the U.S. government, seeking financial compensation and a declaration that the U.S. acted illegally.[22] The lawsuit named, as defendants, then Attorney General **John Ashcroft**, then Secretary of Homeland Security, Tom Ridge, and FBI Director Robert Mueller. Since then, the U.S. government has released only highly censored documents. The Canadian government, also the subject of a lawsuit by Arar, followed

---

[18] Source: *Outsourcing Torture: The secret history of America's "extraordinary rendition" program, Jane Mayer, The New Yorker, February 14, 2005, http://www.newyorker.com/fact/content/?050214fa_fact6.* This is a comprehensive and well-researched article, far greater in scope than can be accommodated in a single entry in this book.

[19] He had once worked with the other person's brother, but otherwise he barely knew him. Obviously, it's quite probable that Arar was on the list solely on the basis of having worked with the brother.

[20] A typical outcome, illustrative of just how useless torture is as a means of discovering the truth.

[21] *60 Minutes II, CBS, January 21, 2004.*

[22] *Arar launches lawsuit against U.S. government, Canadian Broadcasting Corporation, January 22, 2004, updated January 24, 2004, http://www.cbc.ca/stories/2004/01/22/ararsuit040122*

suit until April 21, 2005, when they released over 2000 pages of email messages, memos and handwritten notes to a public inquiry. The documents, including memos written by the Canadian ambassador to Syria, Franco Pillarella, show that the Canadian government was quite happy to benefit from the alleged fruits of Arar's torture. According to other documents, Canada had enough exculpatory information at the time of Arar's "rendition," to allow it to intervene and prevent it from occurring.[23]

Maher Arar is only one of about 150 people caught up in the "extraordinary rendition" program. In July 2005, an interesting memo came to light. It was sent on November 27, 2002, to a senior FBI lawyer by an FBI agent, who happens to be a former New York City prosecutor, and makes the case that even discussing a plan to have detainees interrogated in a country known to practice torture "could be seen as a conspiracy to violate" the U.S. torture statute and that everyone involved could be subject to prosecution.[24,25] As renditions take place on the basis of an executive order issued by George Bush, this could in theory have serious consequences for him.

---

[23] *Documents suggest Canadian involvement in Arar interrogation, CBC News, April 22, 2005, http://www.cbc.ca/story/canada/national/2005/04/21/arar050421.html.*

[24] *Exclusive: Secret Memo—Send to Be Tortured, Michael Issikof, Newsweek, August 8, 2005, http://www.msnbc.msn.com/id/8769416/site/newsweek.*

[25] The FBI has pointed out that the memo is not an "official FBI memo" (and is, therefore, not an official FBI opinion). However, the fact that its author is a former prosecutor adds credibility to its substance.

F

> F is for Fatal, as in *"For every fatal shooting, there were roughly three non-fatal shootings. And, folks, this is unacceptable in America. It's just unacceptable. And we're going to do something about it."*
> —George Bush, Philadelphia, May 14, 2001
> (Teach people to aim better?)

FACA: Federal Advisory Committee Act. This is the act governing committees and task forces, such as Dick Cheney's *Energy Task Force.*

Faith-based Initiative: *See Towey, Jim.*

Falwell, Jerry: Fundamentalist Christian evangelist, who founded the Moral Majority in 1979 and led it until two years before its dissolution in 1989. Until the onset of health problems, Falwell was a frequent guest on TV talk and debate shows (e.g., CNN's now-discontinued Crossfire), on which he showed himself to be incredibly pompous and insufferably rude (often talking, out of turn, over whoever was there to represent the opposing position). He frequently asserted that global warming was a myth (leading a fellow Guest, Lynn Redgrave, on Bill Maher's old *Politically Incorrect* show, to inquire as to whether he was getting enough fiber in his diet[1]). Falwell is also a strong supporter of right-wing Republican causes, such as coercive prayer in schools (misleadingly referred to as "voluntary prayer"— something that is, of course, already permitted under current law and the U.S. Constitution), opposition to all abortions (coupled with opposition to responsible sex education), opposition to the Equal Rights Amendment (or anything associated with feminism), and opposition to some of the rights of homosexuals.

---

[1] Falwell appeared to miss the implication of Ms. Redgrave's subtle comment.

Among Falwell's many unfounded and often hysterical[2] assertions are that *"there is no separation of church and state"* and that Barry Lynn is a *"Christ hater."*[3]

Falwell founded the Thomas Road Baptist Church and Liberty University, in Lynchburg, VA.

Family Research Council (FRC): Extreme right wing think tank, founded by Dr. James Dobson,[4] in 1983, championing "traditional family values." Its current president is Tony Perkins.

The FRC lobbies for state-sponsored prayer in public schools,[5] for *school vouchers*, for abstinence-only *sex education*, and for the right to discriminate against lesbians and gays. A cause they share with somewhat less extreme groups and even with some moderates is the use of filtering software on public library computers.[6] Among their other goals is the elimination of the National Endowment for the Arts (NEA), the Corporation for Public Broadcasting (CPB), and the Department of Education (DOE).

As with similar groups, FRC is obsessed with the idea that same-sex marriages would somehow undermine traditional heterosexual marriages.

FRC was a division of Focus on the Family from 1988, when Gary Bauer took over as president from James Dobson, until October 1992, when they separated for tax reasons. Bauer continued as president until 1999, when he quit to run for a much bigger presidency in the 2000 Republican primaries.

---

[2] Or, perhaps, hysterically funny.

[3] Both these assertions were made on CNBC on February 25, 2004. Barry Lynn is Executive Director, Americans United for the Separation of Church and State, and an ordained minister of the United Church of Christ (a moderate, mainstream Protestant denomination).

[4] James Dobson is much better known, currently, as the leader of **Focus on the Family**.

[5] This is particularly exemplified by their proposal that there be a school prayer amendment to the U.S. Constitution.

[6] The kind and scope of the content that would be filtered varies from group to group. The more moderate proponents of filtering are concerned mainly with violent content.

He was succeeded by Ken Connor, an attorney, who served until 2003, when the current president, Tony Perkins took over.[7]

Typical of the FRC's faith based approach to social (and medical) issues is its opposition to a vaccine (soon to be approved) that will protect women from the very common human papilloma virus (HPV), which causes genital warts and, in some cases, can lead to cervical cancer. In the U.S., it affects something like half of all sexually active women. The FRC's spokeswoman, Bridget Maher, says, *"Giving the HPV vaccine to young women could be potentially harmful, because they may see it as a license to engage in premarital sex."*[8] Like so many statements by religious right organizations, this is simply a quite weak assertion with no evidence to support it. Given the implied caveats (*"could be potentially"* and *"may"*), it provides no justification for withholding the vaccine. Unfortunately, supporters of the FRC's position (including the FRC itself) are inclined to ignore such caveats in the interest of restricting women's choices to those they see as being biblically based.

Fascism: According to Webster, a governmental system led by a dictator having complete power, forcibly suppressing opposition and criticism, regimenting all industry, commerce, etc., and emphasizing an aggressive nationalism and often racism. The definition of fascist obviously follows from that.

George Bush and his administration are governing from the far right. However, do they qualify as fascists? Based on the above definition (which is not the only one), they don't meet all the criteria. However, there are enough similarities to be disturbing. Bush has said how much easier it would be to be a dictator, and many of his actions have certainly

---

[7] Source for most of this entry: *People For the American Way, Right Wing Watch, Right Wing Organizations, Family Research Council, http://www.pfaw.org/pfaw/general/default.aspx?oid=4211.*

[8] *Will cancer vaccine get to all women? Debora MacKenzie, NewScientist.com news service, April 18, 2005, http://www.newscientist.com/channel/sex/mg18624954.500.*

been dictatorial in nature (e.g., his liberal use of Executive Orders, his successful demand that, the U.S. Constitution notwithstanding, the authority to go to war be ceded to him, and more recently, his extra-judicial authorization of wiretaps). On his behalf, the Secret Service has, with the cooperation of local police, been suppressing opposition and criticism (*see* **First Amendment zones**), as did former Attorney General John Ashcroft, with the help of the **USA PATRIOT Act**. His most ardent boosters (including, for example, **Ann Coulter** and right-wing talk-show hosts) have vilified those who criticize him and his administration as unpatriotic and even (in Coulter's case) as traitors. On the other hand, Bush's penchant for deregulation, no-bid contracts, tolerance of companies' use of offshore tax havens, etc. hardly qualifies him as one who wishes to regiment all industry and commerce—quite the contrary. Aggressive and dictatorial nationalism may be a good fit (*see* **Project for a New American Century**) and his opposition to affirmative action and apparent ambiguity on civil rights may possibly qualify as borderline racism (something he and his supporters would, no doubt, vehemently deny).

So, strictly speaking, George Bush and those around him may not qualify as fascist, but what they have brought about may make any distinction merely academic.

fear: *See* **Roosevelt, Franklin Delano**.

Federalist Society for Law and Public Policy Studies: A society of conservative and libertarian lawyers. Its primary purpose seems to be to oppose what it sees as *"a form of orthodox liberal ideology."* It's instructive to note that leading speakers at their National Lawyers Convention included hard-liners like Senate Majority Leader **Bill Frist** and extremists like former Attorney General **John Ashcroft**. The society is usually known by the first two words of its full name. There are Federalist Societies at most (if not all) law schools and, at the state level, in many (if not all) states.

Feith, Douglas Jay: Under Secretary of Defense for Policy, until his resignation on August 8, 2005. From 1984 to 1986, he was Deputy Assistant Secretary of Defense for Negotiations Policy in the Reagan administration, an appointment that was preceded by a stint as Special Counsel to *Richard Perle,* who was then Assistant Secretary of Defense.

Feith is regarded as a neoconservative and is a Richard Perle protégé. He ran the now-defunct *Office of Special Plans (OSP)* for Defense Secretary *Donald Rumsfeld.* The purpose of OSP was to selectively gather intelligence supportive of the administration's plans to attack Iraq, effectively ignoring intelligence that would cast doubt on the wisdom of those plans.

With the help of *Ahmad Chalabi,* whom Jim Lobe refers to as the neoconservatives' favorite exile, Feith collected *"and 'cooked' the most alarmist pre-war intelligence against Saddam Hussein and then 'stovepiped' it to the White House via Rumsfeld and Vice President Dick Cheney, unvetted by the intelligence agencies."*[9] Feith's office was also responsible for post-war planning. However, it rejected the advice of many State Department and CIA Middle East experts, including Iraqis, with consequences that continue to plague the occupying forces. Finally, he and the Coalition Provisional Authority (CPA) created a situation that has led to flagrant profiteering by U.S. contractors, often through no-bid contracts.[10]

felon purge: Although it received scant press coverage, this was almost certainly a significant contributor, in the 2000 Election, to George Bush's dubious victory in Florida. Following an overturned mayoral election in Miami, in which there was evidence of voting by convicted felons and even dead people, the Florida legislature decided in 1998 to purge felons from the voter rolls. To do this, they contracted with an outside firm, Database Technologies, Inc., of

---

[9] *Crisis of Feith, Jim Lobe, TomPaine.com, http://tompaine.com/ feature2.cfm/ID/9390.*

[10] Ibid.

Boca Raton.[11] Database Technologies (DBT) was paid over $3 million to scan the state's voter database for the same kind of people who had improperly voted in the Miami mayoral election—felons and dead people.

State election officials told DBT to use the broadest possible criteria (e.g., match on name only, approximate match on name, etc.) to determine who was ineligible to vote. Despite their warnings that the approach would disenfranchise legitimate voters, DBT was told to go ahead anyway. The result was, according to the May 27, 2001 *Palm Beach Post*,[12] a list of over 42 thousand "probable" and "possible" felons. An article by Greg Palast, in the March 2002 *Harper's Magazine*, cites a higher number—57,700.[13] It also states that Secretary of State **Katherine Harris**, and her predecessor, Sandra Mortham, ordered that those 57,700 "ex-felons" be removed from the voter rolls. Although both Harris and Mortham were protégées of Governor **Jeb Bush**, it is not entirely clear whether he was involved in that decision. Although a significant number of them had never committed a crime, they were required to prove their innocence (usually unsuccessfully) in order to be allowed to vote. Citing the list's unreliability, election officials in twenty counties refused to use it, thus allowing the genuine felons to vote. Other counties used the list, thus prohibiting both the innocent and the genuine felons from voting. The elections supervisor of Madison County, Linda Howell, rejected the list when she found her own name on it.[14]

Palast's article provides actual examples of innocent voters caught up in the purge. The most interesting one is the case of 28-year-old Thomas Alvin Cooper, who was surprised to

---

[11] Now a subsidiary of ChoicePoint of Atlanta.

[12] Available at *http://commondreams.org/headlines01/0527-03.htm*.

[13] The Harpers Magazine article may no longer be available online. However, a December 2004 Salon.com article on the same topic can be found at Greg Palast's own website: *Florida's flawed "voter-cleansing" program—Salon.com's politics story of the year, Greg Palast, December 4, 2004, http://www.gregpalast.com/detail.cfm?artid=55&row=1.*

[14] Ibid.

learn that he had committed a crime in the year 2007. And we all thought time travel only happened in science fiction.

Felonious Five: A name, used by their critics, for the five Supreme Court Justices who voted to stop the recount of the Florida votes in the 2000 Election. In what many legal scholars (and others) regarded as a tortured interpretation of the equal protection provision of the Fourteenth Amendment to the U.S. Constitution, they decided, in effect, that voter rights were best protected by not counting all votes. Incredibly, they also ruled that the basis for their decision was not to be regarded as a precedent for future cases. (In addition to late Chief Justice William H. Rehnquist, the justices were Antonin Scalia, Clarence Thomas, Sandra Day O'Connor and Anthony Kennedy.)

FEMA: Federal Emergency Management Agency, now one of the agencies in the *Department of Homeland Security* (DHS). FEMA is the government agency that has, since President Carter created it by executive order in 1979, responded, one way or another, to many disasters and emergencies. Its role is intended to be proactive (e.g., flood and fire control), as well as reactive. It performed very poorly during the Reagan and George H.W. Bush administrations, but was revived by President Clinton, with his appointment of James Lee Witt, who had worked for him in a similar capacity when he was governor of Arkansas.

> *'Before Witt came along, FEMA was a lackluster agency under abysmal political management. As Donald Kettl of Brookings has written, the old FEMA was a laughing stock: "Every hurricane, earthquake, tornado and flood, the joke went, brought two disasters: one when the event occurred, and the second when FEMA arrived."'*[15]
>
> —*Bruce Reed, Slate, September 4, 2005*

---

[15] *Miracle Worker, Bush longs for James Lee Witt, the Clinton man he should have kept, Bruce Reed, Slate Magazine, September 4, 2005, http://slate.msn.com/id/2125224.*

George Bush managed to return FEMA to its lackluster status (and worse) because, unfortunately, in addition to replacing Witt (in January 2001) with **Joseph Allbaugh** as head of the agency, his administration made drastic cuts in its funding, including 44 percent of funds intended for flood control in New Orleans—something that has been blamed for exacerbating the effects of Hurricane Katrina.[16] With the implementation of the Department of Homeland Security, he also demoted the agency to sub-cabinet-level status. Meanwhile, James Lee Witt thrives as the head of *James Lee Witt Associates*,[17] in which his most prominent senior associates are General Wesley Clark and Rodney Slater, former Secretary of Transportation under President Clinton.

Allbaugh's successor was **Michael D. Brown**, who resigned on September 12, 2005, after failing to perform in response to Hurricane Katrina. Brown's acting replacement is R. David Paulison,[18] who has the appropriate experience and expertise for the job. Whether he can live down the fact that he was the person who suggested the use of plastic sheeting and duct tape to protect against a chemical or biological attack[19] remains to be seen. If his status as acting head of FEMA changes to that of a full appointment, he will have to deal with the fact that, since the beginning of the Bush administration, FEMA has been a dumping ground for a number of political appointees (five in senior positions), who may have been good campaign workers (or helpful to George Bush in other ways), but have no experience in emergency management.[20] As of September 15, 2005, sev-

---

[16] *"No one can say they didn't see it coming,"* Sidney Blumenthal, Salon.com, August 31, 2005, http://salon.com/opinion/blumenthal/2005/08/31/disaster_preparation.

[17] *http://www.wittassociates.com.*

[18] *http://www.fema.gov/about/bios/paulison.shtm.*

[19] *Fear Factor USA: The Duct Tape Defense, ShortNews.com, February 12, 2003, http://www.shortnews.com/shownews.cfm?id=28400.*

[20] It's inevitable (and somewhat distressing) that presidents will make some appointments as a reward for party loyalty. However, it's not unreasonable to expect them to put their friends only in jobs for which they are at least reasonably well qualified. George Bush has not done very

eral of them had decided to beat a hasty retreat.[21] They included Daniel Craig, director of the Recovery Division, and Edward Buikema, acting director of the Response Division. Patrick Rhode, deputy director of FEMA, was also expected to leave, as he had a long-standing poor relationship with David Paulison.

filibuster: A strategy whereby a minority in the U.S. Senate can stand up to the will of a majority whose numbers do not exceed sixty percent of the total.[22] Because of the effort involved (long speeches or an unbroken succession of speeches, around the clock), it is used sparingly. Both major parties have used filibusters when they were in the minority. In the 108th Congress, Senate Democrats used filibusters to prevent a vote on some of George Bush's more extreme right-wing judicial nominees. With Bush resubmitting judicial nominees in his second term who were rejected during his first term, such filibusters were expected to be a fact of life in the 109th Congress.

In May 2005, Senate Majority Leader Bill Frist threatened to eliminate the use of the filibuster to block judicial nominees. (The procedure[23] by which he planned to do so has been referred to as the "nuclear option."[24]) This was in spite of the fact that more than 95% of Bush's judicial nominees, all conservative, had been approved. Three particularly

---

well in this respect. Ideally, of course, every government job should go to the best-qualified and most suitable applicant.

[21] *More FEMA bigs are bailing out, James Gordon Meek, New York Daily News, September 15, 2005, http://nydailynews.com/front/story/346648p-295731c.html.*

[22] The minimum vote count for cloture (ending of debate) on a filibuster is 60 members of the current 100-member Senate.

[23] Frist was threatening a parliamentary maneuver that would have avoided the need for the usual 2/3 majority to change a Senate rule. Once the rule was changed, a filibuster against a judicial nominee's confirmation could be ended with a simple majority of 51. Sixty votes would continue to be required for cloture on other filibusters.

[24] Senator Trent Lott (R-MS) is said to have been the one who first used the term, "nuclear option" with respect to stopping the filibustering of the confirmation of Charles Pickering in 2003. Republicans have since claimed, somewhat childishly, that Democrats invented the term (in 2005).

egregious nominations to federal appeals courts were at stake—Priscilla Owen, of the Texas Supreme Court, Janice Rogers Brown, of the California Supreme Court, and William Pryor, Alabama Attorney General. On May 23, 2005, fourteen Senators (seven Republicans and seven Democrats) reached a compromise in which the confirmations of Owen, Rogers and Pryor would go straight to a floor vote, with filibusters still possible for other nominees, including two others, William Myers and Henry Saad, still pending. All five were confirmed in 2005, with no filibusters taking place.

No equivalent strategy to the filibuster is available to members of the House of Representatives.

First Amendment zones: Because of so-called First Amendment zones, George Bush is rarely exposed to those who wish to exercise their First Amendment rights to peaceably assemble and protest his policies. In advance of any visit to speak to one of his carefully selected audiences, the Secret Service works with local law enforcement officials to set up a restricted area close enough to Bush's planned route to easily herd those with protest signs into it, but sufficiently far away to prevent Bush seeing or hearing them. Those with signs supporting Bush are permitted to line the route or, for an outdoor speech, stand where they can be seen and heard. As if the First Amendment violations were not enough, there are many reported cases of people having nothing to do with a demonstration being manhandled or arrested by the police, simply because they happened to be in the area. In the circumstances, it's hard to accept Bush's claim to be a man of the people. (But, if you want to be picky, you could say that he's a man of his own kind of people.)

flag desecration amendment: Ever since the U.S. Supreme Court, in 1989, struck down all state and local laws prohibiting the burning of the U.S. flag, *neoconservatives* and their fellow travelers in Congress have attempted to reinstate the ban, nationwide, by means of a constitutional amendment. In June 2005, the House of Representatives once again passed a bill that seeks to amend the U.S. Constitution to prohibit flag "desecration."[25] Although almost all Republicans voted in favor of the bill and most Democrats voted against it, there were some Democrats who joined the rush to irrationality and voted in favor, giving the vote a margin of 286 to 130. If eight members had voted against, rather than for the bill, it would not have passed.[26] Until now, enough Senators have demonstrated their sanity by defeating the Senate version of such bills. At the time of writing, this latest attempt has not reached the Senate floor. The last time a vote was taken on such a bill, three Republican Senators still in office voted against it.[27] Nine Democratic Senators are known to favor the amendment (because they are cosponsoring the Senate bill[28]), as are the remaining 52 Republican Senators, giving the bill a potential minimum of 61 votes of the 67 required.

The text of the amendment is, like most of the other amendments to the Constitution, short and concise:

> *"The Congress shall have the power to prohibit the physical desecration of the flag of the United States."*

One of the sponsors of the House bill, the now-convicted former congressman, **Randy "Duke" Cunningham** (R-CA), urged a vote in favor of the amendment by saying, *"Ask the men and women who stood on top of the Trade Center. Ask them and they will tell you, 'Pass this amendment.'"* As all who

---

[25] Webster's second definition of desecration would appear to be the operative one, namely *diversion from a sacred to a profane use or purpose.*

[26] Constitutional amendments require a 2/3 majority in both the House and the Senate, followed by ratification by at least 38 states within the following seven years.

[27] Robert Bennett (R-UT), Lincoln Chafee (R-RI) and Mitch McConnell (R-KY). Lincoln Chafee's late father, Senator John Chafee (R-RI) also voted against a similar bill in 1995.

[28] The Democratic cosponsors are Max Baucus (D-MT), Evan Bayh (D-IN), Ben Nelson (D-NE), Diane Feinstein (D-CA), Tim Johnson (D-SD), Mary Landrieu (D-LA), Blanche Lincoln (D-AR), Senate Minority Leader Harry Reid (D-NV), and John Rockefeller (D-WV). Robert Byrd (D-WV) voted for the amendment in 1995, but against it in 2000. Source: *Daily KOS, http://dailykos.com/story/2005/6/15/131545/032.*

stood on top of the World Trade Center died, asking them might be somewhat difficult. The very reasonable and constitutionally conscious response by Rep. Jerrold Nadler (D-NY) was, *"If the flag needs protection at all, it needs protection from members of Congress who value the symbol more than the freedoms that the flag represents."*

There are several reasons why a flag desecration amendment is neither necessary nor desirable. The following set of reasons does not pretend to be exhaustive:

- It would be a precedent-setting exception to the First Amendment.

- It would be the first restrictive amendment since prohibition, and therefore now the only amendment to deny a freedom.

- It is a supposed remedy for which there is no existing problem. Burning of the U.S. flag (the real target of the amendment) as a protest, on U.S. territory, is extremely rare, even though it is currently a practice protected by the First Amendment. Those contemplating burning a flag in protest are strongly deterred by the prospect of facing an angry crowd.

- Because the amendment implicitly declares the U.S. flag to be sacred, it violates the Establishment Clause (see **Bill of Rights**) by putting the government in the position of defining what is and what is not sacred (a purely religious concept).

- The proposed amendment does not even define what does or does not constitute "flag desecration," although it is obvious that its proponents intend burning as a protest to be part of any definition. It is not clear whether they consider the manufacture and sale of clothing and souvenirs bearing an image of the flag to also constitute desecration.

- The U.S. flag is a symbol. The amendment confuses the symbol with what it represents, which is the United States and, by implication, the U.S. Constitution, including the Bill of Rights. Implicit in that is the fact that what it symbolizes includes one's freedom to protest by burning it (or to adopt a patriotic or even jingoistic posture by wearing it or wrapping oneself in it).

Both Republicans and Democrats (but overwhelmingly Republicans) in Congress appear to be pandering to the least informed of their constituents, rather than taking the trouble (and the risk) of explaining to them the important principles laid out in the Bill of Rights. This is an area in which schools need to do a better job.

Fleischer, Ari: White House Press Secretary from January 2001 to June 2003. During his tenure, Fleischer was known, among other things, as Bush's official liar. Although a press secretary is obliged to toe the official line, one can certainly argue that nobody is obliged to take the job. Until Scott McClellan was named to the position, members of the press were joking that his probable replacement would be Jayson Blair, the New York Times reporter who was fired for fabricating a substantial number of stories.

Focus on the Family: *See Dobson, James.*

Fourteenth Amendment: *See Bill of Rights.*

fox guarding the hen house: Someone who is employed in a position that is supposed to be responsible for the promotion of government policy or the establishment or enforcement of regulations that he or she was formerly employed to oppose.

> *"Republican appointees who oppose the agencies to which they are assigned are a dime a dozen."*[29]
>
> —*Molly Ivins, September 23, 2005*

One clear example (of many) is Michael Grant Young, whom George Bush appointed to the Federal Mine Safety

---

[29] *Government by Temper Tantrum: Bush responds to women's health official's resignation by appointing a veterinarian, Molly Ivins, Alternet, http://www.alternet.org/story/25910.*

Health and Review Commission. Prior to his July 2003 appointment, Young served as Director of Regulatory Affairs for the Pennsylvania Coal Association.[30] Thus, Young is one of many such examples of foxes guarding the henhouse.

Fox News: All-news channel available on basic cable and by satellite. They claim to be "fair and balanced," but appear to be one of the primary propaganda arms of the Bush administration and the Republican Party. Critics of Fox News refer to it as "Faux News."[31] As with all Fox enterprises, the Australian media magnate, Rupert Murdoch, owns it. Murdoch's media empire extends far beyond Fox and, under the *News Corp* banner, includes many TV stations (world wide) and newspapers.

The documentary, *Outfoxed: Rupert Murdoch's War on Journalism,*[32] includes interviews with former Fox employees, who say they were required to promote the right-wing point of view or risk losing their jobs.

See also **Hannity, Sean** *and* **Snow, Tony**.

Free Congress Foundation (FCF): A conservative Washington think tank. In its own words, FCF is not only *"politically conservative,"* but also *"culturally conservative,"* with its main focus on the *"Culture War."* They maintain that, unless the country is returned to its *"Judeo-Christian roots,"* it *"will become no less than a third world country."*[33]

---

[30] His biographical information, at *http://www.fmshrc.gov/young-bio.html,* makes no secret of this fact. The goal of directors of regulatory affairs in industries or industry associations is, of course, to lobby for as little regulation as possible.

[31] Faux, normally pronounced "foe," is French for false.

[32] *Outfoxed: Rupert Murdoch's War on Journalism, Robert Greenwald, Producer and Director, DVD available at www.outfoxed.org, book (ISBN 1932857117) by Alexandra Kitty, available at Amazon.com and Powell's Books (www.powells.com).*

[33] Surely they mean either *"less than a third world country"* or *"no more than a third world country."* But *"will become no less than a third world country"* is what it says on their website. (See *http://www.freecongress.org/about/index.asp.*)

FCF is opposed to multi-culturalism, "judicial activism," Democratic politicians, "moral decay" and "political correctness."

FCF's chairman and chief executive officer is Paul M. Weyrich, who is also national chairman of Coalitions for America. His vision is for cultural conservatives to eventually dominate all aspects of American culture and politics.[34] Not surprisingly, this puts him fairly squarely in the Bush camp. However, he has become very critical of Bush and the House and Senate Republican majorities, accusing them of spending like *"drunken sailors."*[35]

Free Republic: A website for the discussion of conservative (often far right) ideas. In their own words,

> *"The Free Republic forum is intended for Conservative users who wish to have a serious discussion about political events, conservative principles and the elimination of government corruption and abuse."*

It started in the late 1990s and was very active before and during the Clinton impeachment process.

The regular participants are usually referred to as "Freepers."

freedom (of assembly, press, religion, speech): *See Bill of Rights.*

Freeper: *See Free Republic.*

Frist, Bill: Republican Senator from Tennessee and Senate Majority Leader. Frist succeeded *Trent Lott* (R-MS) in the Majority Leader role, following the latter's resignation from the position after acutely embarrassing himself.

Frist appears to be a dedicated Bush loyalist. However, he appears to be less and less successful in pushing Bush's

---

[34] See *People for the American Way (PFAW)* at *http://www.pfaw.org/pfaw/general/default.aspx?oid=4314.*

[35] *"Conservative groups break with Republican leadership,"* Washington Times, January 16, 2004, http://www.washtimes.com/national/20040115-112447-9758r.htm.

agenda in the Senate. Like Trent Lott, he also makes occasional embarrassing statements, although he appears to be unaware of their embarrassing nature.

> *"Get some devastation in the back."*
>
> —Senate Majority Leader Bill Frist,
> to a staff photographer who was taking a picture of
> him before he left tsunami-stricken southern Sri Lanka.
> (Quoted by Associated Press)

Like Bush, he is fond of photo ops. It's apparent, from the above quotation, that his trip to southern Asia following the December 26, 2004 earthquake and tsunami was as much about photo ops as about showing the flag.

Again, like Bush, when he makes a mistake, he is quite prepared to lie about it.

When both the Senate and the House decided very unwisely to intervene in April 2005 in the Terry Schiavo case,[36] Frist said on the Senate floor that he had reviewed a videotape (which was not even recent) of that unfortunate young lady and had concluded that she was responsive.[37,38,39] That was, of course, recorded for posterity by C-SPAN 2. On June 17, one day after an autopsy report showed that Schiavo had suffered irreversible brain damage, Frist took to the Senate floor again, where C-SPAN 2 cameras recorded the following for posterity: *"People said: 'Bill Frist, you're making a diagnosis. Doctor, you're trying to wear your white coat on the floor of the Senate.' I never made a diagnosis. I*

---

[36] Terry Schiavo was a Florida woman who had been in a persistent vegetative state for about 15 years.

[37] Which contradicted expert medical testimony about Terry Schiavo's condition in a series of court cases involving Michael Schiavo's contention that his wife's express wish was to be allowed to die if she were ever in a persistent vegetative state. Michael Schiavo prevailed over Terry's parents and other litigants in every case.

[38] Frist is a medical doctor. However, his specialty is heart-lung transplant surgery.

[39] *Frist Responds on Schiavo, New York Times, June 17, 2005, http://nytimes.com/2005/06/17/politics/17frist.html.*

wouldn't even attempt to make a diagnosis from a videotape."[40] That same evening, Comedy Central's Daily Show played the two relevant C-SPAN 2 clips back to back. The studio audience found it hilarious. It's a good bet that the viewers at home reacted similarly.

Frist is now facing investigation of charges of campaign fund irregularities and of insider trading. The campaign fund story broke on December 2, 2004, in the *Washington Post* and other mainstream papers. It resurfaced on June 27, 2005, when Citizens for Responsibility and Ethics in Washington (CREW), a watchdog group, filed a complaint[41] with the Federal Election Commission (FEC), presenting evidence that Frist's campaign committee (with Frist's knowledge[42]) failed to disclose a $1.44 million loan[43] that was taken out jointly by Frist's 2000 campaign committee and his 1994 campaign committee, making it appear as though the 2000 committee had more money than was, in fact, the case. The complaint asks the FEC to refer the matter to the Justice Department for possible criminal prosecution under the Federal Election Campaign Act (FECA), which requires full disclosure of any loans taken out by campaign committees. The largely dormant 1994 committee made the disclosure, as required. However, the 2000 committee did not. Frist also failed to disclose that he had, in June 2000, invested $1.2 million in contributions to the 2000 campaign in the stock market. Along with so much else that year, the investment lost money from the start. If the FEC does, indeed, refer the matter to the Justice Department and if the Justice Department does, indeed, indict Frist, his days as Senate Majority Leader may very well be numbered. Interestingly, the current Chair of the FEC, Ellen Weintraub, although a

---

[40] Ibid.

[41] *Frist Campaign Committee Failed to Disclose a $1.44 Million Loan,* Citizens for Responsibility and Ethics in Washington, June 27, 2005, *http://www.citizensforethics.org/press/newsrelease.php?view=66.*

[42] Frist signed the loan documents on behalf of his 1994 and 2000 campaigns.

[43] The interest on the loan was about $10,000 per month.

Bush appointee, is a Democrat. Bush appointed her on the insistence of Senator John McCain (R-AZ), who is well known as a champion of campaign finance reform (as evidenced by the McCain-Feingold Campaign Reform Act of 1997).

In June 2005, Frist dumped all of his HCA stock. (His father was the founder of HCA [Health Corporation of America] and his brother is a member of their board.) One month later, a report, by HCA, that admissions of insured patients were lower than expected caused the stock to drop by 9%. Frist had earlier (in 2000) put all of his stocks in a blind trust to avoid the appearance of a conflict of interest, a move that met with the approval of the Senate ethics committee. It was particularly important with the HCA stock, because of his involvement with health care legislation. Unfortunately for Frist, as it turns out, he had an agreement with the trustees of the "blind" trust, permitting them to communicate with him whenever new contributions were made.[44] As contributions were normally in the form of additional HCA stock, statements he made in 2000 that he no longer knew whether or not he still owned HCA stock were decidedly disingenuous.

> *"The notion that you have a blind trust but you can tell your trustee when to sell stock in it just doesn't make any sense. It means you have a seeing eye trust and not a blind trust. It's ridiculous."*
>
> —*Fred Wertheimer, President, Democracy 21,*
> *September 2005*

The Securities and Exchange Commission (SEC) initiated an investigation of both Bill Frist and HCA in September 2005.

---

[44] *Not So Blind Trusts? The Washington Spectator, January 1, 2006.*

G

> G is for Greatness, as in *"I can't tell you what it's like to be in Europe, for example, to be talking about the greatness of America. But the true greatness of America are the people."*
>
> —George Bush, Washington, DC, July 2, 2001
>
> (It really are.)

Gannon, Jeff: Pseudonym of James Dale "J.D." Guckert, the non-journalist who managed to attend White House press briefings and press conferences for two whole years without ever receiving the Secret Service and FBI clearance required of all other reporters in the White House press corps, and after being turned down for a congressional press pass because he didn't work for a recognized news organization. His very strange status was first revealed by bloggers,[1] with the mainstream media largely downplaying the story until it became too hot to ignore. Guckert wrote for Talon News,[2] a web-based operation owned by GOPUSA,[3] which is, in turn, owned by Robert Eberle, a Texas-based Republican Party activist. Guckert/Gannon was, before his hasty resignation, also Talon's Washington Bureau "chief."

Apart from asking softball questions when things got too hot for *Scott McClellan* (the White House Press Secretary) or George Bush,[4] Guckert's main "journalistic" activity seems to have been the copying and pasting of White

---

[1] Bloggers are those who operate and/or participate in Internet discussion forums known as web logs or, increasingly, just as blogs. The web-based virtual environment in which blogs operate is known as the Blogosphere.

[2] *http://talonnews.com.*

[3] *http://gopusa.com.*

[4] He asked George Bush the following question, "You've said you're going to reach out to these people (Democrats). How are you going to work with people who seem to have divorced themselves from reality?"

House press releases and position papers to create very slanted "news stories."

Although not relevant to the main issue, adding to the interest of the Gannon story is the fact that he advertised his services as a male "escort" (for male clients, including military personnel) at a rate of $200 per hour. His advertising included a provocatively posed nude photograph of himself. He has treated the revelation of the existence of his services as an invasion of privacy, which is something that is hard to justify, considering his aggressive promotion of those services at multiple websites.

According to one source,[5] Guckert obtained his first White House press pass four days after Talon News began. Other sources claim he got his press pass as much as two months earlier. What is certain is that he operated using either a series of "daily passes" or, like the better-known members of the White House press corps, a "hard pass," good for ongoing use. There is very little doubt that, if a liberal pseudojournalist had managed to do the same thing in the Clinton White House, there would be a huge hue and cry from the right, accompanied by demands for a congressional investigation of the White House, the Secret Service, the FBI, and other agencies.

gay marriage and civil unions: In his February, 2004 statement, calling for a constitutional amendment banning gay marriage, Bush made the claim that various states (California and New Mexico) and courts (Massachusetts) had forced him to reverse his previous position on the issue.[6] However, a report in the Denver *Rocky Mountain News* gives lie to that claim. The report, which is corroborated by a three-month-earlier report in the *San Francisco Chronicle*, points out that Bush had, in November 2003, pledged to

---

[5] *The strange story of White House reporter 'Jeff Gannon', Donald P. Russo, The Morning Call Online, February 19, 2005, http://mcall.com/ news/opinion/oped/all-columnfeb19,0,4042766.column.*

[6] Source: *Misleader.org: Daily Mislead,* "False Pretenses of Bush's Gay Marriage Reversal March 2, 2004—http://misleader.org/daily_mislead/ Read.asp?fn=df0302204.html.*

Rep. Marilyn Musgrave (R-CO) that he would support a constitutional amendment she was planning to introduce.

Bush's announcement was not only misleading, but also a complete reversal of the position he and Dick Cheney took during the 2000 presidential campaign. In the February 15, 2000 Republican debate in South Carolina, Bush said, about the gay marriage issue, *"The states can do what they wish to."* Again, on May 2, he reiterated that position with, *"... it is going to be up to cities and states to make those decisions."* In October 5, 2000, his running mate, Dick Cheney, said, in response to an August 25 ACLU letter to the Senate, *"the fact of the matter is, of course, that [same-sex marriage] is regulated by the states."* He then added, *"I think different states are likely to come to different conclusions and that's appropriate. I don't think there should necessarily be a federal policy in this area."*[7]

Why the reversal? It seems probable that, by November 2003, Bush was already feeling pressure from his Religious Right constituency. His February 2004 announcement, allegedly justified by the gay-marriage-related events of that month, provided yet another convenient distraction from the real issues being raised in the Democratic Primary debates, the worsening situation on the ground in Iraq, and the escalating tensions and violence in Haiti, the last being a situation he had either neglected for far too long or possibly saw as being consistent with the goals of his neoconservative constituency.[8]

Geneva Conventions: There are four "Geneva Conventions for the Protection of Victims of War." Dated August 12 1949, they were ratified by the United States on July 14,

---

[7] To his credit, Cheney has, unlike Bush, not changed his position.

[8] This is, of course, a simplification, which neglects to take into account Bush's somewhat rudimentary understanding of international issues. A fuller explanation might be that the neoconservatives in and close to the administration saw the ouster of Jean-Bertrand Aristide, President of Haiti, as being conducive to the realization of their goals (*see* **Project for the New American Century**) and advised Bush accordingly.

1955. Under Article VI, Clause 2[9] of the U.S. Constitution, they are, therefore, *"the supreme Law of the Land."* They are:

- **Geneva Convention I**: The Convention for the Amelioration of the Condition of the Wounded and Sick in Armed Forces in the Field;

- **Geneva Convention II** (a variant of Convention I): The Convention for the Amelioration of the Condition of Wounded, Sick and Ship-wrecked Members of the Armed Forces at Sea;

- **Geneva Convention III**: The Convention Relative to the Treatment of Prisoners of War; and

- **Geneva Convention IV**: The Convention Relative to the Protection of Civilian Persons in Time of War.

With respect to many of those being held at Guantánamo Bay, George Bush and Donald Rumsfeld are violating the spirit of and doing an end run around Convention III by labeling the prisoners simply as "detainees, or "unlawful combatants" or *"enemy combatants."* The first term is an obvious example of weasel wording. The second and third have no legal precedent and no recognized legal meaning, either in international or in U.S. law. No matter what they call the prisoners, Bush, **Donald Rumsfeld** and former Attorney General **John Ashcroft** were violating Convention III and could be subject to criminal prosecution for doing so.

Given that many prisoners, especially in the **Abu Ghraib** prison in Baghdad, are civilians, many of whom were simply rounded up on the street without any probable cause, the Bush administration is also in violation of Geneva Convention IV.

*See, also, **Gonzalez, Alberto**.*

---

[9] This Constitution, and the Laws of the United States which shall be made in Pursuance thereof; and all Treaties made, or which shall be made, under the Authority of the United States, shall be the supreme Law of the Land; and the Judges in every State shall be bound thereby, any Thing in the Constitution or Laws of any State to the Contrary notwithstanding.

gerrymandering: Drawing of district lines to maximize the electoral advantage of a political party or faction. The term was first used in 1812, when Elbridge Gerry was Governor of Massachusetts, to characterize that state's redistricting plan, in which one of the districts was shaped like a sala-mander. *For a discussion of the gerrymandering that has taken place (not always successfully) in Colorado, Texas and Pennsyl-vania, see* **redistricting** *and* **Delay, Tom**.

Gilmore, James S: Former Governor and Attorney General of Virginia and former Chairman of the Republican National Committee.

During his tenure as Governor of Virginia, Gilmore re-duced taxes and increased spending, leaving his Democ-ratic successor, Mark Warner, with a $6 billion deficit. The negative economic effects of the 2001 attacks on the World Trade Center and the Pentagon did not, of course, help to avoid a deficit. Gilmore has a reputation as a friend of the tobacco industry, which is not entirely surprising in a to-bacco-growing state.

With Mark Warner's Democratic successor, Tim Kaine, in the governor's mansion, Gilmore is rumored to be eyeing the 2009 gubernatorial race. If Kaine's administration is as popular as Warner's, Gilmore's prospects may not be good.

Gingrich, Newt: Former speaker of the House of Representa-tives and architect of the *Contract with America*. His history, both positive and negative, before and since his time in Congress, is quite well documented on a large number of websites. His relevance, here, is because of the use, by many Republicans and their supporters in the punditoc-racy, of his list of glowingly positive and scathingly nega-tive adjectives. The former are, of course, used to describe other Republicans and Republican programs, policies and legislation; the latter are used to describe Democrats and their programs, policies and legislation. All were contained in a pamphlet, called *Language, a Key Mechanism of Control,* mailed in 1990 by his political action committee (GOPAC) to Republicans throughout the country.[10]

Gingrich's "positive governing words" are:

> *Active, actively, activist,*[11] *building, candid, candidly, care, caring, challenge, change, children, choice, choose, citizen, commitment, common sense, compete, confident, conflict, control, courage, crusade, debate, dream, duty, eliminate good-time in prison, empower, empowerment, fair, family, freedom, hard work, help, humane, incentive, initiative, lead, learn, legacy, liberty, light, listen, mobilize, moral, movement, opportunity, our, passionate, peace, pioneer, precious, premise, preserve, pride, principle, principled, pristine, pro-flag, pro-child, pro-environment, prosperity, protect, proud, provide, reform, rights, share, strength, success, tough, truth, unique, us, vision, we,* and *workfare.*

The negative words or phrases GOP candidates were told to use about their opponents are:

> *"Compassion" is not enough, anti-flag, anti-family, anti-child, anti-jobs, betray, coercion, collapse, consequences, corruption, crisis, decay, deeper, destroy, destructive, devour, endanger, failure, greed, hypocrisy, ideological, impose, incompetent, insecure, liberal, lie, limit, limits, pathetic, permissive attitude, radical, self-serving, sensationalists, shallow, sick, their, them, they, threaten, traitors, unionized bureaucracy, urgent,* and *waste.*

Nearly sixteen years after Gingrich published his list of words, Republicans continue to use many of them, as evidenced during the 2004 election campaign (and subsequently) on TV programs such as CNN's Crossfire (now discontinued).

---

[10] Described at *http://carmen.artsci.washington.edu/propaganda/newt.htm.* Secondary sources, cited on the above website, are: *New York Times September 9, 1990; Orlando Sentinel Tribune, September 14, 1990;* and *Chicago Tribune, September 19, 1990.*

[11] Activist is no longer a "positive governing word," but is now used by Republicans as a negative word, as in "activist judge" (used to describe any judge who makes a constitutionally-based decision they don't like).

More recently (January 2006), Gingrich, who may be throwing his hat in the presidential ring in 2008, has started berating his own party for its culture of corruption. Given that he was the primary founder of the *K Street Project,* one of the goals of which was to ensure that only loyal Republicans would be allowed to lobby Congress, his criticism can only be viewed as hypocritical and self serving.

global warming: A phenomenon in which the average temperature at the Earth's surface and in the oceans is rising every year. If it is not reduced by means of drastic and immediate action to reduce pollution, the polar ice caps will melt (even more than they already have) and coastal areas, worldwide, will be inundated, thus changing the geography of the planet. And that's the good news. The bad news is that other effects could render the planet uninhabitable, at least by mammals (which, of course, includes humans) and many other species. The scientific community is practically unanimous with respect to the reality of the phenomenon, its probable consequences and its possible remedies. *Jerry Falwell* claims that global warming is a myth. George Bush claims that it requires further study.

> *The contempt of the Bush administration for environmentalists and their concerns is well known by now. While evidence of man-made environmental damage mounts, the Bush team resists its implications like a defeated army whose rear guard fights off its pursuers as it retreats. That has been especially true of its handling of the most serious of all environmental issues—global warming.*[12]
>
> —*Walter Cronkite,*[13] *March 15, 2004*

In February and March 2004, both the Pentagon[14] and the world's second largest reinsurance company (Swiss Re[15])

---

[12] *Make Global Warming an Issue, Walter Cronkite, Philadelphia Inquirer, March 15, 2004, http://www.commondreams.org/views04/0315-02.htm.*

[13] In his days as the anchor of CBS News, Walter Cronkite was known as "The most trusted man in America." That trust has not diminished.

[14] *Pentagon Study Looks at Global Climate, http://news.yahoo.com/news ?tmpl=story&u=/ap/20040226/ap_on_go_ca_st_pe/climate_change_wars_1.*

warned of impending catastrophe as a result of global warming. So far, neither George Bush nor anyone in his administration has reacted publicly to either warning. It seems incredible that Bush could ignore the former.

As of May 2006, the Bush administration continued to ignore the problem.

See also **distortion.**

Goat story:[16] The story, "The Pet Goat," to which George Bush was listening, on the morning of September 11, 2001, in a second grade class in the Emma E. Booker Elementary School in Sarasota, Florida, when he was told that a second plane had flown into the World Trade Center. As if it were not disturbing enough that he had even gone into the classroom after hearing of the first plane, it was even more disturbing that he continued to listen to the story and talk to the children for several more minutes before excusing himself—but not before waiting for members of the press to leave, then pausing for a photo-op with the teacher, shaking her right hand and holding his left hand to her back.

Most disturbing of all were the lies he subsequently told, regarding his time there. How do we know they're lies? Because his actual statements and movements, from the time he left his hotel for the school to the time he left the classroom were already on the record.

As he left his hotel, shortly after 8:45 in the morning, a reporter asked him if he knew what was going on in New York. He responded that he did and that he'd have something to say about it later. The lie about this was in a speech, on the evening of the same day, in which he said, *"Immediately following the first attack, I implemented our government's emergency response plans."* At the time, the *Wash-*

---

[15] *Insurer warns of global warming catastrophe, http://www.reuters.co.uk/ newsPackageArticle.jhtml?type=worldNews&storyID=468753&section=news.*

[16] With acknowledgements to *Take Back the Media*™ and their presentation, *"Bush Knew—An American Requiem,"* at *http://www.takebackthe media.com/true911.html.*

ington Post[17] seemed to have bought into that lie, as it had his motorcade leaving the hotel for the school some fifteen minutes before the reporter's question. It appears his response to the reporter was also a lie, in that his Chief of Staff, **Andrew Card**, didn't tell him about the first plane until 9:00, fifteen minutes after the rest of the world knew about it. Apparently, at 8:45, Bush didn't want to admit that he didn't know what the reporter was referring to.[18]

On arrival at the school, Bush was taken into a holding room and given a report on the situation, on the phone, by **Condoleezza Rice**, in the course of which he would have heard of at least two of the other three hijackings. At that point, there is no doubt that he should have canceled what was no more than a photo-op event. But he didn't. There is also no doubt that the Secret Service should have whisked him away without even consulting him. They didn't.

Later, Bush lied (on more than one occasion[19]) about the events of the morning. He said, *"And I was sitting outside the classroom waiting to go in, and I saw an airplane hit the tower — the TV was obviously on, and I used to fly myself, and I said, 'There's one terrible pilot.' and I said, 'It must have been a horrible accident.' But I was whisked off there — I didn't have much time to think about it."*[20] Although this particular lie was incredibly blatant, given the timeline, it had minimal media coverage. First, Bush's arrival at the school and his entry into the classroom were quite some time after the first plane hit the North Tower and 15 minutes after Andrew Card had told him about it. Second, videotape of the scene (not including the impact itself) wasn't available to the TV net-

---

[17] *December 27, 2002 edition.*

[18] This is consistent with Bush's pattern of never admitting either errors or ignorance.

[19] On December 4, 2001 and January 5, 2002. Between those dates, specifically on December 20, 2001, Bush said Karl Rove told him. Source, *Memory: Remember it Right?*, Steve Friess, *Newsweek Periscope*, *http://msnbc.msn.com/id/5970907/site/newsweek.*

[20] *Reported on CNN on December 4, 2001.*

works until much later. Nobody outside New York had seen the first impact.

The following day, CNN reported that, shortly after Bush talked to Condoleezza Rice, reporters asked him if he was aware of the two crashes and explosions. He nodded and said he would talk about the situation later.

Incredibly, pretending nothing was wrong, Bush went to the classroom and started listening to the children read the goat story. While he was there, Andrew Card came in and quietly told him, *"A second plane has hit the World Trade Center. America is under attack."* What followed borders on the unbelievable. With a blank look on his face, at least initially, Bush continued to listen to individual children read the story for something between seven and eighteen minutes. His subsequent excuse was that he didn't want to frighten the children. He could so easily have said, "I'm sorry, children. Something urgent has come up and I have to go."[21]

At 9:30, Bush talked again with Condoleezza Rice, following which he addressed the nation, saying that the country *"has suffered an apparent terrorist attack,"* which was *"a national tragedy,"* promising to chase down *"those folks who committed this act."*

It wasn't until after 9:41, which is when Flight 77 hit the Pentagon, that he gave the authorization[22] to shoot down any planes refusing to turn away from Washington. By then it was too late.[23]

---

[21] The school made a videotape of the event. It illustrates the contradiction between the actual events and the version provided by George Bush, Andrew Card and others. The videotape was eventually made available to the iconoclastic filmmaker, Michael Moore, for a segment in his award-winning documentary film, *Fahrenheit 9/11*.

[22] There is apparently some question as to whether Bush or Cheney gave the order.

[23] The last plane, which crashed into a field in Pennsylvania, may or may not have been shot down. An investigation report came to the conclusion that it had not. However, the investigators and the government have been accused of a cover up. Thus, to many, it remains an open question.

Even Andrew Card grossly distorted the events in the classroom. In a speech on the first anniversary of the attack, he claimed that Bush excused himself from the classroom seconds after he told him of the second plane hitting the South Tower. Technically, it was indeed seconds after—something over 700 seconds!

For a long time, Bush would not agree to answer questions by the 9/11 Commission about the above events or anything else about events before, during and immediately after the attack. He did, however, say he would visit them for an hour. Someone pointed out that that would be about 1.2 seconds for each of the victims. Eventually, with Dick Cheney at his side, he testified privately, and not under oath, to the Commission. Many people drew the obvious inference (whether correct or note) that Bush and Cheney wanted to ensure that their versions did not contradict one another.

An extremely detailed account of the entire day of September 11, 2001, is available, on the Internet, under the heading, *An Interesting Day: President Bush's Movements and Actions on 9/11.*[24]

Gonzalez, Alberto: Attorney General of the United States and former White House Counsel. Just like his predecessor, *John Ashcroft*, Gonzalez squeaked through his Judiciary Committee hearing by a 10 to 8 vote and was confirmed by the Senate, on February 3, 2005, by 60 votes to 36[25]—far from a ringing endorsement, and not much better than Ashcroft's 58 to 42 Senate confirmation vote. He was sworn in on the day of his confirmation.

Gonzalez' nomination was fraught with controversy, for some fairly obvious reasons.

Has Gonzalez been as bad an Attorney General as John Ashcroft? Has he been worse? He has the advantage of not

---

[24] *http://cooperativeresearch.org/timeline/main/essayaninterestingday.html.*

[25] To the disappointment and chagrin of many Democrats, six Democratic senators voted for Gonzalez—Mary Landrieu (LA), Joe Lieberman (CT), Ben Nelson (NE), Bill Nelson (FL), Mark Pryor (AK), and Ken Salazar (CO).

being a religious nut case, but his record on human rights is abysmal.

> *"This new paradigm*[26] *renders obsolete Geneva's strict limitations on questioning of enemy prisoners and renders quaint some of its provisions."*
>
> *—Alberto Gonzalez, January 25, 2002*
> *memo to George Bush*

It was his January 25, 2002, memo (*see, also,* **Yoo, John**) that provided George Bush and **Donald Rumsfeld** with an excuse to skirt the provisions of the **Geneva Conventions** (*see* **Abu Ghraib** *and* **Camp Delta**), some aspects of which Gonzalez described as "quaint" (*see the foregoing quotation*), apparently conveniently forgetting that the United States is a signatory to those conventions, giving them status as the law of the land.

He has also been very zealous in protecting George Bush's secrecy, both when Bush was Governor of Texas and in his first four years as President. As Attorney General, he has enhanced powers to support Bush's assault on the principles of open government, possibly thwarting the public's right to know the details of **Dick Cheney**'s Energy Task Force for another four years.

> *"Based on what I've seen, I don't think concerns about the media enter into [Alberto Gonzalez'] thinking. I think he is going to be even more aggressive than Ashcroft in making sure the executive right to keep secrets is protected."*
>
> *—Lucy Dalglish, Executive Director,*
> *Reporters' Committee for Freedom of the Press*

There was speculation that Gonzalez' appointment was a stepping-stone to his subsequent appointment to the U.S. Supreme Court. However, the fact that he does not apparently have strong "pro-life" beliefs could militate against such a move, given Bush's apparent anxiety to see *Roe v. Wade* overturned. In fact, the nominee for the first Supreme

---

[26] The war on terror.

Court vacancy during the Bush presidency was not Gonzalez, but Judge *John G. Roberts, Jr.*, whom Bush appointed to the D.C. Circuit Court in 2003. Bush's second nominee, after a false start with *Harriet Miers*, was *Samuel Alito*, a very knowledgeable circuit court judge (and, before that, a very knowledgeable attorney), but with a record indicating hostility towards civil liberties and women's *reproductive rights*.

In December 2005 and January 2006, Gonzalez demonstrated his unsuitability for either his current position or an eventual Supreme Court appointment, by attempting to justify George Bush's approval of wiretapping without a warrant, on the grounds that it was covered by Congress's authorization to use force, following the September 11, 2001, attacks on the World Trade Center and the Pentagon. There is no evidence that Congress intended to suspend the Fourth Amendment to the U.S. Constitution, most notably the requirement that *probable cause* be shown.

GOP: Grand Old Party. *See Republican Party.*

Goss, Porter: Director of the CIA, from September 22, 2004, until his sudden resignation on May 5, 2006. He was George Bush's choice to replace George Tenet (who had resigned). Goss was a Republican congressman and was chairman of the House Intelligence Committee, a position from which he resigned immediately after being nominated to the CIA position.

Goss's resignation from his CIA post was rumored to be because of George Bush's dissatisfaction (denied by the White House[27]) with his performance and his frequent disagreements with his boss, *John Negroponte*. Goss told CNN that the reasons would have to remain "a mystery." An intelligence official, who asked to remain anonymous, said that Goss had stood up to Negroponte on behalf of the CIA. Apparently, he objected to having to report to Negroponte,[28] who was appointed to his position after Goss's own appointment.

---

[27] *Bush denies CIA boss forced out, BBC News, May 6 2006, http://news .bbc.co.uk/2/hi/americas/4980676.stm.*

[28] Ibid.

According to congressional sources, both John Negroponte and Bush's Foreign Intelligence Advisory Board had, for some time, been telling him that he should get rid of Goss.[29]

Bush's 2004 nomination of Goss met with a mixed reception among Democrats in the Senate. Nonetheless, his confirmation occurred within two days. Interestingly, Goss's own words would seem to indicate that he didn't think himself qualified for the job with the CIA. In a March 3 interview with Michael Moore, he said:

> *"I don't have the language skills. I, you know, my language skills were romance languages and stuff. We're looking for Arabists today. I don't have the cultural background probably, and I certainly don't have the technical skills, uh, as my children remind me every day: 'Dad you got to get better on your computer.' Uh, so, the things that you need to have, I don't have."*[30]

One can argue, of course, that the Director of the CIA does not require the skills Goss claimed not to have, as those would be more properly associated with a position within the agency. Notwithstanding that, recent CIA directors have been non-partisan and, however even-handed Goss may have been as the Intelligence Committee chairman, his Republican credentials clearly identified him as a partisan.

More significant, though, is the fact the Goss cosponsored legislation in 1995 that called for a 20% cut in a five year period in the total number of people employed by the intelligence community.[31] The same legislation called for the abolition of the Department of Energy, the privatization of the air traffic control system and a number of cuts in government services. Although it was never voted on, it clearly indicated

---

[29] *Behind the Goss Toss, Richard Sisk, New York Daily News, May 7, 2006,* http://truthout.org/docs_2006/050706A.shtml.

[30] Goss can be seen and heard making this statement in a QuickTime® video on Michael Moore's website at *http://michaelmoore.com.*

[31] *Goss Backed '95 Bill to Slash Intelligence, Dana Milbank, Washington Post, August 24, 2004,* http://washingtonpost.com/wp-dyn/articles/A27092-2004Aug23.html.

a misguided sense of priorities, especially in view of the bombing of the World Trade Center two years earlier.[32]

Given that the acting Director of the CIA was quite competent, the timing of the nomination (less than three months before the 2004 Election) was regarded by many as a tactic by Bush to boost an election campaign in which his credibility on security issues was under attack.

After taking over the CIA position, Goss moved some of his former political staffers into senior CIA positions and removed or was instrumental in the resignation of several senior career CIA people.

> *"[W]e support the Administration and its policies in our work ... we do not identify with, support or champion opposition to the Administration or its policies."*[33]
>
> *— Porter Goss, November 15, 2004*
> *(in memo to CIA employees)*

Worst of all, though, he made his partisanship clear, in that he stated that he expected CIA employees to be unconditionally loyal to the administration (as opposed to being loyal to Congress or, as one has a right to expect, to their country).

Goss's top aide at the CIA was his former congressional staffer, Patrick Murray. A former CIA official has said that, when Murray was working for Goss in the House of Representatives, he leaned on him (the CIA official) several times to declassify information so he could use it to *"embarrass the Democrats."*[34]

Greenspan, Alan: Recently retired Chairman of Board of Governors of the Federal Reserve Bank ("Fed Chairman"), a position he held since President Reagan designated him Chairman to take over Paul Volcker's unexpired term on August 11, 1987. George H.W. Bush appointed him to a fourteen-year non-renewable term on the Board, starting

---

[32] George Bush criticized John Kerry for proposing a much less severe cut in intelligence spending at about the same time.

[33] *Destabilizing the CIA, Jason Vest, The Nation, November 24, 2004,* http://www.thenation.com/doc/20041213/vest.

[34] *Newsweek November 21, 2004.*

February 1, 1992, and ending on January 1, 2006. Presidents Reagan, Bush I, Clinton, and Bush II all nominated him to the position of Chairman for four-year renewable terms. The Senate confirmed him on each occasion.

> *"By repeatedly shilling for whatever the Bush administration wants, [Dr. Greenspan] has betrayed the trust placed in Fed chairmen, and deserves to be treated as just another partisan hack."*
> —*Paul Krugman, February 18, 2005*[35]

Every February 20 and July 20, at the latest (in both cases), Greenspan was required to submit to Congress a report on the economy and was called upon to testify before relevant House and Senate committees. His reports and his testimony were always very circumspect, as were his occasional speeches. In many respects, this is necessary, as the slightest misstatement can drastically affect the stock market. However, as Paul Krugman pointed out in his *New York Times* Op-Ed piece,[36] on at least two occasions, Greenspan used some subtle juxtapositions[37] that appeared to lend support to as yet undebated Bush Administration policies, specifically the 2001 tax cut for the wealthy and the 2005 proposed Social Security privatization scheme. In the face of his 2001 testimony, much of the Democratic opposition to the tax cuts evaporated, assuring passage. The same could very well have happened with the Social Security privatization scheme, although, unlike the tax cut, it faced both Democratic and Republican opposition. Needless to say, George Bush took Greenspan's ambiguous comments as an endorsement of his plans.

---

[35] *Three-Card Maestro, Paul Krugman, New York Times, February 18, 2005, http://nytimes.com/2005/02/18/opinion/18krugman.html*

[36] Ibid.

[37] Krugman compares Greenspan's juxtapositions to those used by the Bush administration in the run-up to the 2003 invasion of Iraq. In that context, the prime example was mentioning both 9/11 and Saddam Hussein in the same sentence or in successive sentences. Greenspan's juxtapositions appear to be somewhat subtler, but are similarly misleading.

Ground Zero: This expression dates from the end of World War II, and refers to the area directly below the explosion of a nuclear bomb (which, for maximum effect, is exploded some distance above the ground, unlike a conventional bomb, which explodes when it hits its target). Since September 11, 2001, it has been used to refer to the area on which the World Trade Center used to sit.

Guantánamo Bay: *See Camp Delta.*

Gulag (Гулаг): Acronym for the Russian term (Главное Управление Лагерей [**G**lavnoye **U**pravleniye **Lag**erey]), meaning "Corrective Labor Camps."[38] Alexander Solzhenitsyn wrote extensively on the topic in his book, *"The Gulag Archipelago."* Although its purpose is not corrective,[39] a string of prisons run by the U.S. military, including *Abu Ghraib*, in Baghdad, and *Camp Delta*, at Guantánamo Bay, Cuba, has been compared (with some degree of hyperbole) to the Soviet Gulag.

Gutierrez, Carlos: Secretary of Commerce in George Bush's second term. George Bush nominated the former CEO of Kellogg on November 29, 2004, to succeed *Donald Evans*, who had announced his resignation two weeks earlier. Gutierrez was confirmed, by voice vote in the Senate, on January 24, 2005.

> *"He [Carlos Gutierrez] knows exactly what it takes to make American businesses grow and create jobs."*
>
> —*George W. Bush, November 29, 2004*

On August 15, 1999, under Gutierrez' leadership, Kellogg eliminated about 550 jobs[40] at its Battle Creek, MI, cereal plant. Although it improved Kellogg's financial situation, the company's survival does not appear to have depended on it. Moreover, it contradicted the motto of W.K. Kellogg,

---

[38] The full term, which contains two additional words and describes the entire bureaucracy, means "The Chief Directorate of Corrective Labor Camps."

[39] In reality, the purpose of the Soviet Gulag was not corrective, either.

[40] This was in addition to layoffs starting in 1996.

the company's founder, which was, *"I'll invest my money in people."* One of Gutierrez' justifications for the layoff was *"enabl[ing] greater investment for profitable growth."*

Gutierrez is a Republican contributor, but not a major one. In 2004, he made contributions to Republican candidates and the Republican National Committee, totaling $12,000. The good news is that he doesn't appear to be an ideologue. The bad (but unsurprising) news is that he agrees with Bush's fiscal policy.

H

> H is for Home, as in *"Home is important. It's impor-*
> *tant to have a home."*
> —*George Bush, Crawford, TX, February 18, 2001*
> (Be it ever so humble.)

Hadley, Stephen J.: George Bush's National Security Advisor and successor to *Condoleezza Rice*. Prior to his appointment on January 26, 2005, he was Assistant to the President and Deputy National Security Advisor.

Like his former boss (Rice), Hadley is a firm supporter of missile defense systems. He is, not surprisingly, considered to be a *neoconservative* and is very close to Vice President *Dick Cheney*.

Halliburton: The multinational Halliburton is the world's largest oil field services company.

Through its subsidiaries, including KBR (Kellogg Brown and Root) and Dresser Industries, Halliburton provides a variety of services in addition to those related to the energy industry. Those services include general construction and a large number of military support functions, including food services and the transportation of fuel

Halliburton has become very controversial in recent years, especially during the George W. Bush administration, for a number of reasons, including its use of offshore subsidiaries to provide both tax shelters and a means of conducting business with countries not approved by the State Department, its seemingly endless series of highly profitable no-bid government contracts, and the involvement of Vice President *Dick Cheney*, who became the company's CEO after the end of his tenure as Secretary of Defense at the beginning of 1993. He resigned on becoming Bush's vice presidential running mate in 2000.

At a time when the use of offshore tax havens is coming under increasing scrutiny, or at least criticism, Halliburton's record in that respect is particularly egregious. Because of its numerous government contracts, it has become the beneficiary of billions in taxpayer dollars, while at the same time increasing the burden on ordinary taxpayers by not paying its own share of taxes.

> *"An analysis of Halliburton filings with the SEC indicates that while Dick Cheney was CEO of Halliburton (between 1995 and 2000) the number of company subsidiaries incorporated in offshore tax havens rose from 9 to 44."*
>
> *—Citizen Works, July 31, 2002*[1]

In 1998, Halliburton paid $302 million in corporate taxes. In 1999, its use of tax havens yielded a refund of $85 million,[2] a $387 million reduction from one year to the next.

In 2003, in the nine months following the start of hostilities in Iraq, Halliburton received contracts worth $2.2 billion.[3] This was about 57% more than the total of contracts awarded to the eleven other U.S. companies providing services in Iraq. Only Bechtel had a contract, for construction, that was, at $1.03 billion, even in the same league as Halliburton's. Halliburton's contracts (two) for fuel distribution alone yielded $1.05 billion.

What is most scandalous about Halliburton and its government contracts (with the Defense Department, FEMA, etc.) is the extent to which they appear to have overcharged. One congressman who has been keeping close tabs on Halliburton is Henry Waxman (D-CA), ranking member of the Committee on Government Reform. In

[1] *Halliburton subsidiaries in offshore tax havens increased under Vice President Dick Cheney, Citizen Works: Tools for Democracy, July 31, 2002, http://www.citizenworks.org/admin/press/halliburton-pr.php.*

[2] *Halliburton, Dick Cheney, and Wartime Spoils, Lee Drutman and Charlie Cray, Common Dreams News Center, April 3, 2003, http://commondreams.org/views03/0403-10.htm.*

[3] *Glance at $2.2B Halliburton Iraq Contract, Associated Press, December 12, 2003, http://truthout.org/docs_03/printer_121403D.shtml.*

March 2005, he disclosed that Defense Department auditors found $108 million in fuel-related overcharges for work in Iraq under something called Task Order 5, which was one of several Halliburton task orders for the importation of fuel into Iraq. It appears that Halliburton received payment from Iraqi oil proceeds in the Development Fund for Iraq (DFI). At Halliburton's request the Bush administration concealed the resulting overcharges from the UN-assigned auditors who were monitoring the expenditures from the DFI.[4]

Further audits[5] of Halliburton's Iraqi oil reconstruction work under additional task orders revealed even more overcharges, concealed by withholding information from the auditors at the International Advisory and Monitoring Board (IAMB). References to the overcharges, which totaled $212.3 million (including the previously discovered $108 million), were blacked out over 450 times in the versions of audits the Bush administration sent to the IAMB. The website of the Committee on Government Reform Minority Office includes an interactive feature allowing the visitor to see the redactions in one of the original audit documents and, by clicking on them, to see the original text.[6] It's a revealing example of government and corporate dishonesty of the highest order.

It gets even worse. In the case of six of the task orders under the *Restore Iraqi Oil* contract, Halliburton was eventually told to repay the amount of the overcharges. However, they were able to get away with repaying only 27%. Worse still, Halliburton was paid millions of dollars in bonuses.[7] In the

---

[4] *Iraq Reconstruction, DOD Audits: Halliburton Overcharges Top $212 Million, Committee on Government Reform Minority Office, April 11, 2005, http://democrats.reform.house.gov/story.asp?ID=823.*

[5] Ordered by the National Security Subcommittee of the Committee on Government Reform.

[6] *Administration Withheld Halliburton Overcharges from International Auditors, March 15, 2005, http://democrats.reform.house.gov/story.asp?ID=812.*

[7] *Halliburton got bonuses for overbilling taxpayers by $169 million, Halliburton Watch, December 2, 2005, http://halliburtonwatch.org/news/billings_bonuses.html.*

end, the taxpayers are left holding the bag for the other 73% and nobody in Halliburton is charged with a crime.

Hannity, Sean: Right-wing co-host of *Hannity and Colmes* on Fox News and host of his own afternoon talk radio show.[8] Hannity's virtual monopolization of the dialogue so overwhelms his TV co-host that Al Franken, in his 2003 book, *Lies and the Lying Liars Who Tell Them,*[9] consistently refers to the show as *"Hannity and Colmes."*

Hannity shares a characteristic with **Rush Limbaugh** (and other right-wing talk show hosts), namely carelessness with the truth. On his show of April 13, 2004, he accused a caller of *"not listening,"* then proceeded to insist to her that Saddam Hussein had had weapons of mass destruction, had promised to disclose them, and had broken that promise. This was more than six months after David Kay, the Bush administration's own weapons inspector, testified that his team had *"not uncovered evidence that Iraq undertook significant post-1998 steps to actually build nuclear weapons or produce fissile material"* and had not discovered any chemical or biological weapons.[10] In fact, in the run-up to the war, Saddam Hussein had made a full declaration (in the form of thousands of documents) of the status of his weapons programs and had given inspectors full access. The withdrawal of the inspectors, before they had a chance to complete their work, was a Bush decision.

Like so many on the hysterical right, Hannity is a master of hypocrisy. When President Clinton took action in Kosovo, he said, *"American foreign policy is now one huge big mystery. Simply put, the administration is trying to lead the world with a feel-good foreign policy."*[11] Even though that now appears to

---

[8] The Sean Hannity Show, WABC-AM and affiliated stations.

[9] *Lies and the Lying Liars Who Tell Them: A Fair and Balanced Look at the Right,* Al Franken, E.P. Dutton, August 2003, ISBN 0-525-94764-7.

[10] *Center for American Progress: The Document Sean Hannity Doesn't Want You To Read,* http://americanprogress.org/site/pp.asp?c=biJRJ8OVF&b=91585.

[11] *Crooks and Liars, http://crooksandliars.com/stories/2005/08/17/ heresWhatRepublicansSaidAboutClintonAndKosovo.html.*

be what George Bush is doing, Hannity is strangely silent on the matter (other than excoriating anyone who is critical of the *Bush Doctrine*).

Harris, Katherine: Congresswoman (R-FL), elected in 2002, and Florida's Secretary of State before and during the 2000 election.

Harris is particularly notorious for her role in the 2000 presidential election in Florida. First, she was both Secretary of State and George Bush's Florida campaign manager; a more blatant conflict of interest would be hard to imagine. Second, she was a prime mover (along with her predecessor, Sandra Mortham) in the infamous *felon purge*, which disenfranchised thousands of eligible voters (mostly Democrats, and representing several times the number of votes by which George Bush supposedly prevailed over Al Gore after the Supreme Court stopped the vote counting). Third, she imposed a wholly unrealistic deadline for the completion of a hand recount of the votes.

In 2005, Harris started her campaign to run against Democratic Senator Bill Nelson in the 2006 mid-term elections.

> *"I just don't think she can win."*[12]
>
> — *Florida Governor Jeb Bush, Tallahassee, May 8, 2006*

Her fellow Republicans are not especially enthusiastic about her candidacy and, as of mid-April 2006, she was trailing Nelson in the polls by 30 points (27% to 57%).[13] Jeb Bush is reported to have expressed the hope that Florida House Speaker, Allan Bense (R), would challenge Harris in the primaries.

Hart-Rudman Commission: The official name was *U.S. Commission on National Security/21st Century*. Established in 1998, it was co-chaired by former Senators Gary Hart (De-

---

[12] *Gov. Jeb Bush Says Harris Can't Win, Local6.com, May 8, 2006, http://www.local6.com/news/9177300/detail.html.*

[13] *Florida Senate: Nelson (D) 57% Harris (R) 27%, Rasmussen Reports, April 14 2006, http://rasmussenreports.com/2006/State%20Polls/ April%202006/Florida%20Senate%20April.htm.*

mocrat) and Warren Rudman (Republican). The commission produced Phase I, II and III reports, of which the last, *Road Map for National Security: Imperative for Change,* contained all their recommendations.

In a spirit of bipartisanship (or nonpartisanship) so essential for such commissions, it included former Democratic Congressman Lee Hamilton (later to co-chair the 9/11 Commission) and former House Speaker *Newt Gingrich* (Republican). It also included such people as John R. Galvin, Olin Distinguished Professor of National Security at the United States Military Academy and onetime Supreme Allied Commander Europe, James R. Schlesinger, Secretary of Defense in the Nixon and Ford administrations, Andrew Young, civil rights hero, former Mayor of Atlanta and Jimmy Carter's choice for U.N. Ambassador, and Anne Armstrong, counselor to Presidents Nixon and Ford and former U.S. Ambassador to the United Kingdom. In short, the commission members were broadly qualified to undertake the task with which they were charged.

The commission's report was released on January 31, 2001, just eleven days after George Bush's inauguration and celebration (which, at a cost of about $40 million, was probably the most expensive ever).[14] In addition to providing the White House with the report, Gary Hart and Warren Rudman personally briefed *Condoleezza Rice, Donald Rumsfeld* and *Colin Powell,* warning them of the potential imminence of a terrorist attack.

We now know that, along with all the other warnings (e.g., Presidential Daily Briefings), the recommendations of this report were ignored.

Hastert, Dennis (Denny): Speaker of the House of Representatives and Republican representative from Illinois' 14th District.

---

[14] The celebrations associated with Bush's second inauguration, in January 2005, were equally extravagant. That was, of course, no surprise. However, as the self-styled *"Wartime President,"* Bush should certainly have exercised some restraint, as should those who organized the events.

Hastert has shown himself to be a strong Bush loyalist and a staunch ally of now-indicted former Majority Leader *Tom De-Lay* in ensuring that every possible procedural trick is used to push through legislation favored by both Bush and DeLay and to block legislation favored by Democrats and moderate Republicans.

One of the most egregious examples of the tactics he and DeLay used concerned the *Medicare Drug Bill* (which created Medicare Part D), where he extended the required fifteen minute limit for a roll call vote to almost three hours to allow time for arm-twisting of Republicans opposed to the legislation by him, DeLay, *Karl Rove*, then HHS Secretary Tommy Thompson and George Bush, reversing an initial 218 to 216 vote against the bill to 220 to 215 in favor. Some of the initial 218 planned to vote against the bill if its projected cost exceeded $400 billion. Hastert et al were, no doubt, annoyed that even the phony projection of a lower cost didn't garner sufficient favorable votes.[15]

In March 2005, the *Denver Post* reported on the use, by Hastert and DeLay, of the House Rules Committee to rewrite bills to their own advantage (usually in the middle of the night). They would then waive the rules to move them to a floor vote before anyone could read them. This violated a rule requiring House-Senate conference reports to be published in the Congressional Record and held for at least three days prior to a vote. In the 108th Congress (2003-2004), they did this no fewer than 28 times.

Where Hastert is unable to change a bill he doesn't like, he has used stalling tactics to prevent it from coming to a vote. In November 2005, he delayed a vote on a proposed ban on the use of cruel and degrading treatment of prisoners in US custody, even though it used wording inserted in a Senate

---

[15] Much of the information regarding Dennis Hastert is in an April 6, 2005 press release from the Democratic National Committee, viewable at *http://buzzflash.com/alerts/05/04/ale05051.html*. The press release is composed of excerpts of reports appearing over the preceding year in a large cross section of leading newspapers and on news outlets such as CNN (including cnn.com).

bill by his fellow Republican, Senator John McCain (R-AZ) and approved by the Senate by a vote of 90 to 9.[16] Democrats accused Hastert of trying to save **Dick Cheney** embarrassment at a time when his former aide, **I. Lewis Libby**, was under indictment.

Finally (for the purpose of this entry, anyway), Hastert changed ethics rules and the composition of the House Rules Committee to slow down that committee's actions with respect to Tom DeLay's ethical breaches.

Interestingly, in other deliberative bodies (e.g., the British House of Commons[17]), the speaker is required to maintain a scrupulous neutrality and not be involved in any debate or vote, other than to maintain order.

Hayden, Michael: Director of the Central Intelligence Agency (CIA). Hayden, an Air Force General, was nominated by George Bush, on May 8, 2006, to replace **Porter Goss**. The Senate Intelligence Committee approved the nomination by a vote of 12 to 3 and was confirmed by the Senate, on May 26, by a vote of 78 to 15. Until his confirmation, he remained principal deputy director of National Intelligence. Previously, he was director of the National Security Agency (NSA).

Hayden's nomination was controversial for a number of reasons, one of which is that he is a military officer and would be heading a civilian agency. Some in Congress said that their objection would probably still stand, even if he were to resign his commission, as he would be seen to have an allegiance to the Pentagon, with which the CIA must feel free, if necessary, to disagree.[18] Some members of Congress were uneasy, as all the other intelligence agencies are headed by military men.

---

[16] *House Delays Vote on U.S. Treatment of Terrorism Suspects, Eric Schmitt, New York Times, November 4, 2005, http://select.nytimes.com/ search/restricted/article?res=FB0814F83C5A0C778CDDA80994DD40448 2* (requires subscription).

[17] *The United Kingdom Parliament: The Speaker of the House of Commons, http://www.parliament.uk/works/speaker.cfm.*

[18] To his credit, Hayden has shown a willingness, in the past, to stand up to the Pentagon.

The CIA has been headed by former senior military officers. It has also been headed by serving military offices, including Air Force General Hoyt Vandenberg (June 1946 to May 1947), who was appointed during the final months of World War II, Rear Admiral Roscoe Hillenkoetter (May 1947 to October 1950), and Admiral Stansfield Turner (March 1977 to January 1981), who resigned his naval commission almost two years into his CIA tenure. So, although disquieting, it would not be unprecedented for General Hayden to keep his commission.

> *"So now they're turning the CIA over to a general who not only ran the warrantless wiretap program but still can't figure out that it's unconstitutional."*[19]
>
> *—Molly Ivins, May 8, 2006*

More important, perhaps, than the issue of his military status is his apparent misunderstanding of at least one article of the **Bill of Rights**. In an appearance, on January 23, 2006, before the National Press Club, Hayden defended the National Security Agency's warrantless monitoring of communications involving people suspected of being Al-Qaeda terrorists on the grounds that it is only necessary to show that the action is reasonable. Under polite but persistent questioning by a reporter, he refused to acknowledge that it was necessary to show probable cause, a requirement made very clear in the Fourth Amendment to the U.S. Constitution.[20] He even refused to acknowledge the existence of the probable cause provision. What is really appalling is that he represents himself as a Fourth Amendment expert and should therefore know better, particularly as he has a master's degree in history.[21]

---

[19] *The Best Little Whorehouse in Washington, Molly Ivins, Truthdig, May 8, 2006, http://www.truthout.org/docs_2006/050906A.shtml.*

[20] *Probable Cause for Alarm: Press ignores Ex-NSA chief's ignorance of Constitution, Fairness & Accuracy in Reporting Media Advisory, January 27, 2006, http://fair.org/index.php?page=2808.*

[21] Modern American history, Duquesne University, 1969.

Healthy Forests Initiative: Implemented as the *Healthy Forests Restoration Act,* this exercise in doublespeak was signed into law by George Bush on December 3, 2003.

Rather than being a genuine attempt to improve and preserve forests, it is designed to increase commercial logging in national forests in line with what has always been the Bush administration's stated goal.[22] One of the alleged goals of the "initiative" is to prevent forest fires that would threaten nearby homes by logging smaller and fallen trees, even though the U.S. Forest Service's own fire research lab found that the best method of protecting houses and communities from forest fires is to create a "defensible" space 30 meters wide around an isolated house and 500 meters wide around a community.[23]

The Sierra Club and the Wilderness Society supported an alternative Democrat-sponsored bill that would also encourage the thinning of forests on private land, while at the same time leaving in place environmental safeguards, including an explicit prohibition on logging old-growth trees.[24]

Heritage Foundation: This is the best known of the conservative think tanks. It is also the largest of its kind in Washington, DC. Their own self-description says, "A conservative think tank that publishes research on domestic, economic, foreign and defense policy."

It was founded in 1973 by Joseph Coors (of the well-known beer-brewing family) and Paul Weyrich, both well known for their very right wing views.

Homeland Security: *See Department of Homeland Security.*

Hughes, Karen: Undersecretary of State for Public Diplomacy, with the rank of ambassador. Secretary of State *Condo-*

---

[22] *Bush's Forest Plan Signals Return to 'Logging Without Laws', Matthew Koehler, Native Forest Network, http://nativeforest.org/press_room/release_bfp_8_22_02.htm.*

[23] *House passes forest thinning bill: Bush says measure will help prevent forest fires, CNN, May 20, 2003, http://www.cnn.com/2003/ALLPOLITICS/05/20/bush.forests.*

[24] Ibid.

leezza Rice announced Hughes' nomination by George Bush on March 14, 2005. The Senate confirmed her on July 26. Hughes first worked for George Bush, in the 1990s, when he was Governor of Texas. She was heavily involved in his 2000 presidential campaign and was a very forceful presence during the 2000 Election recount saga. This led to an 18-month stint as a special advisor to Bush. Her new job follows a hiatus of almost three years. The *Dallas Morning News* has described her as "the most powerful woman ever to serve in the White House."

Her new job involves traveling the world, burnishing the image of the United States, and particularly that of the Bush administration. This is consistent with George Bush's emphasis on image, as opposed to substance. As Hughes appears to believe that George Bush can do no wrong, she would seem to be a good fit for the job. On the other hand, her absolute belief in Bush is well known (and documented in her own book), so she could well face skepticism as she pursues her public relations goals. Amazingly, Hughes has spent a fair amount of her time in the Middle East. This is in spite of the fact that she speaks no Arabic and that she seems to have little knowledge of the region.

Apart from some early press coverage, reports of Ms. Hughes' activities seem to be very rare.

Hughes' Views[25]

1. *Pro-choice folks are terrorists*
2. *Only Republicans are normal*
3. *George Bush is our best president ever*
4. *This administration is flawless*

In March 2004, Hughes' book, *Ten Minutes from Normal*, was published. Reviews ran the gamut from gushing praise to scathing derision. One can perhaps judge her credibility (or its absence) from her descriptions of Bush: "laser-like

---

[25] From a reader's review (Ted Bell, Dallas, TX), on Amazon.com, of Karen Hughes' 2004 book, *Ten Minutes from Normal.*

mind," "humble spirit," "moral courage," etc. One particularly scathing review includes the statement, *"Behind this gross-out memoir of gooey sentimentality and jingoism lies a ruthlessness that has no regard for fact or truth and would not hesitate unraveling the intestines of a puppy to advance its Bush agenda."*[26] The puppy image is an obvious bit of hyperbole. However the jingoism and ruthlessness certainly seemed to be present during *Bush v. Gore*. One of the pithiest reviews said, *"Self-aggrandizing drivel. Save your money."*[27] Quite a few echoed that theme. Although many apparent Bush supporters, unsurprisingly, submitted admiring reviews to Amazon.com, many others (i.e., other Bush supporters, who identified themselves as such) wrote quite unflattering comments.

---

[26] Written on November 17, 2004, on the Amazon.com website, by "Loudon," PA.

[27] Written on May 21, 2004, on the Amazon.com website, by Jon de Vos of Winter Park, CO.

I

> I is for Important and Internet, as in *"It's important for us to explain to our nation that life is important. It's not only life of babies, but it's life of children living in, you know, the dark dungeons of the Internet."*
> —George Bush, Arlington Heights, IL, October 24, 2000
> (Dragons, too.)

ideological certainty: Uncertainty is a fundamental characteristic of science and of life in general. Very little can be known for certain. In the vernacular, we talk of the only certainties being death and taxes. Only religious fundamentalists and political ideologues enjoy the certainty that comes with the exclusion of all evidence that might conflict with their comfortable dogma.

Unfortunately for America (and the planet), George Bush exemplifies the worst of all possible worlds, combining religious fundamentalist extremism with political ideology. He appears to be so certain of his own "divinely guided" rightness—seeing things with what he believes to be moral clarity—that he is unable to reconsider any of his decisions.[1]

impeachment: The process by which a public officer may be charged with offences leading to possible removal from office. The U.S. House of Representatives has the power to impeach the President, Vice President, federal judges and members of Congress.

> *The President, Vice President and all civil Officers of the United States, shall be removed from Office on Impeachment for, and Conviction of, Treason, Bribery, or other high Crimes and Misdemeanors.*
> —*U.S. Constitution, Article II, Section 4*

---

[1] On the other hand, it could all be a cover for actions that reward his major corporate contributors.

The House has impeached presidents and federal judges. No vice president has been impeached, and committees are delegated the task of impeaching members of Congress. For a president, once one or more articles of impeachment have received a majority vote, a trial is held in the Senate, with the Chief Justice presiding, and with a two thirds vote required for removal from office.

Of the three presidents who have faced impeachment, two were acquitted (Andrew Johnson and Bill Clinton). Richard Nixon resigned in time to avoid a Senate verdict.

Although the specific citation of treason and bribery provides some kind of setting for how "high crimes and misdemeanors" might be interpreted, the definition of those terms seems to be open to interpretation, although "misdemeanors" is a term that is considered to be more serious in the impeachment context than in the criminal justice system. In the case of Bill Clinton, the bar was set very low when the House's case was built around his lying about a sexual peccadillo.[2]

Impeachment should not be a partisan issue. Unfortunately, though, it is. In a House with a Republican majority, it was relatively easy to bring articles of impeachment against a Democratic president over what was really only a personal matter (its inappropriateness and unseemliness notwithstanding). Even though some of George Bush's actions (e.g., attacking another country on the basis of lies and contrary to international law, bribery, coercion, concealing of information vital to public discussion, etc.) appear to rise to the level of treason (or, at the very least, high crimes), the probability of an affirmative vote on articles of impeachment appears to be zero. Such was not the case with Richard Nixon, where members of his own party (Republican) did, indeed, vote to impeach him. Republicans (most notably

---

[2] Apparently, there is no case (or possibly only a couple of cases) on record of a court convicting someone of perjury for lying about consensual sex.

Senators Howard Baker and Lowell Weicker[3]) were also very prominent in the Senate proceedings.

As of June 30, 2005, a Zogby Poll[4] revealed that 42% of the population would favor impeachment of George Bush if it were proven that he lied about the Iraq War.[5] Other polls indicate that a majority believes that he did, indeed, lie. Breaking down the 42% in the Zogby poll by party reveals that 59% of Democrats would be in favor of impeachment, which is not surprising; what is surprising is that 25% of Republicans agree with them. Both House and Senate Republicans, even those in safe seats,[6] may have some reason to be nervous about the 2006 mid-term elections.

There are several movements seeking impeachment of George W. Bush, along with individual efforts or pro-impeachment statements by people like Congressman John Conyers, Ralph Nader and John Dean. There are also calls for the impeachment of **Dick Cheney, Donald Rumsfeld** and **Karl Rove.**[7] Until his November 2004 resignation, **John Ashcroft** was also a target for impeachment.

incoherence: See the George Bushisms at the beginning of each alphabetical section.

Inhofe, James: Senior Republican Senator from Oklahoma. Inhofe is in his third term and up for re-election in 2006. He is Chairman of the Environmental and Public Works Com-

---

[3] After leaving the Senate, Weicker gave up his Republican Party membership and, in 1990, ran successfully as an independent for the governorship of Connecticut.

[4] *No Bounce: Bush Job Approval Unchanged by War Speech; Question on Impeachment Shows Polarization of Nation; Americans Tired of Divisiveness in Congress—Want Bi-Partisan Solutions—New Zogby Poll, Zogby International, June 30, 2005, http://www.zogby.com/news/ReadNews.dbm?ID=1007.* The poll shows Bush's overall approval rating at 43%. As of mid-September, 2005, it was below 40% and continuing to slip.

[5] A somewhat cautious position, given that the record shows that he lied about Iraq and about many other things.

[6] A consequence of the politicized nature of the redistricting process.

[7] *Wikipedia: Movement to impeach George W. Bush, http://en.Wikipedia.org/wiki/Movement_to_impeach_George_W._Bush.*

mittee, which is one of the most egregious cases ever of the *fox guarding the hen house*.[8]

His opinions are quite interesting, if unsurprising. He believes that global warming is *"the greatest hoax ever perpetrated on the American people"* and that the Environmental Protection Agency (EPA) is a *"Gestapo bureaucracy."*[9] In this respect, he goes even further than **Jerry Falwell**, whose oft-repeated assertion about global warming is that it is *"a myth."* Inhofe appears to be a keen fan of Falwell, and relies on him and ExxonMobil lobbyists, among others, for wisdom on global warming and other environmental issues. Like other FOPs (friends of polluters), he dismisses previous and ongoing research and conclusions by the world's leading climatologists and those in related disciplines, whose work, unlike the faith-based mental processes of Falwell or the coin-operated[10] bias of the lobbyists, is subject to rigorous peer review.

When, thanks to one Republican with a conscience (Lincoln Chafee (RI)), he was unable to push George Bush's inaptly-named and polluter-friendly Clear Skies Act (*see* **Clear Skies Initiative**) through his committee in the Senate, he turned petulant and ordered the two primary organizations opposing the plan (and representing 48 state and 165 local air pollution control agencies) to turn over all their financial and tax records.[11] Interestingly, the two organizations have accepted no money from environmental activists or any other private interests, unlike Inhofe himself, who is the runner up to Senator John Cornyn (R-TX) in terms of the

---

[8] George Bush cannot, of course, be blamed for this one, as Senate committee chairmanships are Senate controlled and are based on seniority (and, of course, on being a member of the majority party).

[9] *Inhofe's Idiocy, The Nation, Blog, Daily Outrage, February 22, 2005, http://www.thenation.com/blogs/outrage?bid=13&pid=2211.*

[10] Coin-operated is a term used (sometimes tongue in cheek, sometimes seriously) to characterize people whose primary motivation is money. In vendor organizations, for example, it sets the commissioned sales people apart from the support people.

[11] *Inhofe's Idiocy, The Nation, Blog, Daily Outrage, February 22, 2005, http://www.thenation.com/blogs/outrage?bid=13&pid=2211.*

amount of campaign money received from big oil and gas companies.[12] In the words of the final paragraph of the *Inhofe's Idiocy* article,[13] talk about a hoax!

Interior, Department of: *See Norton, Gale.*

international terrorism: *See terrorism.*

Iraq Group: *See Card, Andrew H., Jr.*

Issa, Darrell: Republican Congressman for California's 49th District (San Diego). His voting record reveals him to be quite conservative, in which respect he typifies most House Republicans.[14]

NARAL Pro-Choice America gives him a zero rating on the question of reproductive choice. He is opposed to same sex marriage and in favor of the *flag desecration amendment*, having voted in favor of the last three attempts (2001, 2003, 2005) to pass it. On the environment, he voted in favor of the misleadingly named Healthy Forests Restoration Act (*see* **Healthy Forests Initiative**). On gun control, he doesn't like it, as evidenced by his "A" rating from the NRA.

On public health, the American Public Health Association (APHA), has given him a miserable 12% rating. In 2003, he voted against the reimportation of prescription drugs, while at the same time voting for the 2003 Medicare bill that prohibited the government from negotiating prescription drug prices.

In 2003, Issa bankrolled the recall campaign against California Governor Gray Davis, seeing himself as the probable winner of the post-recall vote. However, he withdrew, somewhat tearfully, when Arnold Schwarzenegger announced his candidacy. Although his name was never on

---

[12] Ibid.

[13] Ibid.

[14] For a comprehensive breakdown of the views and voting record of every American political leader, including Darrell Issa, you may want to visit the *On The Issues* website at *http://issues2000.org*. In spite of the 2000 in the URL, the site is up to date.

the ballot (as he withdrew his name before ballots were printed), his website (*issaforgovernor.com*) was still active and soliciting contributions as late as mid-January, 2004. The website, which contained his official biography, had disappeared by March 2004. A copy of the site, including a still-active contribution form, continued to be viewable at the UCLA Library site until well into 2005.

Prior to his election to Congress, Issa had a checkered past, with arrests on illegal-weapons charges (including a misdemeanor conviction) and car theft. Interestingly, he subsequently became a millionaire running his own high-tech car alarm company (with a payroll of about 150 people).

Istook, Ernest J., Jr.: Republican Congressman from Oklahoma (5th District). In 2000, he was one of six people on the "Emergency Committee to Defeat Al Gore" and the "Emergency Committee to Stop Hillary Rodham Clinton."[15] Gore ended up being defeated by a Supreme Court decision (*see Felonious Five*) and Hillary Clinton won her Senate seat by a comfortable margin in New York State.

In November 2004, Istook sneaked a provision into a 3000-page $388 million spending bill that would have allowed chairmen of appropriation committees and their staff members to look at the tax returns of any U.S. taxpayer. When it was discovered, he and other involved Republicans claimed that their motives were misread and that there was no intention to invade the privacy of taxpayers. House and Senate leaders (including House Speaker Dennis Hastert) agreed to remove the provision, after expressing (or feigning) outrage.

On June 4, 1998, the House defeated, by 61 votes, Istook's proposed constitutional amendment that would have authorized tax aid to faith-based private schools and various forms of hitherto prohibited religious activities in public schools.

---

[15] The other members of both committees were Morton C. Blackwell, a conservative activist, former California Congressman Bob Dornan, Alan Keyes, Reagan's Attorney General Ed Meese, and Lyn Nofziger, the well-known political operative.

J

> J is for jobs, as in *"And if one of those jobs are cre-ated, we must have a system which trains people for the jobs which actually exist."*
> —George Bush, on employment training, June 17, 2003
> (Apparently.)

James, Daniel: Lieutenant General Daniel James III was nomi-nated, on October 2, 2001, by George Bush, to the position of Director, Air National Guard. In the process, he was promoted from Major General to Lieutenant General, mak-ing him the highest-ranking officer to serve in that capacity. The Senate confirmed the appointment by voice vote on May 16, 2002.

Why is this interesting? James was previously Adjutant General of the Texas Air National Guard, where the Na-tional Guard records of George W. Bush were apparently "scrubbed."

According to Lieutenant Colonel Bill Burkett, (Texas Air National Guard, ret.), he (Burkett) *"was outside the Adjutant General of Texas office when I overheard a call from Joe All-baugh[1] and Dan Bartlett[2] that told General James to 'make sure there is nothing embarrassing in the Governor's file' in prepara-tion for his reelection run and a run for the presidency. I was pre-sent when James and Asst. AG General Marty told a state ser-vices employee to do the same. I was there when the retained re-cords person surrendered files under order of Col. William Good-win, Chief of Staff, for the scrub of the Governor's files."[3]

---

[1] Joe Allbaugh was appointed by Bush to head FEMA, from which he re-signed, effective March 1, 2003.

[2] Dan Bartlett was subsequently appointed by Bush as White House Com-munications Director.

[3] Source: *http://buzzflash.com/analysis/2002/05/28_Scrubbed.html*. Bur-kett is also a Contributing Writer for Online Journal (*http://online journal.com*).

Burkett's credibility regarding the above events is very high, as he lodged a complaint, at the time, in a letter to a member of the Texas Senate. This did not, of course, stop the Bush campaign from claiming, in the run-up to the 2004 election, that he was politically motivated.

Unfortunately, Burkett's overall credibility has since been challenged, because of his involvement, in 2004, in supplying copies of typewritten memoranda, signed by Bush's commanding officer, to CBS's *60 Minutes II* for their program on the gaps and other problems in Bush's Texas National Guard service. An inquiry fell short of declaring them to be forged, but was unable to authenticate them.[4] Unfortunately, the controversy overshadowed the already-known and well-researched facts about Bush's service (or non-service) and the Bush campaign changed the subject by impugning candidate John Kerry's service in Vietnam.

> *"Does nothing stick to this guy, who has yet to come clean about his alkie, Vietnam-evading past? After all, the basics of the CBS story were true, reported five years ago by Greg Palast and other real don't-just-play-one-on-TV reporters."*[5]
>
> —*Antonia Zerbisias, September 21, 2004*

jingoism: Pseudo-patriotism, usually based on talking points, slogans, or the desire to portray dissenters as "traitors" or "un-American."

Johanns, Mike: Secretary of Agriculture in George Bush's second term, replacing Ann Veneman. He was nominated on December 2, 2004, unanimously confirmed by the Senate on January 20, 2005, and sworn in on January 21. Formerly, he was the Republican Governor of Nebraska.

---

[4] The secretary of Bush's commanding officer said that the views of Bush expressed in the memoranda were, indeed, those of her boss, regardless of whether the copies were of the genuine article.

[5] *CBS's Memo Becomes a Free Pass for Bush,* Antonia Zerbisias, *Toronto Star,* September 21, 2004, http://www.commondreams.org/views04/0921-09.htm.

As Governor, Johanns promoted the production of ethanol in his state, well known for its corn production. Corn-based ethanol, as a gasoline additive, is controversial, partly because growing the corn from which it is produced is highly subsidized, partly because of the amount of fossil fuel consumed in growing and harvesting it, and partly because its use results in only a small reduction in the emission of greenhouse gases. As Secretary of Agriculture, Johanns is expected to continue to promote corn-based ethanol production. [6]

Johnson, Stephen L.: Administrator of the Environmental Protection Agency (EPA) in George W. Bush's second term. Bush nominated him on March 4 2005, while he was acting Administrator. He was confirmed on April 29 and sworn in on May 2. Although he had a 24-year career with the EPA, his confirmation was not without controversy, based on his support, during Bush's first term, of the testing of pesticides on people. Specifically, he had said, *"We are willing to consider that such studies can be useful."* This was in spite of the fact that an EPA-convened panel of scientists and ethicists had, in 1998, determined that such trials were not only unethical, but also unsuitable for estimating the safety of chemicals. The studies in question, conducted in 2001, had given paid volunteers pesticide doses that were hundreds of times greater than the amount considered safe for the public.[7] In April 2005, during the confirmation process, Johnson changed his position (and, therefore, that of the EPA), thus removing the objection to his confirmation.

Given his long and apparently unblemished career, Johnson appears to be one of the better Bush appointees.

---

[6] *Mikey Likes It, Bush's pick to head the USDA is a big ethanol booster, Amanda Griscom Little, Muckraker, Grist Magazine (environmental news and commentary), December 9, 2004, http://grist.org/news/muck/2004/12/09/little-johanns.*

[7] *E.P.A. Nominee Supports Testing of Chemicals on Human Subjects, http://u.webring.com/forum?forum=badgovernment;did=99#here.*

K

K is for Killers, as in *"Wait for us to succeed peace. Wait for us to have two states, side by side—is for everybody coming together to deny the killers the opportunity to destroy."*
—George Bush, to travel pool reporters, June 15, 2003
(If he says so.)

Kempthorne, Dirk: Secretary of the Interior, replacing *Gale Norton*. He was previously Governor of Idaho. George Bush announced his nomination on March 16, 2006, a week after Norton's resignation. His nomination was sent to the Senate on April 24, where he was confirmed on May 26.

> *"Gov. Kempthorne has built his career by pushing an anti-environmental agenda and catering to the oil, mining, and timber industries. Kempthorne is cut from the same cloth as Gale Norton. He will be a cheerleader for the Bush administration's efforts to open public lands to industrial development."*
> *—Todd True, Staff Attorney, Earthjustice*[1]

Kempthorne is not highly regarded by environmentalists, with the League of Conservation Voters, giving him a 6 out of a possible 100 in his first year as a Senator, and zero thereafter.[2]

> *"The president could not have chosen a more divisive nominee."*
> *—Philip E. Clapp, President, National Environmental Trust*[3]

Like Norton, he appears to be in the role of the *fox guarding the henhouse*.

---

[1] *Bad choice to head Department of Interior,* EARTHJUSTICE, March 16, 2006, http://earthjustice.org/news/display.html?ID=1131.

[2] *Idaho Gov. Chosen for Interior,* James Gerstenzang and Julie Cart, Los Angeles Times, March 17, 2005, http://www.latimes.com/news/nationworld/nation/la-na-interior17mar17,1,2245822.story.

[3] Ibid.

Kerik, Bernard: Nominated by George Bush on December 3, 2004 to replace Tom Ridge as Secretary of Homeland Security. Kerik was New York City's Police Commissioner at the time of the attack on the World Trade Center on September 11, 2004.

> *"[Kerik is] a personal and professional time bomb the Bushies will learn to regret."*
>
> *— Ellis Henican, Newsday, December 4, 2004*

Only eight days later, on December 11, Kerik withdrew himself from consideration for "personal reasons." It appears that the time bomb exploded prematurely. His stated reason was that he had employed an illegal alien as a nanny and that he had not withheld (and paid) taxes from her wages. He claimed, implausibly, to have just discovered those facts after looking into his finances in preparation for his Senate confirmation hearing.

It appears that the nanny issue, which had previously been a problem for both Bush and Clinton cabinet nominees, might have been the least of his confirmation worries. He had had at least two mistresses, including publisher Judith Regan (who published his book), which although perfectly legal, might have brought his judgment into question. While Police Commissioner, he had used New York City policemen to do research for his autobiography. After he had resigned as Police Commissioner, he had accepted a six-month assignment in Iraq to train new Iraqi police, but had returned to the U.S. after only three and a half months. According to those who saw him in Iraq, he spent much of his time joining South African mercenaries[4,5] on raids against "bad guys." His screensaver on his laptop computer was a photograph of his $1.2 million house, in New Jersey, that was being renovated. He told his colleagues that he planned to be in Baghdad for the three months or so it

---

[4] The mercenaries were serving as bodyguards to U.S. officials.

[5] *A Tough Guy Tumbles, Newsweek National News, http://msnbc.msn.com/ id/6700947/site/newsweek.*

would take to complete. An official said, *"So, you're here because you needed a place to go while they're doing renovations on your house."* According to the official, Kerik cocked a finger and grinned, which the official interpreted as *"You got it."* A Kerik spokesman (who was, presumably, not there at the time) dismissed the story as absurd.[6] If that was, indeed, Kerik's reason for leaving Iraq halfway through his assignment, he was presumably derelict in his duty to meet his commitment.

Regardless of the accuracy of those and other revelations,[7] it seems obvious that the person responsible for supervising the vetting of Kerik prior to his nomination, **Alberto Gonzalez**, did a very poor job. To be fair to Gonzalez, George Bush was an ardent admirer of Bernard Kerik, who had vigorously campaigned for him in the 2004 election, and was probably not interested in hearing anything negative about him.

It appears that Kerik, along with George Bush and former boss[8] Rudy Giuliani, has no shame. Bush invited him to attend the January 20, 2005, Inauguration and Giuliani invited him to attend a private inaugural party. He attended both.

Keyes, Alan: Candidate for the Republican nomination in the 2000 presidential primaries.

In May 2004, Keyes made the strange claim that women who undergo abortions and the physicians who perform the procedures are essentially terrorists, because *"the evil is the same."*[9] This was a follow up to his bizarre claim that the

---

[6] *Ibid.*

[7] Including alleged mob connections, alleged kickbacks, etc.

[8] Giuliani was twice Kerik's boss, first when Kerik was New York's Police Commissioner and second at Giuliani Associates, from which Kerik resigned not long after his withdrawal from consideration of his nomination.

[9] *Keyes likens abortion to terrorism, Natashi Korecki and Scott Fornek, Chicago Sun Times, August 17, 2004, http://www.suntimes.com/output/news/cst-nws-sen17.html.*

attacks of September 11, 2001, were a warning from God to wake up and stop the *"evil of abortion."*

Keyes made more news in early August, 2004, by accepting his party's nomination to oppose Barack Obama, a Democratic State Senator,[10] in the 2004 U.S. Senate race in Illinois. Not only did Keyes fail twice in his bid for the U.S. Senate in his home state of Maryland, but he also roundly criticized Hillary Clinton when she ran for the U.S. Senate in New York State.[11] In March of 2000, he said to Fox News, *"I deeply resent the destruction of federalism represented by Hillary Clinton's willingness to go into a state she doesn't even live in and pretend to represent the people there, so I certainly wouldn't imitate it."*[12] In Keyes' case the word "hypocrite" seems to spring readily to mind.

Barak Obama beat Keyes in a landslide. Rather than slinking back to Maryland, it appears that Keyes will attempt to save face by staying in Illinois.

Both Keyes and Obama are Harvard alumni.

---

[10] Obama, who was born in Kenya, gained national prominence as a result of a brilliant keynote address at the Democratic National Convention in July 2004.

[11] To her credit, Senator Clinton did at least move to New York State in time to become familiar, in some detail, with the issues of her constituents. She is now considered, even by many Republican senators, to be one of the most effective members of the U.S. Senate.

[12] *Keyes vs. Obama? Residents React To Possible Matchup*, Nicole Sack, *The Southern Illinoisan, August 6, 2004, http://southernillinoisan.com/rednews/2004/08/07/build/top/TOP002.html.*

L

L is for Listen, as in *"I promise you I will listen to what has been said here, even though I wasn't here."*
    —*George Bush, Waco, TX, August 13, 2002*
(And listen good.)

Leavitt, Michael O.: Secretary of Health and Human Services in Bush's second term, replacing *Tommy Thompson*. George Bush announced his nomination on December 13, 2004. The Senate confirmed him by voice vote on January 26, 2005.

Leavitt is a former Governor of Utah and was Administrator of the Environmental Protection Agency (EPA) in the final year of Bush's first term,[1] a position in which he replaced Marianne Horinko, the Acting Administrator, who had filled in since the resignation of *Christine Todd Whitman*, whose tenure in the position was said to have been somewhat stressful—something she has denied.

In nominating Leavitt to the EPA, Bush referred to his environmental record as "strong." Carl Pope, of the Sierra Club, was quick to point out that this was a distortion of reality, in that Leavitt had opened up Utah's formerly protected wilderness to heavy industry. When he learned of his confirmation (which had required a number of compromises in response to Democratic objections), Leavitt said the following to reporters:

"I continue to be optimistic that I can make a contribution. I accepted this responsibility because I believe the President is committed to substantially more progress on the environment, and doing it in such a way that does not compromise our place in the world competitively."

The problem is, of course, that the Bush administration is committed to giving the short-term interests of its contribu-

---

[1] He was sworn in as EPA Administrator on November 6, 2003.

tors priority over environmental considerations almost every time.

Leavitt showed his true colors in his defiant February 16, 2004, response to a unanimous decision on February 3, by the Second U.S. Circuit Court of Appeals, in which they ruled that allowing massive destruction of fish and other aquatic organisms by power-plant cooling systems, then attempting to replace them in the ecosystem, does not fulfill the Clean Water Act requirement to mitigate environmental damage. Their ruling mandated what is known as closed-cycle cooling (or better) in new plants. In response, the EPA issued a rule that allows power plants to do exactly what the court ruled they could not do (i.e., substitute restoration for mitigation).[2] (*See, also,* **Clear Skies Initiative.**)

Given this seeming lack of concern for people's health, there was some concern about how Mr. Leavitt would handle his Health and Human Services responsibilities, notwithstanding assurances he gave at his confirmation hearing and to the press.

Libby, I. Lewis, Jr. ("Scooter"): Until October 28, 2005, Dick Cheney's Chief of Staff and Adviser to George Bush. Libby resigned after being indicted on one count of obstruction of justice, two counts of perjury and two counts of making false statements, resulting from the investigation of the "outing" of Valerie Plame Wilson[3] (wife of Ambassador Joseph Wilson) as a covert CIA agent. Libby had claimed, before a grand jury, that he first heard of Valerie Wilson from Tim Russert, host of NBC's *Meet the Press* program. Unfortunately for Libby, the prosecutor, Patrick Fitzgerald, had evidence that he, Libby, had no fewer than seven conversations about her with government officials prior to the al-

---

[2] For the full story, see *http://www.bushgreenwatch.org/mt%20archives/ 000054.php*.

[3] In retaliation for the publication, in the New York Times, of an article by Joseph Wilson, debunking the Bush administration's claim of a yellow-cake uranium purchase from Niger by Iraq. Wilson had been sent to Niger to determine the truth or otherwise of the claim, which turned out to be based on forged documents.

leged conversation with Russert. Not only that, Valerie Wilson's name was never even raised in that conversation.

Libby, a founding member of *Project for the New American Century,* is a well known *neoconservative,* a philosophy no doubt nurtured by one of his professors at Yale, *Paul Wolfowitz,* former Undersecretary of Defense under *Donald Rumsfeld* and now head of the World Bank.

Libby now has the distinction of being the first senior White House official in over 130 years to have been indicted. He may not be the last.

On April 5, 2006, sources indicated that the leak probe involving Libby (but not only Libby) was "winding down." At the same time, Patrick Fitzgerald made a court filing, which revealed that Libby had testified that *Dick Cheney* had specifically authorized him to disclose "key judgements" in a classified National Intelligence Estimate (NIE) briefing to Judith Miller of the *New York Times.*

Libby's lawyers have tried to have charges against him dismissed, using the argument that Patrick Fitzgerald had been given too much power. However, on April 27, 2006, U.S. District Court Judge Reggie B. Walton (a George Bush appointee) turned down their request in a 31-page ruling, which included a discussion of why Fitzgerald's appointment and authority were perfectly proper.

Libby's trial is scheduled for January 2007. His conviction or acquittal may depend on how the Bush administration responds to repeated requests, by his defense team, for classified government documents, including presidential briefings. The administration's denial of requests and the admissibility of documents will, of course, by adjudicated by the courts.

In the meantime, Fitzgerald continues to hold grand jury hearings, at which *Karl Rove* and others have testified. An indictment against Rove is considered to be a strong possibility.

liberal: Webster's Dictionary provides a large number of definitions for this word. It also provides the following synonyms: *progressive, broad-minded, unprejudiced, generous, beneficent, charitable, open-handed, munificent, unstinting,* and *lavish.* Most of these appear to be good qualities. Among the antonyms are *reactionary, regressive* and *intolerant*—normally considered to be quite negative qualities.

Inexplicably, Republicans and other conservatives use the word as an insult or as a derisive description. They have managed to define the discourse—and the language—solely for their own ends, to the extent that otherwise reasonable people are reluctant to admit to being liberal. At the very least, those so labeled expect to reach an agreement on the definition[4] before making such an admission.

This situation was exemplified in the most startling manner in the Democratic Primary debate on CBS, on February 29, 2004, when Elizabeth Bumiller of the *New York Times* demanded, implicitly, that John Kerry give a one-word answer to the question, *"Are you a liberal?"* Subsequently, Dan Rather asked Dennis Kucinich, *"Congressman, do you consider Senator Kerry a liberal by your definition?"* Kucinich's initial response was, *"I think it's important to hear how the senator describes himself."*

Dan Rather subsequently asked the same question of Rev. Al Sharpton and Senator John Edwards. Sharpton's response was, in part, *"I don't think anybody in America cares about what some inside-Washington publication says about your ideology."* In repeating the question, Rather (who is by no means a conservative) showed that even he had allowed himself to be influenced by right wing rhetoric.

David Michael Green, a professor of political science at Hofstra University in New York, has suggested that liberals eschew the *liberal* label, at least for a generation, in favor of the

---

[4] With emphasis, presumably on the synonyms *progressive, broad minded* and *unprejudiced.*

term *progressive*.[5] Moreover, he suggests that today's Republicans would be more appropriately labeled *regressives*. The latter will, no doubt, disagree with his suggestions.

Liddy, G. Gordon:[6] Ultra-conservative radio talk show host, best known, at least to those who were around at the time, for his role in the infamous Watergate burglary and other Nixon-era dirty-tricks operations. As a member of CREEP (Committee to **RE**-Elect the **P**resident) and Richard Nixon's "White House Plumbers,"[7] Liddy led the break-in to the Democratic National Committee headquarters in the Watergate building, which is just across the Potomac from Washington, DC. He served five years for his crimes and was eventually pardoned by President Jimmy Carter.

lies: Josef Goebbels, the Minister of Propaganda for Germany's Third Reich, considered it axiomatic that, if one lies to the people consistently and often, they will eventually accept what is said as the truth. Unfortunately, the German people proved him right. After World War II, they decided they would never be hoodwinked again. Sadly, the German resolve to engage, henceforth, in critical thinking does not seem to have spread to the United States.

Lying in the Bush administration is so pervasive that people are being punished for telling the truth. In an article[8] on the TomDispatch.com website, which is a project of *The Nation*

[5] *What's In A Name? Everything: How Progressives Can Start Winning Again By Renaming Their Opponents and Reframing The Debate,* http://commondreams.org/views05/0208-21.htm.

[6] His full name is George Gordon Battle Liddy.

[7] Ironically, the White House Plumbers unit, which was set up to prevent the leaking of information from the White House, ended up manufacturing a leak in the DNC's offices, in the form of stolen documents. They also conducted dirty-tricks operations against various Democrats and broke into the office of Daniel Ellsberg, best known for *The Pentagon Papers* (out of print). A more recent book by Ellsberg is *Secrets: A Memoir of Vietnam and the Pentagon Papers,* reissued in paperback in 2002 by Viking Books, ISBN 0-67-003030-9.

[8] *The Fallen Legion: Casualties of the Bush Administration,* Nick Turse, October 14, 2005, http://truthout.org/docs_2005/101405P.shtml or http://tomdispatch.com/index.mhtml?pid=28817.

magazine's *Nation Institute*, Nick Turse provides a list of forty people in government, some well known, some not, who have either been fired or demoted, or felt compelled to resign because they told the truth when the Bush administration either wanted the truth withheld or its own lies to go unchallenged.

For example, Richard Clarke, a 30-year veteran of government service under several presidents and chief adviser on terrorism to both Clinton and Bush, had pointed out in a memo that there was no connection between Al-Qaeda and Saddam Hussein. He received a memo in return, saying *"Wrong answer. Do it again."* George Bush had previously said to him, in an intimidating manner, *"Iraq! Saddam! Find out if there's a connection."* Clarke finally quit in January 2003.

Paul O'Neill, who was Secretary of the Treasury in the first two years of Bush's first term, was also a permanent member of the National Security Council, where he found himself under pressure from Bush, from the start, to find a way to get rid of Saddam Hussein. He was fired on December 6, 2002, not for failure to respond to the Iraq issue, but for opposing Bush's tax cuts.

Ann Wright was a career diplomat and an Army Reserve colonel. She resigned on March 19, 2003, the day the Iraq War started. Her letter of resignation to **Colin Powell** included the following statement:

> *"I believe the Administration's policies are making the world a more dangerous, not a safer, place. I feel obligated morally and professionally to set out my very deep and firm concerns on these policies and to resign from government service as I cannot defend or implement them."*

Two generals, one retired and one active, expressed assessments that were at odds with the war plans of George Bush and **Donald Rumsfeld**, but which were subsequently proved to be right. In his first term, Bush made Anthony Zinni, a retired Marine Corps general, his special envoy to the Middle East. However, Zinni disagreed with Bush's plans to go to war and forecast a prolonged aftermath. Bush rewarded his candor by failing to reappoint him, as was originally planned, in March 2003. Zinni later made the following statement in a book he co-wrote with Tom Clancy and Tony Koltz:[9]

> *"In the lead up to the Iraq war and its later conduct, I saw at a minimum, true dereliction, negligence and irresponsibility, at worst, lying, incompetence and corruption."*

The other general was Eric Shinseki, the Army's Chief of Staff. His apparent sin was telling Congress that Iraq's occupation would require several hundred thousand troops. Deputy Secretary of Defense **Paul Wolfowitz** publicly derided his statement and, worse, Donald Rumsfeld announced, shortly thereafter, that Shinseki would be leaving the Army in June 2003, right at the end of his term as Army Chief of Staff.

See also **Bolton, John; Bush Doctrine; Bush, George Walker; distortion; Fleischer, Ari; Frist, Bill; gay marriage and civil unions; Gingrich, Newt; Goat story; Limbaugh, Rush; McClellan, Scott; Medicare Drug Bill; Misleader.org; Mission Accomplished; Nicholson, Jim; Republican Party; Republican Rhetoric; Rice, Condoleezza; Rove, Karl;** *and* **trifecta.**

Limbaugh, Rush: The most financially successful of the right wing radio talk show hosts. Limbaugh claims that his show is simply "entertainment." However, his opinions, supposedly supported by "facts" that, in many cases, turn out not to be facts at all,[10] have an enormous influence on his uncritical audience, most of whom apparently rely on him as their only source of political news and opinion. Many of his fans proudly refer to themselves as "dittoheads," based on their unquestioning agreement with everything he says. As

---

[9] *Battle Ready, Tom Clancy, Tony Zinni and Tony Koltz, 464 pages, Berkley Trade, May 2005, ISBN 0425198928 (paperback—there are other editions).*

[10] Some of Rush Limbaugh's false claims are documented in Al Franken's *Rush Limbaugh is a Big Fat Idiot,* published by Dell, ISBN 0-44-050864-9.

Limbaugh is a supporter of George Bush and the *Republican Party*, so are his fans. In fact, Limbaugh is so vehemently pro-Bush that he has opined that, if anyone but Bush is in the White House,[11] the terrorists will have won. It remains to be seen whether the revelations of Richard Clarke and, subsequently, others about the Bush administration's pre-9/11 preoccupation with matters other than terrorism will ever cause Rush to modify his position. Based on his track record, it seems unlikely.

One of Limbaugh's well-known positions used to be his hard-line stance on drug offenses. In his view, all drug offenders should be locked up. It was ironic, therefore, when it was revealed, in late 2003, that he had been buying massive (and illegal) quantities of the prescription painkillers, hydrocodone, Lorcet® and OxyContin®. His housekeeper, who had been buying the drugs for him, was the one who blew the whistle on him. Apparently he had prescriptions for all the drugs, but they were overlapping ones, acquired by what is known as doctor shopping. Although it's almost never prosecuted, doctor shopping can be punished by a jail sentence of up to five years. Limbaugh has retained a good lawyer, Roy Black, and is obviously not anxious to go to jail. However, in view of his tough position on drugs, he is now viewed as a hypocrite of the highest order (although not by those who call themselves dittoheads). Having a good lawyer is no guarantee, of course, that Limbaugh will prevail. For example, the State of Florida had, with a search warrant, seized his medical records. On October 6, 2004, the Fourth District Court of Appeal rejected Roy Black's argument that his client's privacy rights had been violated by the seizure. Black also argued that a search warrant was insufficient and that the proper process would have been the issuing of a subpoena.

On April 28, 2006, Limbaugh turned himself in at the Palm Beach County Jail to face a fraud charge. He was immedi-

---

[11] This was, of course, in the context of the 2004 election, where the choice was between George Bush and John Kerry.

ately released on $3000 bail. As a result of a plea bargain, he will remain free for eighteen months, subject to continuing treatment for his addiction, breaking no laws, and being able to pass drug tests. If he meets that requirement, all charges will then be dismissed. He paid $30,000 in costs (which, for him, is chump change).

Given Limbaugh's hypocrisy, a conviction would have been poetic justice and would have given some satisfaction to many of his opponents. However, from a civil liberties point of view, it would have been inappropriate.

Lott, Trent: Republican Senator from Mississippi and former Senate Majority Leader. He stepped down from his majority leader position[12] on January 6, 2003, after things got out of hand following a racially divisive remark he made at the December 6, 2002, hundredth birthday and retirement celebration for the now late Senator *Strom Thurmond*. The offending remark was, *"I want to say this about my state: When Strom Thurmond ran for president,[13] we voted for him. We're proud of it. And if the rest of the country had followed our lead, we wouldn't have had all these problems over all these years, either."* Both Democrats and Republicans were offended by the remark. Even William F. Buckley, Jr. was moved to write, *"Not the kind of thing that goes well with birthday-cake festivities, but Lott got into this mess, and has now to get out of it."*[14] Approval came, not surprisingly, from the CEO of the *Council of Conservative Citizens,* Gordon Baum, who said, *"God bless Trent Lott."*[15]

---

[12] Ironically, he had just regained the position of Senate Majority Leader, following the restoration of the Republican majority in the 2002 mid-term elections.

[13] Thurmond ran in 1948, on a segregationist ticket (Dixiecrat Party), against Harry S. Truman (D) and Thomas Dewey (R).

[14] *National Review Online, Birthday-Cake Exegesis, http://www.national review.com/buckley/buckley121302.asp.* To be fair, it should be noted that Buckley also claimed that Lott's remarks had been misinterpreted.

[15] *Washington Post, December 10, 2002, Lott Decried For Part Of Salute to Thurmond, http://www.washingtonpost.com/ac2/wp-dyn?pagename=article &node=&contentId=A20730-2002Dec6.*

In his youth, Lott was an ardent segregationist, having been a leader in a successful battle to prevent his college fraternity at Ole Miss[16] from accepting black students in any of its chapters.[17]

After stepping down as Senate Majority Leader, Lott became the Chairman of the Senate Rules Committee.

---

[16] University of Mississippi.

[17] *Time Magazine, December 12, 2002, Trent Lott's Segregationist College Days: At Ole Miss, the Senator helped lead a fight to keep blacks out of his national fraternity, http://www.time.com/time/nation/article/0,8599, 399310,00.html.*

M

M is for Money, as in *"It's your money. You paid for it."*
—*George Bush, LaCrosse, WI, October 18, 2000*
(You get what you pay for—apparently.)

Machiavelli, Nicolo (1469-1527): Political philosopher, whom many regard as the first great political philosopher of the Renaissance. His famous treatise, *The Prince*, focuses on the practical problems of a monarch wishing to stay in power. George Bush and, especially, **Karl Rove** have been compared to Machiavelli. One of the most telling comparisons was possibly that made by John DiIulio (*Jim Towey's* predecessor) in an interview for an article in the January 2003 issue of *Esquire*. In describing how, in the White House, politics trumped principle every time, he said:

> *"There is no precedent in any modern White House for what is going on in this one: a complete lack of a policy apparatus ... What you've got is everything, and I mean everything, being run by the political arm. It's the reign of the Mayberry[1] Machiavellis."*

Major Combat Operations: *See **Mission Accomplished.***

mandate: A command or authorization to act in a particular way on a public issue given by the electorate to its representative.[2] One might think that a landslide victory in an election would be necessary to assert a claim of a mandate, and that having about half the country against one would clearly invalidate such a claim. After the 2000 Election, it was expected (naïvely, as it turns out) by at least some

---

[1] For those unfamiliar with the television situation comedies of the 1960s, Mayberry was the fictitious North Carolina town portrayed on the Andy Griffith Show, on which Griffith played Sheriff Andy Taylor and Don Knotts played his hopelessly incompetent and non-self-aware deputy, Barney Fife. Some of the other characters on the show were also a few bales shy of a complete load, intellectually speaking.

[2] *Webster's New Universal Unabridged Dictionary.*

moderates that, given his shortfall in the popular vote, George W. Bush would be compelled to govern from the center (or reasonably near the center). As it turned out, Bush treated the favor done for him by the *Felonious Five* on the U.S. Supreme Court as a mandate. The way he decided to govern—for the rich, powerful and bellicose, at the expense of almost everyone else, and with utter disregard for the U.S. Constitution and international law—is now, of course, a matter of record. Even if one assumes that his popular vote majority in the 2004 Election was legitimate, his margin of victory still didn't warrant a claim of a mandate. This opinion is obviously one that the *Republican Party* would not currently favor, although it's safe to assume that a Democratic victory in a future presidential election could easily modify that view.

mandate, unfunded: *See unfunded mandate.*

marijuana, medical: *See medical marijuana.*

marriage, gay: *See gay marriage and civil unions.*

Marriage Amendment: Proposed amendment to the U.S. Constitution, which would define marriage as being solely between a man and a woman, implicitly denying states the right to define marriage in any other way. If such an amendment were to pass, the Constitution would include, for the first time, the explicit denial of a right.[3] George Bush has asked Congress for such an amendment. Will it pass? Probably not. It requires a 2/3 vote in both the Senate and the House and ratification by 38 states—a process that could take several years, during which everyone will have time to consider the contradictory implications with respect to the First Amendment.

Mayberry Machiavellis: *See footnote for Machiavelli, Nicolo.*

---

[3] The 18th Amendment, prohibiting the manufacture, sale and use of alcoholic beverages, removed a freedom and could be said, depending on one's definition, to have denied a right. However, it was at least egalitarian, in that it did not discriminate against a group or class of people.

McClellan, Scott: The White House's hapless former Press Secretary and successor to *Ari Fleischer.* He continued the Fleischer tradition of being George Bush's official liar, although the lies were perpetrated mostly through omission and obtuseness. His sometimes comical[4] evasiveness provided both entertainment and frustration for the White House press corps.

medical marijuana: The use of marijuana for the alleviation of nausea and other kinds of suffering in cancer patients undergoing chemotherapy, end-state AIDS patients, etc. In spite of much higher priorities (e.g., terrorism), the U.S. Justice Department, under former Attorney General *John Ashcroft,* attempted to override the will of the people of California, Oregon, and several other western states, who voted to legalize the therapeutic use of marijuana. Whether Ashcroft's successor, *Alberto Gonzalez,* will exhibit the same zeal remains to be seen. In the meantime, though, the U.S. Supreme Court ruled that federal law trumps state law and that it's up to Congress to determine whether or not medical marijuana use should be legal (*see Ashcroft, John*).

Medicare Drug Bill: Passed in November 2003, this bill,[5] which is supposed to provide prescription drug benefits to seniors, took effect in January 2006. Quite apart from its merits and deficiencies,[6] it exemplifies Bush administration disinformation, Republican strong-arm tactics, and the victory of politics over policy.

First, let's look at the bill itself. Senator Edward Kennedy (D-MA) had criticized it as a step on the way to privatization of Medicare, and because it provided the pharmaceutical industry with a massive giveaway in the form of a pro-

---

[4] But not intentionally comical.

[5] Medicare Prescription Drug and Modernization Act of 2003 (H.R. 2473).

[6] Although it provides coverage to many who had none before, it has doubled the cost of coverage for many who were already covered (e.g., members of Kaiser Permanente's Senior Advantage plan). Also, because there are so many providers, people have had considerable difficulty choosing the most economical (for them) from a bewildering array of plans.

vision prohibiting Medicare from negotiating drug prices with suppliers. Individual plan providers can negotiate; however, they don't have same clout as a large government program like Medicare.

Second, let's look at how the bill was passed in the House. A roll call vote defeated the bill 218 to 216. That should have been an end to it. However, majority leader *Tom Delay* and Speaker *Dennis Hastert* refused to close voting, even though there is a fifteen-minute time limit for roll call votes. After almost three hours of arm-twisting, phone calls to recalcitrant Republicans from George Bush and *Karl Rove*, and browbeating by Tommy Thompson (HHS Secretary), the vote turned around to 220 to 215 in favor of the bill.[7] This has been described as nothing less than thuggery.

Finally, let's look at the disinformation (or, to be blunt, lies) involved. The estimated cost of the bill was represented by the administration to be $395 billion over the decade following its passage. Several Republicans in Congress, whose vote was crucial, had said they could support the bill only if the cost did not exceed $400 billion. More than three months after the bill's passage (by 5 votes in the House and by 10 votes in the Senate), it was revealed that the cost would be about $534 billion. That's a rather large discrepancy, but it could be due to mere incompetence on the part of the administration, right? Wrong! The real estimate was $551 billion.[8] However, Richard Foster, the chief actuary for Medicare at the Department of Health and Human Services, was threatened by his boss, Tom Scully,[9] the Medicare administrator, with dismissal or forced resignation if he revealed the true figure. The threats were not revealed until March 2004, when Richard Foster told of a handwritten note, from Scully, telling him not to answer questions from Democrats.

---

[7] Evidently, participation in the vote increased by 1.

[8] Revised again in the first half of 2005 to $724 billion.

[9] Scully has since left HHS and is now a top lobbyist for the healthcare industry.

On March 13, 2004, then Senate Minority Leader Tom Daschle[10] (D-SD) called for an investigation into whether the disinformation was a criminal act or simply an ethical violation. He also called for a revote on the bill. Unfortunately, he was unsuccessful on both counts.

Mehlman, Ken: Chairman of the Republican National Committee (RNC). Mehlman assumed that position on January 19, 2005, the eve of George Bush's second inauguration. Mehlman, who headed Bush's reelection campaign in 2004, announced his "durable majority" plan, which includes support for Bush's second-term agenda (obviously) and strategies, not only for the 2008 presidential election, but even for the redistricting that will take place in 2011, following the 2010 decennial census. He represents a formidable challenge for Democrats and the Democratic National Committee (DNC), who seemed to have lost their focus during the 2004 campaign.[11]

Miers, Harriet: George W. Bush's old friend, former personal lawyer, current White House Counsel,[12] and his nominee to replace Sandra Day O'Connor on the U.S. Supreme Court. Bush announced her nomination on October 3, 2005.

Miers was apparently helping Bush put together a short list of possible candidates when Bush asked he if she'd like to be the nominee. Given how long she has known Bush and the fact that she seems to be astonishingly unqualified for the position, it appeared to be the ultimate exercise in cronyism, with even Republicans expressing doubts. She is a member of a fundamentalist church in Texas, with regular attendance for 20 years (prior to moving to Washington in 2001). The position of her church on issues like abortion and homosexuality is completely consistent with that of other fundamentalist Christian churches. Given that fundamentalists believe their Bible to be inerrant, including the story of creation

---

[10] Daschle was defeated by John Thune in the 2004 election.

[11] The DNC is hoping to regain its focus under its new chairman, Howard Dean.

[12] As of October 6, 2005, when this entry was written.

in Genesis, it seems unlikely that she would uphold the separation of church and state by ruling against the teaching of creationism or its pseudo-respectable manifestation, intelligent design, in public schools.

> '[W]e are now beset by people who insist on dragging religion into governance—and who themselves believe they are beset by people determined to "drive God from the public square."'
>
> —Molly Ivins, October 5, 2005[13]

Her judicial experience is non-existent and her track record as a lawyer, although it has some notable highlights (e.g., first woman president of the Texas Bar Association), does not place her among the country's leading lawyers, whether conservative or otherwise. It came as no surprise (except, apparently, to some in Washington, who were reported by the Associated Press as being "stunned") when Miers, not wishing to embarrass herself or George Bush any further during her Senate Judiciary Committee hearings, withdrew her nomination on October 27.[14,15] An additional factor in her withdrawal may have been the announcement, two days earlier, by conservative activists, that they had opened two websites and were planning a TV ad campaign to oppose her nomination.[16]

Miller, Zell: Former Republican-leaning Senator in Democrat clothing. Miller, who was, until January 2005, one of the two senators from Georgia and a member of the Democratic Party, consistently voted with the Republicans in the

---

[13] *The Unification of Church and State, Molly Ivins, AlterNet, October 5, 2005, http://www.alternet.org/story/26404.*

[14] *Bush's Embattled Nominee to Supreme Court Withdraws, Associated Press, October 27, 2005, http:// truthout.org/docs_2005/102705Z.shtml.*

[15] In fact, although her letter of withdrawal was dated October 27, Miers informed George Bush at 8:30 pm on October 26 of her intention to withdraw.

[16] *Conservatives Escalate Opposition to Miers: Web Sites and Ad Campaign Seek Nominee's Withdrawal, Michael A. Fletcher and Charles Babington, Washington Post, October 25, 2005, http://www.washingtonpost.com/wp-dyn/content/article/2005/10/24/AR2005102401744.html.*

U.S. Senate. He also endorsed George W. Bush for President in the 2004 election. Miller, himself, did not seek re-election. Prior to the 2002 mid-term elections, Miller's membership of the Democratic Party did at least contribute to a Democratic majority in the Senate, allowing Democrats to chair all Senate committees. Miller, who is also a former Governor of Georgia, has published several books, of which the latest (2003) bears the title, "A National Party No More," and apparently, among other things, presents his views on the current state of the Democratic Party. The other Republican Senator from Georgia, prior to the 2004 elections, is *Saxby Chambliss*. Miller was replaced, in the 2004 elections, by a bona fide Republican and former three-term congressman, Johnny Isakson, described by *On the Issues* as a "libertarian leaning conservative."[17]

On September 1, 2004, Miller gave the keynote speech at the Republican National Convention. It was nothing if not scathing and vitriolic. He wrapped himself in the flag (figuratively), excoriated the Democratic Party (mainly by misrepresenting their positions and those of John Kerry,[18] both in the past and currently), praised George W. Bush as the one man to whom he was willing to entrust his family's future, and more or less accused John Kerry of treason for daring to run against the Commander in Chief in a presidential election in a time of war. Incredibly, he had high praise for Kerry as recently as 2000.

Shortly after Miller's speech, Chris Matthews interviewed him on his MSNBC show, *Hardball*. Matthews considered Miller's speech to be over the top and said so, to which Miller responded by challenging Matthews to a duel. Matthews' reaction was a combination of incredulousness and laughter.

---

[17] *On the Issues, Johnny Isakson, http://www.issues2000.org/GA/ Johnny_Isakson.htm.*

[18] Among other things, Miller criticized Kerry for voting in the Senate against a number of weapons and weapons systems. What he failed to note was that, at the time, then Secretary of Defense, Dick Cheney, was calling for the elimination of exactly the same weapons as Kerry.

In August 2005, Miller participated in an evangelical event called *Justice Sunday II,* where he said, regarding the Supreme Court's finding against displaying the Ten Commandments, *"How is it that the government thinks we need a no smoking sign by gas pumps to remind us of that danger, but does not think we need a reminder of the danger of a sinful lifestyle?"* Apparently he doesn't know the Ten Commandments too well; they say nothing regarding the consequences of ignoring any of the "Thou shalt nots."

Mineta, Norman: Secretary of Transportation and the only Democrat in the Bush Cabinet.

Mis-Leader of the Free World: George W. Bush. The hyphenation of the title (as opposed to "Misleader") makes the deliberately unsubtle point that Bush has squandered his opportunity to qualify for any legitimacy as the Leader of the Free World.

Misleader.org: A website,[19] dedicated to the publication of examples of actions (or lies) by George Bush and/or members of his administration that are or appear to be intended to mislead the public. In their own words, their purpose is to be "a daily chronicle of bush administration distortion." (Yes, they do use all lower-case letters for that statement.) They also publish an email newsletter, called "The Daily Mis-Lead."

Mission Accomplished: On May 1, 2003, George Bush landed on the aircraft carrier U.S.S. Abraham Lincoln, as one of three passengers in a Navy S-3B Viking. He appeared in a green flight suit with a white helmet and strutted across the deck to salute and shake hands with several of those on the flight deck. Later, he gave a speech in which he declared that "major combat operations" were over. Stretched across the carrier's superstructure was a banner with the words "Mission Accomplished."

---

[19] A project of MoveOn.org.

The following day, CNN reported that Bush had flown in by plane because the Lincoln "was too far off the California coast for a helicopter to bring him aboard."[20] Meanwhile, several alternative sources of news, on the Internet, were revealing that San Diego was clearly visible from the deck and that the ship was steaming south, with the TV cameras facing west, away from San Diego, to give the impression of being far out at sea. In short, the whole exercise was a stunt, at taxpayer expense, designed to portray Bush as a resolute Commander in Chief and, quite probably, to provide material for 2004 campaign commercials.

As the months passed and it became very clear that the mission in Iraq was far from being accomplished, and that U.S. and British troops were being killed and wounded in alarming numbers, Bush was asked about the "Mission Accomplished" banner. He claimed, initially, that the sailors on the carrier had made it and had put it up themselves. Caught in a lie, he changed his story and admitted that it was a White House project (just like the backdrops he uses for all his speeches). Unwittingly, of course, he provided the Democrats with some excellent potential clips for their own campaign commercials.

Mohler, R. Albert, Jr.: President of the Southern Baptist Theological Seminary. The most radical of the active Christian fundamentalists look to him as their guru, as they attack the rights of women and gays and work to destroy the public education system. Attacking public education is, in fact, Mohler's main focus, and he has called on Southern Baptists to lead an exodus from public schools.[21]

---

[20] *Commander in Chief lands on USS Lincoln, http://www.cnn.com/2003/ALLPOLITICS/05/01/bush.carrier.landing.*

[21] *Under The Revival Tent: Beyond the aging Billy Graham, some new faces on the Christian right, James Ridgeway, Village Voice, June 28, 2005, http://villagevoice.com/news/0526,ridgeway,65361,2.html.*

N

> N is for Nations, as in *"See, free nations are peaceful nations. Free nations don't attack each other. Free nations don't develop weapons of mass destruction."*
> —George Bush, Milwaukee, WI, October 3, 2003
> (France, Israel, Britain and America aren't free?)

National Policy, Council for: *See Council for National Policy.*

Negroponte, John: National Intelligence Director. Bush nominated him on February 17, 2005 to the position that had been recommended by the 9/11 Commission. He received Senate confirmation, by a vote of 98 to 2,[1] on April 21, 2005. Until his nomination, he was U.S. Ambassador to Iraq[2] (since June 30, 2004) and was formerly the U.S. Ambassador to the United Nations. As National Intelligence Director, he oversees fifteen intelligence agencies, which have both overlapping and conflicting activities.

His diplomatic skills notwithstanding, Negroponte was characterized, at the time of his nomination to be Ambassador to Iraq, as "a torturer's friend"[3] and "a rogue for all seasons."[4] There was a good reason for this. During the Reagan Administration, as U.S. Ambassador to Honduras, he ignored reports of the torture and disappearance of Honduran leftists, even though there were at least 318 reports of such activity in Honduran newspapers.[5]

---

[1] Sen. Tom Harkin (D-IA) and Sen. Ron Wyden (D-OR) voted against confirmation.

[2] His position as Ambassador to Iraq has been referred to by some critics of the Iraq débacle as "Viceroy of Baghdad."

[3] *Negroponte, a torturer's friend, Matthew Rothschild, The Progressive,* April 20, 2004, http://www.progressive.org/webex04/wx042004.html.

[4] *Negroponte: Nominee for Baghdad Embassy a Rogue for all Seasons,* Press Release: Council On Hemispheric Affairs, quoted on Scoop, April 23, 2004, http://www.scoop.co.nz/mason/stories/WO0404/S00250.htm.

[5] Ibid.

neo: A prefix, from the Greek, meaning new or recent.

neocon: Abbreviated form of *neoconservative*. Usually used disparagingly.

neoconservative: Literally, new conservative, so called because neoconservatives are all former liberals. However, defining them by their former status is not very instructive. In a special feature, called *Empire Builders: Neoconservatives and their blueprint for U.S. Power,*[6] the Christian Science Monitor, one of the world's most respected newspapers, has the following implicit and scary definition of neoconservatives:[7]

Neoconservatives …

- Want the US to be the world's unchallenged superpower
- Share unwavering support for Israel
- Support American unilateral action
- Support preemptive strikes to remove perceived threats to US security
- Promote the development of an American empire
- Equate American power with the potential for world peace
- Seek to democratize the Arab world
- Push regime change in states deemed threats to the US or its allies

Some of today's most influential neoconservatives and some the positions they hold or have held[8] are:

- Irving Kristol, sometimes known as the Godfather of the neoconservative movement, who started out as a Trotskyite and moved, over the years, all the way to the right.

---

[6] *http://www.csmonitor.com/specials/neocon*
[7] *http://www.csmonitor.com/cgi-bin/neoConQuiz.pl.*
[8] Most hold or have held more positions than are listed here.

- Norman Podhoretz, member of the Council on Foreign Relations.

- *Paul Wolfowitz*, former Deputy Secretary of Defense, military analyst in the Reagan Administration, and a leading participant in the *Project for the New American Century*.

- *Richard Perle*, former chairman and now former member of the *Defense Policy Board*.

- *Douglas J. Feith*, Undersecretary of Defense for Policy and protégé of Richard Perle.

- *I. Lewis ("Scooter") Libby*, former assistant to the President and Vice President Cheney's former Chief of Staff.[9]

- *John Bolton*, U.S. Ambassador to the United Nations. Formerly Under Secretary of State for Arms Control and International Security.

- *Elliott Abrams*, member of George Bush's National Security Council, former Assistant Secretary of State under Ronald Reagan, and one of the signers of the *Project for the New American Century* letter that was sent to President Clinton.

- Robert Kagan, cofounder, with William Kristol, of the *Project for the New American Century*, senior associate at the Carnegie Endowment for International Peace and, in the Reagan administration, Deputy for Policy in the State Department's Bureau of Inter-American Affairs.

- Michael Ledeen, fellow at the *American Enterprise Institute* and former employee of the Pentagon, the State Department and the National Security Council.

---

[9] Libby resigned on October 28, 2005, following his indictment in connection with the 2003 "outing" of Valerie Plame Wilson as a CIA agent.

- William Kristol, Editor of the *Weekly Standard,* son of Irving Kristol, and founder of the *Project for the New American Century.*

- Frank Gaffney, Jr., founder and president of the Center for Security Policy, columnist for the Washington Times, and contributor or columnist for several other mostly-conservative papers.

Nicholson, Jim: Secretary of Veterans Affairs, nominated by George Bush on December 9, 2004, to replace Anthony Principi. Nicholson was previously (from August 10, 2001) the U.S. Ambassador to the Holy See (i.e., to the Vatican). From January 1997 until the 2000 election, he was Chairman of the Republican National Committee (RNC).

As RNC Chairman, Nicholson was as active as anyone in spreading lies about Al Gore. One of the greatest lies was the statement that Gore had claimed to have invented the Internet. What Gore had in fact claimed (truthfully) was that he had taken the initiative in making the Internet available to everyone, not just universities, defense contractors and government agencies. His initiative involved holding hearings, writing and sponsoring enabling legislation, etc. One very silly lie was to the effect that Gore had said that he and his wife, Tipper, were models for the novel, *Love Story.* What Gore in fact said was that an article in the *Nashville Tennessean* had said that Eric Segal, *Love Story's* author, had made such a statement. In fact, the Tennessean had slightly misquoted Segal, who said that Gore and his college roommate, Tommy Lee Jones, were models for the male protagonist. He had said nothing about Tipper.

Through the distorted use of such stories, Nicholson and others were able to create an image of Gore, rather than Bush, as being a stranger to the truth. Gore's minor gaffes[10]

---

[10] Such as when Gore, in talking about his visit to a Texas disaster, said that he had accompanied James Lee Witt, then the head of FEMA. He had, in fact, accompanied Witt's deputy. His statement was reported as a

were treated as the most venal of lies. Unfortunately for Gore, the press (including the *Washington Post* and the *New York Times*) simply parroted the lies.

No Child Left Behind: Slogan, used by George Bush for political purposes, in particular the No Child Left Behind Act.[11] Its similarity to the Children's Defense Fund's (CDF) official motto, "Leave no child behind" (which is protected as a registered trademark), may or may not be coincidental.

Norquist, Grover: *See Safavian, David H.*

North, Oliver: *See Council for National Policy; Earl, Robert; and Poindexter, John.*

Norton, Gale : Until her March 2006 resignation, Secretary of the Interior (DOI) and former Attorney General of Colorado. The White House website refers to her as *"a lifelong conservationist, public servant and advocate for bringing common sense solutions to environmental policy."*

The Secretary of the Interior is responsible for national parks and public lands, and for the administration of the Endangered Species Act. Norton's appointment to that position was a matter of great concern to a large number of environmental groups, based on her previous involvement in defending several companies against environmental lawsuits and her role as National Chairwoman of the Coalition of Republican Environmental Advocates, which is funded by Ford Motor Company and BP Amoco, among others.[12]

Shortly after her appointment as Colorado's Attorney General, she decided to run, in 1996, for Colorado's vacant U.S. Senate seat. About a third of the total of about $800,000 con-

---

"boast," rather than being acknowledged for the simple slip of the memory it really was.

[11] One of many unfunded mandates.

[12] *Presidential Profile: George W. Bush's Cabinet,* http://www.opensecrets.org/ bush/cabinet/cabinet.norton.asp.

tributed to her unsuccessful campaign came from the oil and gas industry.[13]

Some people refer to Norton as *"James Watt in a skirt."* James Watt, a Christian fundamentalist, was Ronald Reagan's Interior Secretary. His view was basically that protection of the environment wasn't really necessary, as the "end times" were coming anyway. Gale Norton was a member of his staff. According to a January 2001 article by Doug Kendall,[14] *"Norton's absolutist views on property rights and her hostility to environmental protections place her far outside the mainstream of even conservative legal scholarship on these issues."*

According to BushGreenwatch[15] (and, apparently, others), since Gale Norton took the top job, *"the Department of Interior has become a wholly owned subsidiary of the mining industry."*

NRA: National Rifle Association. Colonel William C. Church and General George Wingate, Union Army Civil War veterans, started the organization in 1871 to *"promote and encourage rifle shooting on a scientific basis."* They were dismayed, during the Civil War, by the lack of marksmanship among the troops.

Over the years, not merely satisfied with improving the competence of hunters and target shooters, the NRA has developed into a very powerful lobbying organization for what they see as gun owners' rights under the Second Amendment to the U.S. Constitution (*see **Bill of Rights***). The Second Amendment does support the right to keep (which can obviously include owning) and bear arms, but this right is subject to a very clearly stated qualification, namely, *"A well regulated Militia, being necessary to the security of a free State, ..."* Those thirteen words, defining the cir-

---

[13] Ibid.

[14] *Gale Norton is no James Watt; She's Even Worse, Doug Kendall, Los Angeles Times, January 9, 2001,* (still available on *Common Dreams* website at *http://www.commondreams.org/views01/0109-07.htm*).

[15] *Bush GreenWatch (Tracking the Bush Administration's Environmental Misdeeds), http://bushgreenwatch.org.*

cumstances under which keeping and bearing arms are permitted, are never uttered by the leaders of the NRA. From their point of view, the words might just as well not exist. Not only that, the "right of the people," a collective right, is always treated by the NRA as the "right of individuals," a personal right.

It should be noted that, at the time the Second Amendment was passed (along with the other nine articles of the Bill of Rights), the guns used by the individual members of militias were single-shot flintlock rifles. It seems very unlikely that the authors of the amendment anticipated today's sophisticated weapons, which can be used with devastating effect on multiple human targets. Even short of that alarming possibility, today's ammunition, not available in the eighteenth century, allows guns to be used instantly—by criminals, angry spouses, curious children, those contemplating suicide, and others.

Although the U.S. Supreme Court does not appear to have ruled on collective versus personal rights in the context of the Second Amendment, it has been consistent with respect to the limitations expressed in the first thirteen words. For two landmark cases, see *Article II,* under *Bill of Rights.*

Nothing daunted, the NRA continues to lobby for the elimination (or the defeat) of laws requiring child-proof trigger locks, gun purchaser background checks, regulation of gun show sales, the banning of assault weapons, and on and on.

In 2000, the NRA was heavily involved in promoting George Bush as their candidate for president. Their astonishing arrogance was revealed in a leaked video from a closed NRA meeting in Los Angeles. In it, the NRA's number two man is revealed as saying (somewhat ungrammatically and with tortured syntax), *"If we win, we'll have a president where we work out of their office—unbelievably friendly relations."* This was taken to mean that the NRA would actually have an office in the White House,[16] something even George Bush would not be dumb enough to allow.[17]

In 2004, the NRA managed to block renewal of a 10-year ban on assault weapons.

On October 1, 2005, a law went into effect that must have gladdened the heart of the entire gun lobby, and the NRA in particular. That law is known as Florida's "Shoot First Law." It stands in stark contrast to a well established rule that anyone killing someone in self defense (against a real or perceived danger) must have employed all possible means, consistent with personal safety, to avoid the necessity of taking another's life. This means taking, if at all possible, a safe avenue of retreat.[18] The new law allows someone to *"stand his ground"* and use deadly force simply if he or she *"reasonably believes it is necessary to do so to prevent death or great bodily harm to himself or herself or to another person or to prevent the commission of a forcible felony."* Having done so, he or she is given immunity from both criminal prosecution and civil suits. The recklessness of such a law is mind-boggling. It is also very self-destructive for the State of Florida, given that state's heavy dependence on tourism. Although tourists are not being specifically warned to stay away, they are being warned by a number of organizations to avoid any kind of behavior someone (including the mentally unbalanced) could perceive as even remotely threatening.

On October 20, 2005, the House of Representatives passed an unbelievably irresponsible bill, called the *Lawful Commerce in Arms Act*, granting the gun industry blanket immunity from lawsuits brought by the victims or the families of victims of gun violence. As the measure had already passed in the Senate and as George Bush was in favor of the

---

[16] *Gun lobby claims it would 'work out of President Bush's office,' Julian Borger, The Guardian, May 5, 2000, http://guardian.co.uk/US_election_race/Story/0,2763,217390,00.html.*

[17] However, experience shows this could be a wrong assumption.

[18] *Shoot first, ask questions never ..., http://shootfirstlaw.org/law.*

bill, the probability of a veto was nil.[19] Six days later, Bush signed the bill into law.

Wayne LaPierre, Vice President of the NRA, appeared to gloat when he said, *"I think the air is out of the gun control balloon and I think what popped the balloon is politics and elections."* He was right about politics and elections, as quite a few Democrats from southern states voted for the bill, with the obvious purpose of protecting their seats in future elections. Maryland Democrat Chris Van Hollen, who voted against the bill, said it would *"strip innocent victims of crimes of their rights and instead extend protections to those unscrupulous dealers who put guns into the hands of criminals."*

> *"This bill is an unprecedented attack on the due process rights of victims injured by the misconduct of an industry that seeks to escape the legal rules that govern the rest of us."* [20]
>
> —*Dennis Henigan, director of the Brady Center's*[21]
> *Legal Action Project, October 20, 2005*

The Brady Center said it would challenge the constitutionality of the bill in court.

Wayne LaPierre's gloating may have been premature, in that there was finally some good news for supporters of gun control in the November 8, 2005, odd-year elections. The Republican candidates for Governor in New Jersey and Virginia, both heavily backed by the NRA, lost to Democrats with a very strong gun-control message. Also in Virginia, two NRA-backed candidates for the Virginia House

---

[19] *House passes gun lawsuit shield legislation, Joanne Kenen, Reuters, October 20, 2005, http://reuters.myway.com/article/20051020/2005-10-20T171940Z_01_MOR021735_RTRIDST_0_NEWS-CONGRESS-GUNS-DC.html.*

[20] Ibid.

[21] The Brady Center is a gun control organization, originally called the Center to Prevent Handgun Violence (founded in 1983 and renamed on June 14, 2001). James Brady, Ronald Reagan's press secretary, was crippled by gunshot wounds on March 30, 1981, during the assassination attempt on his boss. Brady's wife, Sarah, became involved in the fight for sensible gun control laws in 1985.

of Delegates were defeated. In San Francisco, a ballot measure to ban the ownership of handguns in the city passed by a wide margin. Finally, unrelated to the election, NRA lobbyists failed to muster enough votes in the Illinois House to override Governor Rod Blagojevich's veto of three recent NRA-sponsored bills.

In the meantime, in the United States, something like 30,000 people die each year from gun violence. About 13,000 of that total were homicides, some of them unintentional. Some sensible gun laws and an overall decrease in crime appear to be responsible for reducing this from about 40,000 per year in the mid 1990s. However, the rate (about 10 per 100,000 of population) is still vastly higher than that of other industrialized nations and even of most developing nations.

If we look just at gun-related murders, we see that the 1996 figure for the United Kingdom was 30. Adjusting for population, that is equivalent to about 180 in the United States, which had a total, in the same year, of almost 9400—about 52 times the U.K. rate.[22]

The NRA will argue, no doubt, that it isn't responsible for the high murder rate. To the extent that guns make murder much easier (allowing killing from a distance, for example), such an argument would be disingenuous. The policies for which they lobby certainly appear to make the country a much more dangerous place than it need be.

---

[22] *Join Together Online, Gun Violence, Overview—Comparison with Other Countries, http://www.jointogether.org/gv/issues/problem/global.*

O

> O is for Optimistic, as in *"The march to war affected the people's confidence. It's hard to make investment. See, if you're a small business owner or a large business owner and you're thinking about investing, you've got to be optimistic when you invest. Except when you're marching to war; it's not a very optimistic thought, is it? In other words, it's the opposite of optimistic when you're thinking you're going to war."*
> —George Bush, Springfield, MO, February 9, 2004
> (The optimist believes this is the best of all possible worlds. The pessimist believes he may be right.)

Office of Special Plans (OSP): *See Feith, Douglas Jay.*

Olson, Barbara: Attorney, spokesperson for the Independent Women's Forum (an organization funded by *Richard Mellon-Scaife*), and wife of former United States Solicitor General, *Theodore Olson*, who was appointed to that position by George W. Bush. Olson was unlucky enough to be a passenger on the plane that crashed into the Pentagon on September 11, 2001. She was a strong supporter of George Bush and of right-wing causes generally, and was one of Bill Clinton's shrillest detractors. The fact that much of her income came from Mellon-Scaife sources led to her inclusion, by her critics, in the group known as the *Scaifettes*.

Olson, Theodore Bevry: United States Solicitor General in George Bush's first term. His confirmation, by a very narrow margin (51 to 47), took place on May 24, 2001.[1]

---

[1] Two Democrats, Ben Nelson (NE) and Zell Miller (GA) voted for him. A third Democrat, Jay Rockefeller (WV), did not vote. Jim Jeffords (R-VT), who had not yet defected from the Republican Party, also did not vote. If all Democrats had voted against him, it would have taken a no vote by Sen. Jim Jeffords to avoid a tiebreaking vote by Dick Cheney.

One of the really contentious issues in Olson's confirmation hearings was his involvement in the **Arkansas Project**, whose sole purpose was to discredit President Bill Clinton (long before the Monica Lewinsky fiasco). Under questioning by the Democrats on the Senate Judiciary Committee, Olson denied any involvement. However, in written responses to written questions by Senator Patrick Leahy (D-VT), he apparently regained the use of his memory and was unable to categorically deny his role in the project.[2]

> *Ted Olson's defenders say the Clinton-bashing effort was protected by the First Amendment—and besides, Olson didn't know much about it anyway. They're wrong on both counts.*
>
> *—Joe Conason, May 22, 2001*[3]

Olson's other well known role was as the advocate for George Bush in the disputed 2000 election, including his arguments, before the U.S. Supreme Court, against counting all the ballots in Florida. Unfortunately for Al Gore, Olson's opposing counsel, Harvard law professor Lawrence Tribe, was surprisingly ineffectual.

Olson announced his resignation on June 24, 2004, to take effect in July, following the end of the Supreme Court session. His stated reason was that he wanted to return to private law practice.

ongoing legal proceeding: Standard excuse by **Scott McClellan**, former White House Press Secretary, when refusing to provide an answer to a question.

> *"There is no way for me to separate that question and talk about this issue without discussing an ongoing legal proceeding. And I can't do that. We have a policy that's been established, and I'm obligated to adhere to that policy."*
>
> *—Scott McClellan, April 7, 2006*

---

[2] *The Arkansas Project wasn't journalism*, Joe Conason, Salon.com, May 22, 2001, http://dir.salon.com/news/col/cona/2001/05/22/olson/?pn=1.

[3] Ibid.

P

P is for Power, as in *"The California crunch really is the result of not enough power-generating plants and then not enough power to power the power of generating plants."*
—George Bush, NY Times interview, January 14, 2001
(Power to power the people!)

Padilla, José: *See enemy combatant.*

Paige, Rod: Secretary of Education in George Bush's first term and part of his second term. He was also the Texas secretary of education when Bush was the governor.

On September 17, 2005, it was reported that Paige had accepted the chairmanship of the Chartwell Education Group, a New York firm founded by him and at least four former top aides to offer high-priced advice on the policies they helped create.[4] Those policies include the *No Child Left Behind Act*, from which *Neil Bush*, George Bush's brother, is already profiting.

Although many former government officials find employment or business opportunities in the private sector, the Chartwell Education Group is unusual in that it has so many people from the same government agency. Their CEO is John Danielson, who is Paige's former chief of staff.

partial-birth abortion ban: The first thing to note about "partial-birth abortion" is that, medically, there is no such term.[5] The correct term for the procedure, described both mislead-

---

[4] *Paige, former aides join consulting firm, Associated Press,* http://usatoday.com/news/nation/2005-09-17-paige-consulting_x.htm?csp=15.

[5] The term does, however, now have legal meaning, as a result of attempts to ban the procedure, as defined in several bills introduced and passed in the House and Senate. Until the most recent one (November, 2003), such bans have been vetoed (by President Clinton). The U.S. Supreme Court has ruled similar bans, at the state level, unconstitutional.

ingly and in excruciating detail by those who oppose all abortions, is intact dilation and extraction (I-DX), although the legislation enacted by Congress uses language more limiting than that used in medical guidelines for the use of I-DX.

In signing the November 2003 ban into law, the only one in U.S. history to prohibit a specific medical procedure, George Bush must expect eventual action by the Supreme Court, on which a majority still supports the inclusion of a clear exception for the life or health of the relatively small number of women who need to undergo the procedure.

patriot: This word has a dictionary definition and a highly-partisan right wing definition. Webster's defines a patriot as a person who loves, supports, and defends his country and its interests with devotion. The important object in this definition is "country." The definition says nothing about being supportive of or uncritical of a rogue administration. Republicans, who went after President Clinton with a vengeance, with respect to both his private behavior and his foreign policy decisions, did not see their own behavior as unpatriotic. However, they question the patriotism of any non-Republican (e.g., Democrat, Independent, Green—but especially Democrat) who has the temerity to question George Bush's actions before and on September 11, 2001, his invasion, contrary to international law, of Iraq, or his despoiling of the environment.[6]

Patriot Act: *See USA PATRIOT Act.*

Perkins, Tony: President of the *Family Research Council*.

Perle, Richard: *Neoconservative* former chairman of the *Defense Policy Board*, original signatory of the *Project for the New American Century*, fellow of the *American Enterprise Institute*, and close friend of former Deputy Secretary of Defense, *Paul Wolfowitz*.

---

[6] Early 2006 has seen a change in attitude by a fair number of Republicans, with many now openly criticizing Bush's policies and actions.

Perle was a hawk during the Vietnam War. However, like so many who also became neoconservatives, he did not serve.[7]

After his resignation from the Defense Policy Board, in a November 2003 speech in London, Perle admitted that the invasion of Iraq violated international law. However, this was not an real admission of the culpability of the Bush administration, as he also opined that to follow international law and "leave Saddam Hussein alone," would have been "morally unacceptable."[8]

According to a number of reports, Perle's service on the Defense Policy Board was marked by a number of conflicts of interest,[9] including the time when he sought $750,000 from Global Crossing in return for getting them Pentagon approval to sell one of their units to a Chinese-owned company. He also helped Loral Corporation's reinstatement as an exporter of satellite equipment and expertise after it had made illegal technology transfers to China.[10]

photo op: Photo opportunity, an occasion beloved of politicians and exploited to the maximum by George W. Bush. The ideal photo op, for those opposed to the use of taxpayer funds for the purpose, is incidental to the occasion at which it occurs. Unfortunately, most of George Bush's photo ops are manufactured events, set up ostensibly for some other purpose. The most blatant example was his multimillion-dollar *Mission Accomplished* stunt on the aircraft carrier Abraham Lincoln on May 1, 2003. His admirers saw him as a hero. Others saw him as something of a

---

[7] *Richard N. Perle, Sourcewatch, http://sourcewatch.org/index.php?title= Richard_N._Perle.*

[8] *War critics astonished as US hawk admits invasion was illegal, Guardian Unlimited, November 20, 2003, http://www.guardian.co.uk/Iraq/Story/ 0,2763,1089158,00.html.*

[9] The primary reason for his resignation.

[10] *Richard Perle: high price for bad advice, William D. Hartung, Global Beat Syndicate, January 26, 2004, http://www.bu.edu/globalbeat/syndicate/ hartung012604.html.*

clown, with his still-buckled safety harness[11] giving the impression that he was wearing an enormous codpiece. It was not only a grossly irresponsible use of taxpayers' money; the mission that had supposedly been accomplished was not then accomplished, nor has it been since.

Pickering, Charles: *See recess appointments.*

Pioneers: *See Bush Pioneers.*

Plamegate: Nickname for the scandal involving the illegal outing of Valerie Plame Wilson, the wife of Ambassador Joseph Wilson, as a CIA operative *(see Cheney, Dick, Libby, I. Lewis and Rove, Karl).*

Since the Nixon-era burglary of the Democratic Party headquarters in the Watergate complex (which includes a hotel, apartments and offices), the media and others have occasionally used "gate" as a suffix for real or alleged government and government-related scandals (e.g., Whitewatergate,[12]).

plutocracy: Webster's has three definitions:

1. the rule or power of wealth or of the wealthy,

2. a government or state in which the wealthy class rules,

3. a class or group ruling, or exercising power or influence, by virtue of its wealth.

George Bush's America would seem to fit nicely into definition 3. Although the power of the wealthy to shape government policy is not new, the extent to which that power overrides almost all other considerations is probably greater than at any time in the last hundred years. Bush, of course, hides

---

[11] Military pilots normally unbuckle their safety harness immediately after leaving the plane—something one would have expected Bush to have learned in the Texas Air National Guard.

[12] Whitewater was the name of a real estate project in which Clintons invested when Bill Clinton was governor of Arkansas. The Clintons were accused of financial improprieties, but were eventually cleared of wrongdoing.

the truth about the current plutocracy by calling it an "ownership society." What he fails to mention is that relatively few get to do the owning. [13]

What the Founding Fathers had in mind for the country was, of course, a representative democracy, or republic.

plutocrat: A member of a plutocracy.

Poindexter, John, Admiral: Appointed by George Bush, on February 12, 2002, as Head of the Information Assurance Office, at the Defense Advanced Research Projects Agency (DARPA). He resigned exactly 18 months later, on his 67th birthday (August 12, 2003), amid controversy about the Total Information Awareness (TIA) project,[14] for which he was responsible. (*See **TIA**.*)

Although he has strong academic credentials (including a Ph.D.[15]) he was one of several convicted felons[16] appointed by Bush to high-profile positions. He was indicted, on March 16, 1988, on seven charges, all connected with the Iran-Contra scandal (in which, while serving as Ronald Reagan's National Security Advisor, he was the leading figure), and convicted of the following crimes on April 7, 1990:

- Criminal conspiracy[17] with Col. *Oliver North,* Air Force Maj. Gen. Richard V. Secord (Ret.) and Albert Hakim
- Two counts of obstruction of Congress

---

[13] Ken Stump, of Seattle, WA, deserves credit for this, which is based on the definition of Ownership Society he submitted to the *Republican Dictionary* project of *The Nation* magazine.

[14] Subsequently named *Terrorism Information Awareness.*

[15] Nuclear physics, California Institute of Technology (CalTech).

[16] His conviction was later overturned on, by now, familiar grounds— namely that he had previously testified before Congress with a grant of immunity. The three-judge panel found that his congressional testimony might have influenced the testimony of witnesses against him. The Government appealed the decision to the U.S. Supreme Court, which declined to hear the case.

[17] Obstruction of congressional inquiries and proceedings, false statements, falsification, destruction and removal of documents.

- Two counts of making false statements

In spite of Poindexter's record, George Bush said he thought he was *"an outstanding American and an outstanding citizen who has done a very good job in what he has done for our country, serving in the military."* Until Iran-Contra, Poindexter does, indeed, appear to have been outstanding.[18]

Portman, Rob: Director of the Office of Management and Budget (OMB), and formerly U.S. Trade Representative. He replaced the former U.S. Trade Representative, **Robert B. Zoellick**, in the fourth month of Bush's second term. George Bush nominated him OMB Director, replacing **Joshua Bolten**, on April 18, 2006. The nomination is subject to Senate confirmation.

Prior to his earlier appointment, Portman was the Congressman for Ohio's second district.

Although Portman's confirmation as U.S. Trade Representative was by voice vote, indicating very little controversy within the Senate, there was outside opposition, based on his record in the House of Representatives. In October 2004, the United States Business and Industry Council[19] (USBIC) issued its scorecard[20] on the performance of the eighteen Ohio members of the House of Representatives, ranking them on their record for supporting U.S.-based manufacturing companies and American jobs. Portman was dead last, with a score less than half that of the second last. That was not a good recommendation for someone who was supposed to look out for U.S. interests in international trade.

Bush's choice of Portman for OMB Director is unsurprising. Portman supports making Bush's tax cuts for the very wealthy permanent, as do most Republican true believers.

---

[18] For a brief biography of John Poindexter, see *"Who is John Poindexter?"* at *http://www.warblogging.com/tia/poindexter.php.*

[19] The USBIC's motto is "Fighting for American companies and American jobs since 1933."

[20] *http://www.usbusiness.org/files/public/USBICOhio.pdf.*

Powell, Colin: Secretary of State in George Bush's first term. He resigned on November 12, 2004. A few days later, Bush announced that his nominee to replace Powell was National Security Advisor *Condoleezza Rice.*

Powell is reputed to have had a distinguished military career.[21] It culminated in his appointment as Chairman of the Joint Chiefs of Staff.

His reputation as Secretary of State was marred, at least for those who knew the facts,[22] by his February 5, 2003, presentation to the United Nations Security Council, in which he was purportedly making the case for the invasion of Iraq.[23] The hope was that the U.N. would build on the November 8, 2002, Resolution 1441, which called on Iraq to disarm, by passing a new resolution authorizing the U.S. and its small so-called *coalition of the willing* to take military action. He has since voiced regret for the considerable amount of misinformation contained in his presentation, much of it attributed to an informant known as *Curveball.* What was really regrettable, though, was that the uncritical mainstream press took him at his word, in spite of considerable misgivings by experts both within and outside the intelligence community.

Powell cited the presence of "decontamination vehicles" close to bunkers as evidence that those bunkers contained chemical or biological weapons. It turned out that some of the vehicles were fire trucks and some were trucks that had been unused for so long that they had cobwebs inside. There were no decontamination vehicles.[24]

Although it had already been discredited, months before, Powell identified aluminum tubes that had been found by

---

[21] Some writers have questioned the credibility of Powell's reputation, citing a number of reasons, including involvement in the attempted cover-up of the My Lai massacre during the Vietnam War.

[22] Which included ordinary people who had been paying attention to the ongoing disagreements between the experts and the politicians.

[23] *Transcript of Powell's U.N. Presentation, CNN, February 6, 2003,* http://www.cnn.com/2003/US/02/05/sprj.irq.powell.transcript.

[24] *Powell's Widening Credibility Gap, Robert Parry, Consortiumnews.com,* September 17, 2005, http://consortiumnews.com/2005/091605.html.

weapons inspectors as potential components of centrifuges used in the uranium enrichment process. Given their dimensions, they were in fact perfectly suited for use as artillery rocket casings and, according to nuclear experts, totally ill-suited for use in centrifuges. However, the centrifuge story suited the agenda of George Bush, **Dick Cheney**, **Paul Wolfowitz**, and **neoconservatives** in general, and Powell was nothing if not loyal to the Bush administration.

> *"On Monday, former Secretary of State Colin Powell told me that he and his department's top experts never believed that Iraq posed an imminent nuclear threat, but that the president followed the misleading advice of Vice President Dick Cheney and the CIA in making the claim. Now he tells us."*[25]
>
> *—Robert Scheer, Friday, April 11, 2006*

His April 7, 2006, statement to Robert Scheer tells us what many of us long suspected, both at the time of his UN speech and subsequently.

He now makes speeches at $100,000 or more per occasion, is a director of several companies, has a multi-million dollar stock portfolio, and has apparently retired from politics.

press, freedom of: *See Bill of Rights.*

Project for the New American Century (PNAC): In their own words,[26] they are *"a non-profit educational organization dedicated to a few fundamental propositions: that American leadership is good both for America and for the world; and that such leadership requires military strength, diplomatic energy and commitment to moral principle."*

In the words of *Sojourners* magazine,[27] they are an organization with *"a strategy of maintaining and strengthening unchallenged U.S. military superiority against a potential future super-*

---

[25] *Robert Scheer: Now Powell Tells Us, Truthdig, April 11, 2006, http://www.truthdig.com/report/item/20060411_bush_leak_plame_libby_powell.*

[26] *Project for the New American Century, http://newamericancentury.org.*

[27] *http://www.sojo.net.*

power rival and against unrest around the world, through pre-emption rather than containment and unilateral military action rather than multilateral internationalism." They point out that *"Bush Sr. administration officials rejected it as too radical."*[28] On close examination, the PNAC website reveals the truth of that statement, although their objectives are couched in somewhat less explicit terms. Experience now shows that *Sojourners* seems to have it right when it says that *"their principles are now the governing foreign and military policy of the Bush administration."*

None of this is surprising when one considers the key PNAC participants, most of whom are well-known **neoconservatives.** They include **Elliott Abrams**, Deputy National Security Advisor and former Iran-Contra plotter; Richard Armitage, Deputy Secretary of State and another former Iran-Contra plotter, **John Bolton**, whose job during Bush's first term was as Undersecretary of State for Arms Control and National Security (now U.S. Ambassador to the United Nations); Vice President **Dick Cheney**, who was CEO of **Halliburton** at the time of PNAC's inception; **I. Lewis Libby, Jr.**, Dick Cheney's recently-indicted former chief of staff; Peter Rodman, Assistant Secretary of Defense for National Security and a Henry Kissinger protégé; **Donald Rumsfeld**, Secretary of Defense; **Paul Wolfowitz**, former Deputy Secretary of Defense and now head of the World Bank; and James Woolsey, former CIA Director.

> *"Their plan is for nothing less than securing U.S. global domination for decades to come—and that's according to their own testimony."*
>
> *—Duane Shank, Sojourners*[29]

Project for the Old American Century (POAC): This is a website[30] whose main purpose is to be one of the many alterna-

---

[28] *The Project for a New American Empire: Who are these guys? And why do they think they can rule the world? Duane Shank, Sojourners, September-October 2003, http://www.sojo.net/index.cfm?action=magazine.article&issue=soj0309&article=030911.*

[29] Ibid.

[30] *http://oldamericancentury.org.*

tive sources of news on the Internet. The founder of the website sums up his purpose in the sentence, *"Dissent IS patriotic and I will dissent by spreading the truth from any non-biased reputable source I can find to as many people as possible."* Not surprisingly, he includes a section on the Project for the New American Century, containing some limited parody and numerous extremely informative links.

Pryor, William: *See filibuster and recess appointments.*

pussy: According to George W. Bush, at the 1988 Republican National Convention, what his father talks about when not discussing politics.[31]

---

[31] As reported by Jake Tapper, in *Salon.com, September 4, 2000.*

Q

Q is for Quality, as in "And if you're interested in the
quality of education and you're paying attention to
what you hear at Laclede, why don't you volunteer?
Why don't you mentor a child how to read?"
—George Bush, St. Louis, MO, January 5, 2004
(Or just be a tormentor of the English language?)

quid pro quo: One thing in return for another. Customarily,
the one has about the same value as the other. However, in
politics, the one is often considerably more valuable than
the other—and is usually misappropriated.

According to a March 2004 Public Citizen report, ninety
percent of Bush *Pioneers* and *Rangers* represent the special
interests of America's corporations. In return for the contributions they amass,[1] the Bush administration provides favorable tax breaks, lenient regulations (especially with respect to the environment), legislative favors and plum appointments. For the corporations and for those who receive
the plum appointments, the payoff is enormous—and is, of
course, at the expense of the majority of taxpayers. The
amazing thing is that about half of middle- and working-
class voters (predominantly the male ones) continue to vote
for Republican candidates and believe that Bush is the right
man for the presidency, even though a good portion of their
taxes ends up subsidizing the big corporations.

Given the need, in the absence of 100% public financing of
elections, to raise money for campaigns, Democrats are not
entirely innocent in this respect. However, the Bush administration has taken this kind of corruption to unprecedented levels. Frank Clemente, director of Public Citizen's
Congress Watch, said, *"This report shows the insidious influence of money in politics. The Bush campaign's unprecedented*

---

[1] Pioneers raise $100,000 or more; Rangers raise $200,000 or more.

fundraising has made this administration more indebted to spe-cial interests than any in recent times."

The Public Citizen report[2] highlights six major categories of donor—the financial industry, real estate developers, elec-tric utilities, oil and gas companies, mining companies and the pharmaceutical industry.

---

[2] *Bush's Campaign Ads Brought to You By Special Interests, http://www. whitehouseforsale.org/contributorsandpaybacks/page.cfm?pageid=519.*

R

> R is for Redefining, as in *"Redefining the role of the United States from enablers to keep the peace to enablers to keep the peace from peacekeepers is going to be an assignment."*
> —George Bush, NY Times interview, January 14, 2001
> (Glad he cleared that one up.)

Racicot, Marc: Former Governor of Montana and former lobbyist for Enron. In 2001, George Bush appointed him to head the national **Republican Party**. While in that position, he continued to lobby for very high fees, although he claimed he was no longer lobbying for Enron.[1] After **Ed Gillespie** replaced him, he was made Bush's 2004 campaign chairman.

At the time of the 2002 vote, in Congress, authorizing George Bush to use the threat of military action to get Saddam Hussein to comply with U.N. resolutions, Racicot revealed himself to be a chickenhawk when he labeled as unpatriotic those members of Congress, many of whom were wounded in the Vietnam War, who voted against the authorization. Racicot was of draft age at the time of the Vietnam War, but apparently nobody has been able to find any evidence of him registering for the draft.[2,3]

On July 28, 2004, the *Houston Chronicle* reported that Racicot had been accused of funneling corporate money (specifically from Burlington Northern Santa Fe Corp., where he is a director) into Congressman **Tom DeLay**'s political action committee, **TRMPAC**. Delay refused to help residents of Clear Lake, TX, fight a proposed freight train line through their

[1] *Of deregulation, Enron and Chickenhawks, Pat Dawson, Montana Unplugged, The Billings Outpost, http://billingsnews.com/story?storyid=3182&issue=98.*

[2] Ibid.

[3] It's hard to fault anyone who, as a matter of conscience, does not want to fight in a war. However, to have taken that position and, subsequently, to question the patriotism of those who want to avoid a war is highly hypocritical and provides ample justification for the "chickenhawk" label.

neighborhood. That line would be used for the transportation of many tons of potentially lethal chemicals. Interestingly, one of Burlington Northern's partners, Lyondell Chemical Company, has also contributed to TRMPAC.[4] If the accusation against Racicot turns out to be true, this would be just one more example of a Bush ally favoring a large corporation over the rights of the majority of voters.

Rangers: *See* **Bush Pioneers.**

reapportionment: *See* *redistricting.*

recent surge in violence: This is the phrase that was used with puzzling consistency in news reports of at least 38 separate fairly significant periods of violence Iraq from September 2003 to March 2006.[5] If the use of the synonymous *"recent wave of violence"* is also considered (discounting reports from places other than Iraq), the count is much higher. In quite a few cases, it appears to have been used by or to have originated with people in the Bush administration. Press and TV network correspondents now appear to be in the habit of using it in questions posed at White House press conferences. It's probable, of course, that they are simply using a phrase that **Scott McClellan** already used in his briefing.

No doubt the Bush administration would like people to have short memories and to believe that all surges in violence in Iraq are just recent, rather than frequent occurrences.

recess appointments: Presidential appointments, normally requiring Senate confirmation, made while the Senate is in recess. In many cases, such appointments seem to be unconsti-

---

[4] *DeLay's $51,000 Reasons to Abandon Clear Lake, http://Richard morrisonfordistrict22.com/blog/comments.php?id=48_0_1_0_C.* Also, *Taking on Tom Delay: Delay, Railroads, Racicot and TRMPAC, July 28, 2004, http://takingontomdelay.com/archives/000064.html.*

[5] *"A Recent Surge in Violence ...", Democratic Underground, posted by EarlG, March 4, 2006, http://journals.democraticunderground.com/ EarlG/13.*

tutional. This is based on the wording of Article II, Section 2, Clause 3 of the U.S. Constitution:

The President shall have Power to fill up all Vacancies that may happen during the Recess of the Senate, by granting Commissions which shall expire at the End of their next Session.

Although lawyers may parse this statement in a variety of tortuous ways, the intent seems to be quite clear: if a critical vacancy occurs during a Senate recess and it would be demonstrably harmful to await the Senate's reconvening, then the President is entitled to make a temporary appointment without delay. Absent tortuous parsing, it would be hard to claim that a vacancy that existed prior to a recess should be filled during that recess.

George Bush has made a considerable number of recess appointments, most of them controversial, including the appointment of *John Bolton* as U.N. Ambassador. However, apart from Bolton's, the most controversial are the judicial ones, specifically Charles Pickering (5th Circuit) and William H. Pryor (11th Circuit). In March 2005, the Supreme Court declined to hear three cases opposing Pryor's appointment on constitutional grounds. Given that the opposition to Pryor was based on his extreme right wing positions, including opposition to civil rights, the Supreme Court decision was very bad news for progressives. What was worse news was that, following an agreement in the Senate in which the Democrats agreed not to *filibuster* three judicial appointments, Pryor was confirmed on June 9, 2005, by a 53 to 45 vote, to a lifetime appointment.[6] His recess appointment would only have lasted until the end of 2006.

Since George Washington's time, judicial recess appointments have occurred, on average, less than twice per year (for a total of about three hundred). However, after Dwight D. Eisenhower (Ike) made three recess appointments to the

---

[6] *Three More Appellate Court Judges Confirmed by Senate, Charles Babington, Washington Post, June 10, 2005, http://washingtonpost.com/wp-dyn/content/article/2005/06/09/AR2005060900214.html.*

Supreme Court, the Senate passed a non-binding resolution urging him not to do it again. Since that time, Jimmy Carter and Bill Clinton made one recess judicial appointment each.

What makes Bush's appointments so controversial is that, until now, no president has appointed a rejected judicial nominee to the Federal bench. It's not as though Bush was having trouble getting judicial nominees confirmed. As of April 2004, out of 176 nominated, 173 had been confirmed.[7] The three who were rejected were considered too extreme and too much out of the mainstream by Democrats.

red state: A state that has been marked on an electoral map of the United States as having its Electoral College votes decided in favor of the Republican candidate for president. Unfortunately, the media, and now the public, have come to treat red states as wholly Republican and blue states as wholly Democrat. California, which for Electoral College purposes is shown as blue, has a fairly strong Democrat majority, as does New York. Utah has a very clear Republican majority. However, most states, especially those referred to as "swing" or "battleground" states, are fairly evenly split or at least not lopsidedly one way or the other. Although there is a fairly clear ideological split, that split is within states, rather than between them. Within states, much of the split can be accounted for by differences between urban and rural voters.

None of this, of course, deters right-wing demagogues from pointing to the Electoral College map to boast about their alleged hold on the vast "red" middle of the country.

Why the TV networks chose red to represent Republicans and blue to represent Democrats is something of a mystery. Traditionally, red has been the color of the left wing. The Soviet army used to be referred to as the "Red Army"; the

---

[7] This did not stop former Senate Judiciary Committee Chairman, Orrin Hatch (R-UT), and others from accusing Senate Democrats of unfairly obstructing Bush judicial appointments. As Senate Republicans refused to confirm a large number of Clinton judicial nominees, Hatch appears to be short on memory and somewhat long on hypocrisy.

Peoples' Republic of China used to be "Red China"; the de facto national anthem during the Chinese Cultural Revolution was "The East is Red"; and British Labour Party candidates and their supporters sport red rosettes[8] at election time. Their Conservative counterparts wear blue rosettes.

redistricting: Sometimes referred to as reapportionment, this is a process that takes place (usually), following each decennial U.S. Census. The original purpose was to take into account the growth (or shrinkage) and distribution of the population. It is supposed to be an objective (i.e., non partisan) process in which congressional district boundaries (and/or their state-level counterparts) within a state are redrawn, along with the possible addition of new districts or a reduction in the total number of districts. Unfortunately, the process has become highly politicized, not only for the decennial redistricting, but also at other times, with what can only be described as tampering with district boundaries. The politicization is unsurprising, as all states leave redistricting activities in the hands of the state legislature, rather than with a boundaries commission (or similar body), as in the United Kingdom. The practice of registering voters by political party exacerbates the situation. Redrawing boundaries to favor a political party or other groups is often referred to as *gerrymandering*. Historically, both major parties have engaged in gerrymandering, but the recent activities of Republicans have reached predatory proportions.

> *Mid-decade redistricting is part of a national Republican strategy to leverage newly achieved control in a state legislature by redrawing the Congressional map in a way that favors Republicans.*[9]
>
> —*Linda Greenhouse, New York Times, June 8, 2004*

---

[8] The applicable definition of rosette (in Webster's) is *a rose-shaped arrangement of ribbon or other material, used as an ornament or badge.*

[9] *Colorado Republicans Lose Redistricting Effort, Linda Greenhouse, New York Times, http://www.theocracywatch.org/redistricting_colo_times_june8_04.htm.*

In the closing days of the Colorado legislature's 2003 session, Republicans pushed through a redistricting plan that would favor their candidates in future elections. This was in spite of the fact that the post-2000 Census redistricting had already taken place the previous year. The Democrats appealed to the Colorado Supreme court, which ruled that the Colorado state constitution prohibited any redistricting in addition to the routine once per decade process. Even though it was a state matter, the Republicans appealed to the U.S. Supreme Court, which voted 6 to 3 not to hear the case. (Acceptance of a case requires four votes in favor.) The dissenting votes, not surprisingly, were those of the usual suspects, Rehnquist, Scalia and Thomas.

A redistricting plan pushed through by Republicans in the Pennsylvania General Assembly had a very different outcome. Richard and Norma Jean Vieth, both citizens and registered voters in Pennsylvania, successfully filed a complaint in district court (*Vieth v. Pennsylvania*), alleging that the plan was an unconstitutional gerrymander. In upholding their complaint, the court invalidated the plan.

Robert C. Jubilerer, the President of the Pennsylvania Senate appealed that decision to the Supreme Court of Pennsylvania (*Vieth at al v. Jubilerer*). Quite a few progressive organizations (e.g., ACLU, Public Citizen, Texas House Democratic Caucus, etc.) filed *amicus curiae*[10] briefs in support of the original complainants. In spite of their arguments, the three sitting judges upheld the plan.

The Pennsylvania court's decision was appealed to the U.S. Supreme Court, which accepted the case and upheld the lower court's decision, 5 to 4, on the grounds that, although gerrymandering claims were justiciable,[11] there was no real standard for adjudicating such claims (other than, for example, in racially motivated cases). The decision was an-

---

[10] Friend of the court. Sometimes *amici curiae*, meaning friends of the court.

[11] Capable of being settled by law, or in a court.

nounced by Justice Antonin Scalia, who also wrote the majority opinion.[12]

It was no surprise that Chief Justice Rehnquist and Justices O'Connor and Thomas joined in that opinion, with Justice Kennedy filing a concurring opinion. All of the other four Justices (Breyer, Ginsburg, Souter and Stevens) expressed their strong disagreement by filing dissenting opinions.

> *'Sometimes purely political "gerrymandering" will fail to advance any plausible democratic objective while simultaneously threatening serious democratic harm.'*
>
> — *Supreme Court Justice Steven Breyer, April 28, 2004, in his dissent in Vieth et al v. Jubilerer*

In the 2004 Election, the 32-member Texas delegation in the House of Representatives changed from 16 Republicans and 16 Democrats to 21 Republicans and 11 Democrats. One might assume that Republicans had suddenly become vastly more popular than Democrats in that state. However, that assumption would be wrong. After the 2000 Census, the Texas legislature took up the question of redistricting (as must and as did all states). At the time (2001[13]), the legislature was divided, with the Republicans controlling the Senate and Democrats controlling the House. That division led to a deadlock on the redistricting issue, leading to a panel of federal judges putting together a compromise plan that reflected that fact that, at the time, the Texas congressional delegation consisted of seventeen Democrats and thirteen Republicans. The plan also increased the number of congressional districts from 30 to 32, and the 2002 mid-term elections saw Democrats and Republicans each taking sixteen of those districts. At the same time, Republicans became the majority in the Texas House of Representatives, giving them

---

[12] For the entire decision, see *http://jenner.admin.hubbardone.com/files/ tbl_s18News/RelatedDocuments147/787/02-1580_decision.pdf*.

[13] The Texas legislature meets only in odd years, with the regular session starting on the second Tuesday in January and lasting a maximum of 140 days. The governor may call additional special sessions to deal with urgent legislation.

control of the legislature. It appears that ***Tom Delay,*** the congressman from Sugar Land (in the Houston area) and the former House Majority Leader in Washington, saw a golden opportunity to increase and lock in the Republican majority in Congress—another round of redistricting. Encouraged by DeLay, the Republicans in the Texas legislature took on the task in their 2003 session, creating new districts that, overall, favored Republican candidates. Worse still, some Democratic members of Congress found themselves living in a district other than the one they represented, presenting them with a problem in the 2004 Election.[14]

The Democrats came close to stopping the redistricting, twice going out of state, en masse, to ensure there would be no quorum, thus preventing a vote. On the first occasion, Tom Delay and his friends in Austin improperly used the ***Department of Homeland Security*** to track them down,[15] based on the movements of a Piper turboprop aircraft owned by one of them.

> *"[T]he use of the Homeland Security Department for partisan political purposes should alarm all Americans. It deserves a full, complete and independent investigation."*[16]
>
> *—Glenn W. Smith, Common Dreams News Center*

Eventually the Democrats got tired of running and the Republicans were able to railroad the plan through a special session of the legislature, with the bill being signed by Governor Rick Perry on October 12, 2003.

The story doesn't end there. In an attempt to invalidate the redistricting, a number of groups filed a lawsuit in federal

---

[14] 24-year Congressman Charles Stenholm, a conservative Democrat, lost his seat as a result of the redistricting.

[15] Something Tom DeLay admitted and for which the House Ethics Committee admonished him; *see Homeland Security Department Used to Track Texas Democrats, Glenn W. Smith, Common Dreams News Center, May 14, 2003, http://commondreams.org/views03/0514-07.htm.*

[16] Ibid.

district court, at least one of which (*Session v. Perry*) was based on the following (and other) positions:[17]

1. Texas may not redistrict in mid-decade.
2. The plan is a product of unconstitutional racial gerrymandering.
3. The plan is an unconstitutional partisan gerrymander.
4. Various districts in the plan dilute the voting strength of minorities in violation of the Voting Rights Act.

Despite what appear to be the obvious merits of all four points, a three-judge panel rejected all the lawsuits.

The next step was an appeal by the plaintiffs to the U.S. Supreme Court. In a surprise move, on October 18, 2004, that court sent the case back to the district court for review. It was only a partial victory for the Democrats, as the district court was not required to review the case before the election, the following month.

On March 1, 2006, the Supreme Court finally began hearing arguments in the case, with the four conservative justices (Samuel Alito, Chief Justice John Roberts, Antonin Scalia and Clarence Thomas) asking questions that seem to indicate their support for the redistricting, the four more liberal justices (Stephen Breyer, Ruth Bader Ginsburg, David Souter and John Paul Stevens) telegraphing the opposite point of view, and Justice Anthony Kennedy asking difficult questions of both sides. Thus, it appears that Kennedy's vote may be the deciding one when the court hands down its decision in the summer of 2006. Key to that vote may be Kennedy's view that, in at least one area, the redistricting might have involved a violation of the civil rights of Hispanic voters.

If the case is ultimately resolved in the Democrats' favor, a number of Republican members of the Texas congressional delegation could lose their seats.

religion, freedom of: *See Bill of Rights.*

---

[17] *The Campaign Legal Center, Redistricting, Court Cases, Summaries, Session v. Perry, http://campaignlegalcenter.org/redistricting-224.html.*

rendition: *See extraordinary rendition.*

reproductive rights: Umbrella term for the right of women to control when, how and if they will have children. It includes the right to birth control advice, birth control devices, pre- and post-natal care, and abortion.

Establishment of reproductive rights can be viewed as a repudiation of the historical dominance of women by men. The Vatican and the religious right both take a position that the restrictions they wish to impose are biblically based, although they disagree with respect to the details.[18]

The right to contraception wasn't firmly established, even for married couples, until June 1965. In *Griswold v. Connecticut (381 U.S. 479 (1965)),*[19] the U.S. Supreme Court overturned a Connecticut law prohibiting the use of contraception and the abetting of those wishing to use it. Seven and a half years later, in *Roe v. Wade (410 U.S. 113 (1973)),* the justices found a right to privacy based on the 14th Amendment (see **Bill of Rights**) and overturned a Texas law banning abortions.

Republican politicians, who claim to want as little government as possible, have adopted the position of the religious right (of which many are members) and constantly seek, both at the state level and nationally, to make it as difficult as possible for women to obtain abortions.[20] Inconsistently, through the support of abstinence-only *sex education*, they make it difficult for women to avoid pregnancy. There is now, in many states, a severe shortage of clinics willing to perform abortions and of doctors qualified to perform the procedure. In March 2006, in a direct challenge to *Roe v.*

---

[18] The Vatican opposes all forms of contraception (although most Catholics appear to disagree). The religious right doesn't appear to oppose contraception, but doesn't want those who attend sex education to know about it (especially about condoms).

[19] *http://caselaw.lp.findlaw.com/scripts/getcase.pl?court=us&vol=381&invol=479.*

[20] There are exceptions, including Sen. Arlen Specter (R-PA). Some Democrats, including Senate Minority Leader Harry Reid (D-NV), also oppose abortion, although there is of course no concerted Democratic Party effort in that direction.

Wade, South Dakota enacted a law criminalizing abortion except in cases where the life of the mother is in danger. In June 2006, Louisiana passed a similar law, which is expected to be signed by the Governor (who is a Democrat).[21]

Republicans are even willing to impose their abortion views on other countries. The Reagan administration and those of both Bushes have blocked U.S. aid to overseas family planning agencies if they so much as approve of abortion. Such anti-choice policies have caused the deaths of thousands of women and children, an increase in the abortion rate, and the exacerbation of the world's population problem.[22] The restrictions were lifted by President Clinton, but reinstated when George W. Bush came to power.

See also **Alito, Samuel** *and* **Concerned Women for America (CWA)**.

Republican Party: Also known as the GOP (Grand Old Party), this has been known historically as the party of Lincoln. Interestingly, it's more the party of Lincoln than most Republicans (or, for that matter, Democrats and others) realize. Lincoln favored big government.[23] The GOP has for years claimed that it was for limited and small government. It still makes that claim. However, under George W. Bush, it has expanded government, and government spending, beyond all recognition.

> *"I have determined that the GOP has always been, from its very beginning, a party of big government and a plague on freedom."*[24]
>
> *— Anthony Gregory, Research Analyst,*
> *The Independent Institute, Oakland, CA*

---

[21] *Strict abortion bill expected to be signed by La. governor, requires Roe's overturning, Catholic Online, June 7, 2006, http://catholic.org/national/national_story.php?id=20108.*

[22] *"Is Government in America Becoming Faith-Based?", Edd Doerr, President of Americans for Religious Liberty, in a platform address to the New York Society for Ethical Culture, May 8, 2005, published in the June 2005 issue of Human Interest, http://hagsa.org/newsletter/2005/nl2005-06.html.*

[23] *Government Growth, the Party of Lincoln, and George W. Bush, Anthony Gregory, http://lewrockwell.com/gregory/gregory40.html.*

[24] Ibid.

The main objective of today's Republican Party seems to be to win at any cost. In the process, truth is the main casualty, while hypocrisy, chicanery and mendacity seem to be standard operating procedure.

> *"Gerrymandered congressional districts are an affront to democracy and an insult to the voters. We oppose that and any other attempt to rig the electoral process."*[25]
>
> *—Statement from 2000 Republican platform*

Gerrymandering is a process also not unknown to Democrats. However, the hypocrisy of the above statement is evident in three subsequent major redistricting efforts by Republicans. The most egregious, demonstrating chicanery of the highest order, was the one engineered, in Texas, by ***Tom DeLay*** and his associates. All three are discussed under ***redistricting***.

> *"The First Amendment enshrines in our Constitution and guarantees indispensable democratic freedoms of speech, press, and association, and, the right to petition our government. The Republican Party affirms that any regulation of the political process must not infringe upon the rights of the people to full participation in the political process."*[26]
>
> *—Statement from 2000 Republican platform*

One only has to consider the use of ***First Amendment zones***, designed to keep even the most orderly protestors away from George Bush at all of his appearances, to realize the rank hypocrisy of the above statement. As for full participation in the political process, that was denied in Florida in the 2000 election, not just by way of the notorious ***felon purge***, involving the Republican governor and the Republican secretary of state, but also by the deliberate failure to count numerous allegedly "spoiled votes," which were not in fact spoiled at all. They were optically mark-readable ballots on which voters

---

[25] This and other 2000 Republican campaign statements can be found at *Revisiting the 2000 GOP Platform: 20 Outrageous Assertions, Shameless Lies and Broken Promises*, Maureen Farrell, June 2, 2004, *http://buzzflash.com/ farrell/04/06/far04018.html*.

[26] Ibid.

had selected Al Gore and had, in addition, written his name (just to be sure) in the write-in-vote area.[27]

The malefactions of today's Republican Party could fill a very long book (just as they occupy a good part of this book). However, some are more extreme, and therefore more interesting, than others. Just as a sampler, see the entries for *Jack Abramoff, John Ashcroft, Haley Barbour, Saxby Chambliss, Tom DeLay, Dennis Hastert, James Inhofe,* and *Swift Boat Veterans for Truth*.

Republican rhetoric: *See Gingrich, Newt and talking points.*

revolving door syndrome: The propensity of some people to move in and out of the private sector and political or appointed government office. Under the Bush administration, many of those moving into senior government jobs go into agencies whose aims they were previously employed to thwart (e.g., going into the EPA[28] after representing, as a lobbyist or as an attorney, a fossil fuel company seeking relaxed environmental standards). (*See fox guarding the hen house.*)

Many of those leaving government, even from elected office (e.g., *Billy Tauzin*), become highly paid lobbyists. Others become senior executives with companies who do business with the government. *Dick Cheney,* with no private sector experience, moved from being *George H.W. Bush*'s Secretary of Defense to being CEO of *Halliburton,* where he was able to use his considerable inside knowledge and contacts to secure contracts for that company and its subsidiaries. It will be interesting to see if he returns to Halliburton after he leaves office in 2009 (assuming he doesn't run successfully for President in 2008[29]).

---

[27] *One million black votes didn't count in the 2000 presidential election: Its not too hard to get your vote lost—if some politicians want it to be lost, Greg Palast, San Francisco Chronicle, June 20, 2004, http://gregpalast.com/ detail.cfm?artid=342.*

[28] Environmental Protection Agency.

[29] It seems unlikely that Cheney will run, let alone win.

Billy Tauzin's case is particularly egregious, as he was one of the primary supporters in the House of Representatives of the 2003 Medicare prescription drug bill[30] that includes a provision prohibiting Medicare from negotiating prices with pharmaceutical manufacturers. His new job, which he started in January 2005, immediately following his final term as a congressman, is as head of the Pharmaceutical Research and Manufacturers of America (PhRMA), which serves 48 pharmaceutical companies and is one of the largest and most influential lobbying organizations in Washington. His compensation package, for overseeing about twenty staff lobbyists and several PR firms under contract, is supposedly about $2 million per year. One of the PR firms is Barbour, Griffith and Rogers, one of whose former principals,[31] **Haley Barbour**, is the Republican governor of Mississippi and the former Chairman of the Republican National Committee.

> *"It's a sad commentary on politics in Washington that a member of Congress who pushed through a major piece of legislation benefiting the drug industry gets the job leading that industry."*[32]
>
> *—Joan Claybrook, President, Public Citizen*

In Billy Tauzin's case, the issue is not whether or not he should be able to put his experience to work (at least eventually) for a lobbying firm. It is, first, that he was in violation of the legally required one-year waiting period, and second, that it is possible (although not proven) that he was in negotiations with his new employer at the time the 2003 Medicare prescription drug bill[33] was being considered (and passed) in the House. In the first case, he appears to be

---

[30] Medicare Prescription Drug and Modernization Act of 2003 (H.R. 2473).

[31] Barbour Griffith and Rogers was sold in 1999 to the Interpublic Group of Companies, with a requirement that the name be preserved, even though Barbour was to no longer have a financial stake in the company

[32] *Tauzin switches sides from drug industry overseer to lobbyist, William H. Welch, USA Today, December 16, 2004, http://usatoday.com/money/industries/health/drugs/2004-12-15-drugs-usat_x.htm.*

[33] Medicare Prescription Drug and Modernization Act of 2003 (H.R. 2473).

criminally in violation of the Ethics Reform Act of 1989;[34] if the second case is true, that compounds the violation.

rhetoric, Republican: *See Gingrich, Newt and talking points.*

Rice, Condoleezza: Secretary of State. In George Bush's first term, she was National Security Advisor. She is a loyal Bush ally (apparently a stronger prerequisite than competence for a cabinet appointment in Bush's second term), a former child prodigy, former member of the board of Chevron, and former Provost at Stanford University.

> *"I don't think anybody could have predicted that these people would try to use an airplane as a missile, a hijacked airplane as a missile."*
>
> *—Condoleezza Rice, post 9/11*

Dr. Rice apparently forgot that, at the July 2001 G8 Conference in Genoa, Italy, the Italians had responded to such a warning by installing a missile defense system and anti-aircraft guns, in addition to keeping fighter planes in the air, to protect the conference site. During that conference and for that reason, George Bush was an overnight shipboard guest of the U.S. Navy, on an aircraft carrier moored offshore. [35]

Condi (as she is almost universally known) performed extremely poorly in some critical areas as National Security Advisor,[36] which is completely at odds with her record of success in other fields. She exhibited potential as a concert pianist at the age of three and has played publicly numerous times. She is also, apparently, an accomplished figure skater. She entered university at fifteen, holds a master's

---

[34] Senator Robert Byrd (D-WV) proposed an amendment, which failed to pass, to increase the waiting period to two years.

[35] Sources include *Center for Cooperative research, http://cooperative research.org/context.jsp?item=a0701summit.*

[36] She won praise, however, for being a discreet, low-key, diplomatic and effective negotiator in settling differences, particularly between George Bush and Dick Cheney *(Newsweek, Vol. 20, No. 151—U.S. Politics: The quiet power of Condi Rice).* This does not, of course, mean that she helped Bush and Cheney to make good decisions.

degree and a Ph.D. in international studies[37] (plus some honorary doctorates), and successfully managed a $1.5 billion budget at Stanford University. Chevron named their largest oil tanker after her (although they discreetly changed its name after she joined the Bush cabinet). She has been a member of the Council on Foreign Relations since 1986 and served as Senior Director of Soviet and East European Affairs in the George H.W. Bush administration. She also appeared frequently on TV news and discussion programs as an expert on the Soviet Union and China.

As it turned out, events in the Soviet Union in the 1990s, including its breakup, turned out to be very different from her predictions.

In a *Slate Magazine* article,[38] Fred Kaplan referred to Rice, with respect to her performance as National Security Adviser, as *"passive, sluggish, and either unable or unwilling to tie the loose strands of the bureaucracy into a sensible vision or policy."* He went on to say, *"... she has not done what national security advisers are supposed to do."* One of the things they are supposed to do (or would, by any reasonable person, be expected to do) is to take the initiative on issues of national security. Instead, she waited for others to tell her what ought to be done. This was exemplified by her statement, in her testimony on April 8, 2004 before the National Commission on Terror Attacks ("9/11 Commission"), in which she said that if she needed to do anything (with respect to warnings of possibly imminent terrorist acts), *"I would have been asked to do it. I was not asked to do it."* With that one statement, she diminished her role to that of an obedient flunky.

Apparently not having learned anything from 9/11, Rice missed no fewer than three opportunities to eliminate *Abu Musab Al-Zarqawi*, a known terrorist operating in northern Iraq (in an area not controlled by *Saddam Hussein*). Ac-

---

[37] In addition to a bachelor's degree, with honors, in political science.

[38] *Condi Lousy: Why Rice is a bad national security adviser, Slate, April 8, 2004, http://slate.msn.com/id/2098499.*

cording to NBC,[39] the Pentagon, in June 2002, responded to intelligence reports of Al-Zarqawi and members of Al Qaeda having set up a chemical weapons lab in northern Iraq by drafting plans to attack them with cruise missiles and air strikes and sending those plans to the White House for approval. It appears that the National Security Council debated the matter to death and thus failed to approve the plans. A second Pentagon plan was also killed, probably because the White House was, by then, much more interested in attacking Iraq. It doesn't take too much cynicism to suppose that the WMD case for attacking Iraq could be reinforced if al-Zarqawi were left in place and, through innuendo, linked to Saddam Hussein.

The National Security Council refused to approve yet another Pentagon plan in January 2003, after London police discovered a ricin lab connected to al-Zarqawi's lab in northern Iraq. Military officials in the Pentagon were convinced they had an airtight case. However, it was reported that destruction of the camp and lab could weaken the administration's case for war. By the time the camp was attacked (at the beginning of the war), it was too late, as al-Zarqawi and most of the others had left. The procrastination of the administration, and particularly of the National Security Council under Condoleezza Rice, has quite probably cost the lives of over 1000 Iraqis, all or at least most of them innocent. As of this writing, al-Zarqawi is still going strong.

In her new role, Rice is supposed to be the country's leading diplomat. Far from being diplomatic, she can best be described as crass. In her confirmation hearing before the Senate Foreign Relations Committee, she characterized the monumentally disastrous south Asian earthquake and tsunami of December 26, 2004 as providing *"a wonderful opportunity"* for the United States to show compassion with relief

---

[39] *Avoiding attacking suspected terrorist mastermind: Abu Musab Al-Zarqawi blamed for more than 700 killings in Iraq*, NBC Nightly News, March 2, 2004, http://msnbc.msn.com/id/4431601.

efforts that reaped *"great dividends"* on the diplomatic front.[40] Technically, she was correct, but her statement betrayed immense cynicism and a staggering lack of sensitivity. In view of the enormous and tragic loss of life,[41] it was something that was best left unsaid.

According to Sidney Blumenthal, Rice's first trip to Europe after taking over the State Department was refreshingly marked by an apparent willingness to listen, as opposed to her usual style, which is lecturing. He goes on to say, though, that, on her second visit in December 2005, she was the enforcer of George Bush's torture policy. [42]

> *"Condoleezza Rice's contradictory, misleading and outright false statements about the U.S. and torture have taken America's moral standing—and her own—to new depths."*[43]
>
> —Sidney Blumenthal, December 8, 2005
> (subheading of Salon.com article)

In a speech at a press conference with the new German chancellor, Angela Merkel, Rice indulged in what can only be described as either the most cynical doublespeak or outright lies about the ***extraordinary rendition*** and torture of captured terrorist suspects.

> *"Rice has yet to master the art of diplomacy but she certainly excels in double talk."*[44]
>
> —Helen Thomas, Hearst Newspapers,
> December 13, 2005

---

[40] *Condi Rice: Tsunami Provided "Wonderful Opportunity for US," Agence France Presse, January 18, 2005, http://www.commondreams.org/headlines05/0118-08.htm.*

[41] The death toll was estimated to be about 168,000 at the time. That figure has since been revised to over 200,000.

[42] *Condi's trail of lies: Condoleezza Rice's contradictory, misleading and outright false statements about the U.S. and torture have taken America's moral standing—and her own—to new depths, Sidney Blumenthal, Salon.com, December 8, 2005, http://salon.com/opinion/blumenthal/2005/12/08/condi.*

[43] Ibid.

[44] *Reduced to double talk in defending torture policy, Helen Tomas, San Francisco Chronicle, December 12, 2005, http://chron.com/disp/story.mpl/editorial/outlook/3517584.html.*

Her remarks followed, by only a few days, a Washington Post report of the rendition to a jail in Afghanistan of a German citizen, who underwent five months of imprisonment and torture until it was realized that it was a case of mistaken identity. Chancellor Merkel said later that Rice had apologized for the fact that the U.S. had made a "mistake." Rice denied having done so, embarrassing Merkel and undermining her own credibility, at least with the skeptical German press.

For those close to George Bush, loyalty and a love of truth would appear to be incompatible virtues.[45]

right wing organizations: Organizations that attempt to roll back or impede social justice progress and to reshape government and society to their liking.[46] People for the American Way (PFAW), a progressive advocacy organization, has identified over 800 right wing organizations, including the following:[47]

> **Alliance Defense Fund**, *American Center for Law and Justice, American Conservative Union,* **American Enterprise Institute**, *American Family Association, American Legislative Exchange Council, American Life League, FRCAction, Americans for Tax Reform, Lynne and Harry Bradley Foundation Campaign for Working Families PAC, Cato Institute, Christian Coalition, Club for Growth,* **Concerned Women for America**, *Eagle Forum,* **Family Research Council, Federalist Society for Law and Public Policy Studies, Focus on the Family**, *Free Congress Research and Education Foundation,* **Heritage Foundation**, *Hoover Institution on War, Revolution, and Peace, Independent Women's Forum, Institute for Justice, Leadership Institute, Pioneer Institute for Public Policy Research, Mackinac Center for Public Policy, Madison Project, National Center for Policy Analysis, National Right to Life*

---

[45] Leaving aside the question of whether loyalty to Bush qualifies as a virtue.

[46] *People for the American Way, Right Wing Watch: Right Wing Organizations, http://www.pfaw.org/pfaw/general/default.aspx?oid=3147.*

[47] Ibid.

Committee, National Taxpayers Union, State Policy Network, Traditional Values Coalition.

Some of them, such as the American Center for Law and Justice (ACLJ) and the Traditional Values Coalition, are mainly or exclusively religious right organizations. One of them, the Cato Institute, is specifically Libertarian and sees itself as supportive of Jeffersonian or market liberalism. However, its push for the privatization of government services is consistent with the aims of the right wing, generally, and the Republican Party, in particular.

rights, civil: *See civil rights.*

Roberts, John G., Jr.: Chief Justice of the U.S. Supreme Court, replacing the late William H. Rehnquist. He was originally George Bush's nominee to replace Justice Sandra Day O'Connor. However, when Chief Justice Rehnquist died, Bush upped the ante. Roberts was confirmed on September 29, 2005, by a 78 to 22 vote in the Senate, and sworn in about four hours later.

In 2003, Bush appointed Roberts to the D.C. Circuit Court. He was also a Justice Department official in the Reagan administration and deputy solicitor general in the George H. W. Bush administration.

Roberts is 50 years old, good looking, married with two adopted children, an extremely competent and very smooth talking lawyer with excellent academic credentials—and very conservative. George Bush promised to nominate people with a judicial philosophy like that of associate justices Clarence Thomas and Antonin Scalia and, in Roberts, he may have found that. Because he has replaced a very conservative Chief Justice, his presence should have little effect on near-term Supreme Court decisions. However, his youth ensures that there is unlikely to be a change in the leadership of the court for a generation.

Robertson, Pat: Well known televangelist, ardent Republican, supporter of George W. Bush, constant violator of the Establishment Clause of the First Amendment (*see **Bill of***

Rights) and, based on his numerous outrageous statements, a religious nut case.

Robertson is the founder of the Christian Broadcasting Network (CBN), which carries his *700 Club* program, the Christian Coalition, the inaptly named American Center for Law and Justice, Operation Blessing, and similar organizations.

In 1988, he ran in the Republican presidential primaries, during which he claimed that Hurricane Gloria (1986) spared Virginia Beach, the site of his headquarters, because he had asked God to intervene. He failed to mention that Gloria had gone on to cause about $320 million in damage to Long Island and Boston. Although he was not victorious in the primaries, he managed to build a mailing list of three million names, something that would be very valuable in both his non-profit and profit-making enterprises.[48]

Robertson can, of course, well afford to buy whatever mailing lists he might need. His net worth is estimated to be something between $200 million and $1 billion.[49] He has, of course, donated millions to his own causes, including Regent University. On the other hand, he has raised money by somewhat dubious means, including his implicit claim of being instrumental (with "the Lord's help," of course) in healing viewers of the 700 Club as they watch the program.

Robertson's most dubious venture was the one he undertook, with the cooperation of Mobutu Sese Seko, the late brutal dictator of Zaire (formerly the Belgian Congo and now The Democratic Republic of the Congo, or simply Congo). It was a diamond mining operation, which would have been fine (apart from Mobutu's involvement) if it had not been supported by one of his charities, *Operation Blessing*. He had solicited funds for the charity to acquire aircraft to ship medical supplies in and out of Goma, a refugee camp in Zaire. Those who flew the planes can only recollect

---

[48] *Pat Robertson: 'I don't have to be nice to the spirit of the Antichrist',* Greg Palast, *Observer (London), August 23, 2005, http://gregpalast.com/ detail.cfm?artid=49&row=1.*

[49] Ibid.

one occasion on which they were used for that purpose. All other flights were used for the transfer of mining equipment. Robertson claimed to be unaware of that, which might be credible had he not been on one of the flights.[50]

Sadly for Robertson, he wasn't able to turn a profit from his diamond mining operation and closed it down.

All of the above hardly begins to scratch the surface of Robertson's activities. He is, apparently, one of the people from whom George Bush seeks advice, although even Bush has felt compelled to disavow at least some of Robertson's pronouncements, including his call for the assassination of Hugo Chavez, the president of Venezuela, something Robertson at first tried to deny and subsequently tried to categorize as innocuous.[51]

Roosevelt, Franklin Delano (FDR): Three-term president, Democrat, father of the New Deal, and architect of America's recovery from the Great Depression. (Contrast with *Bush, George Walker,* father of the Big Deal and architect of the post-9/11 Great Repression.) FDR also said, *"We have nothing to fear but fear itself."* George Bush's interpretation of this appears to be, *"Fear is good."* FDR was Teddy Roosevelt's fifth cousin. (First Lady Eleanor Roosevelt was Teddy Roosevelt's niece.)

Roosevelt, Theodore (Teddy): Two-term socially progressive Republican president, who would probably be appalled by the current Republican sell-out to corporate interests, pandering to the wealthy, and the destruction of the environment. Far from giving tax breaks to the wealthy, he attacked them at every opportunity. He also sided with striking mine workers against their employers. Very significantly, he is said to have read a book a day. By way of contrast, George

---

[50] Ibid.

[51] Although Robertson calls himself a Christian, many Christians (including most of those who would characterize themselves as main-line Christians) regard much or even most of his rhetoric as un-Christian.

Bush boasts that he reads no more than newspaper headlines.[52]

> *"To announce that there must be no criticism of the presi-*
> *dent, or that we are to stand by the president right or*
> *wrong, is not only unpatriotic and servile, but is morally*
> *treasonable to the American public."*
>
> — *Theodore Roosevelt*

Roosevelt won the Nobel Peace Prize for ending the Russo-
Japanese War, although his record on other fronts would have
endeared him to today's **neoconservatives**. He did, after all,
intervene in the Dominican Republic, Honduras, Nicaragua
and Venezuela. He also perpetuated the U.S. presence in the
Philippines, where the U.S. occupation was said to be responsible for the deaths of something like 200,000 civilians.[53]

Because of his immense popularity and even though he was
no angel, TR's 1904 election to his second term was by an
overwhelming majority.

Rove, Karl: Senior political adviser to George W. Bush and former White House Deputy Chief of Staff. It was reported, on
May 13, 2006, that Rove had been indicted the previous day
for perjury and lying to investigators in the Valerie Plame
Wilson case.[54] He may or may not also be indicted for obstruction of justice, as was *I. Lewis Libby.* There was no
comment from the White House and nothing appeared in
the mainstream media, so the report remains unconfirmed.

Given Bush's penchant for nicknames, it's not surprising
that he has one for Rove. However, the one he uses, "Turd
Blossom," is quite revealing—and, given what is known
about Rove, appears to require no explanation.

Many who are unfamiliar with Rove have assumed that
George Bush is something of a puppet and that *Dick Che-*

---

[52] As told to Brit Hume, in an hour-long interview on *Fox News.*

[53] *Government Growth, the Party of Lincoln, and George W. Bush,* Anthony
Gregory, *http://lewrockwell.com/gregory/gregory40.html.*

[54] *Karl Rove Indicted on Charges of Perjury, Lying to Investigators,* Jason Leopold,
Truthout, May 13, 2006, *http://truthout.org/docs_2006/051306W.shtml.*

ney is the puppeteer (in addition to being the *de facto* president). Whatever Cheney may or not be, Rove certainly seems to be a very clever strategist and is the architect of Bush's rise, via the governorship of Texas, to the presidency. Given Bush's many flaws, including his disturbing lack of curiosity, that was no mean feat. Even prior to that, he helped Bush's father when he was the vice presidential candidate. Still earlier, according to Bill Clinton's former Labor Secretary, Robert Reich, Rove was a mole in the Nixon administration, specializing in the infiltration of Democratic organizations.[55]

Rove has often been described as amoral, an adjective that seems to crop up repeatedly in the political arena. A synopsis of the book, *Bush's Brain*,[56] contains the following somewhat chilling statement:

> "… *Moore and Slater expose the brutal and sometimes morally questionable, but invariably effective ways in which Karl Rove—and America's political system—actually operate.*"

Rove got an early start in the dirty tricks department. In 1970, when he was only 19, he managed to obtain sheets of the letterhead of Alan Dixon, an Illinois Democrat, and proceeded to distribute them at a campaign rally, bearing a message advertising "free beer, free food, girls, and a good time for nothing."[57] It's a stunt that Rove has since admitted to having perpetrated.

He was named to the Deputy Chief of Staff position on February 8, 2005. In that job, he was in charge of coordinating domestic policy, economic policy, national security and homeland security, which are all activities in which was in-

---

[55] *The Rove Machine Rolls On, Robert B. Reich, The American Prospect, February 1, 2003, http://prospect.org/print/V14/2/reich-r.html.*

[56] *Bush's Brain: How Karl Rove made George W. Bush Presidential, James Moore and Wayne Slater, John Wiley & Sons, December 2003, 395 pages, ISBN 0471471402.*

[57] *Karl Rove, Deputy White House Chief of Staff, Highlights and Quotes, Right Web, http://rightweb.irc-online.org/profile/1343.*

volved, behind the scenes, since the beginning of George Bush's first term. The new title simply made that official.[58]

> *"Empowering Rove in this way shows that Bush cares more about political positioning than honest policy discussions. Bush knows that Rove is neither an economic nor a national security expert; he's simply an ideological strategist who has a history of bending the truth and using dirty tricks to get his way."*[59]
>
> —*Terry McAuliffe, Chairman, Democratic National Committee, February 8, 2005*

After **Josh Bolten** took over from **Andrew Card** as Chief of Staff, Rove lost his status as deputy chief, with instructions to concentrate on the 2006 mid-term elections.

Rove has been a constant source[60] of daily **talking points** for right wing pundits, Republican operatives, Bush Cabinet members, and Republicans in Congress. For those who assiduously follow the news, the talking points were obvious, in that most of those who use them seem to have memorized them by rote and to be too lazy to even modify the wording or, worse still, to even check whether or not they are factual. What is dangerous is that such constant parroting is much less obvious once it gets into secondary news reports, leading the majority of the population to believe they are hearing or reading facts, rather than partisan propaganda.

> *"The most brilliant propagandist technique will yield no success unless one fundamental principle is borne in mind constantly—it must confine itself to a few points and repeat them over and over."*
>
> —*Dr. Paul Josef Goebbels, Minister of Propaganda, Third Reich*

---

[58] *Rove is Promoted to Deputy Staff Chief: Job Covers a Broad Swath of Policy, Peter Baker, Washington Post, February 9, 2005, http://www.washingtonpost.com/wp-dyn/articles/A9308-2005Feb8.html.*

[59] Ibid.

[60] Probably the sole source.

However vile Josef Goebbels may have been, there can be no denying that he was a brilliant propagandist—possibly the most brilliant ever. The above quotation has sometimes been rendered more basically as, "If you throw enough mud at a wall, eventually some will stick." Whether or not Rove is consciously following Goebbels' example (and some have claimed that he is), he appears to be adhering to the same principles.

Goebbels' life and career ended simultaneously.[61] Rove's life doesn't appear to be in any danger, but his career seems to be coming to an end as a result of what has come to be known as *Plamegate*—the apparently vengeful outing of Valerie Plame Wilson as a covert CIA agent.[62] One of those involved, *I. Lewis Libby, Jr.*, was also indicted, not for that offense, but for perjury and making false statements about the matter—the same charges now facing Rove. Following Libby's indictment, the prosecutor, Patrick Fitzgerald, declined to respond in any way to speculation about further indictments. Many in the press regarded both Karl Rove and Dick Cheney as possible targets. Their names came up many times during Fitzgerald's investigation, even if Fitzgerald himself avoided mentioning them. Could Dick Cheney be next?

(*See, also, **Machiavelli, Nicolo**.*)

Rumsfeld, Donald ("Rummy"): Secretary of Defense.

Rumsfeld is one of the co-founders of the *Project for the New American Century*, but he is probably best known as the most prominent of the retreads from *George H.W. Bush's* cabinet, where he was also Secretary of Defense. Prior to that, he was Ronald Reagan's special Middle East envoy, in which capacity he visited Baghdad, in March 1984, to reassure Iraq's Foreign Minister, Tariq Aziz, that in spite of U.S.

---

[61] Goebbels was in Adolf Hitler's bunker at the end. He had a doctor administer lethal injections to his six children, then had an SS guard shoot him and his wife.

[62] In retaliation for Ambassador Joseph Wilson's newspaper article revealing as false George Bush's reference to Saddam Hussein acquiring yellowcake uranium in Africa (specifically in Niger). Documentation allegedly supporting Bush's assertion turned out to be a very crude forgery that should have been instantly recognizable as such.

statements in opposition to the use of chemical weapons, the U.S. desire *"to improve bilateral relations, at a pace of Iraq's choosing"* remained undiminished. This followed a December 1983 visit, which was reported to have been to persuade Iraq to resume diplomatic ties with the United States. Throughout the 1980s, while publicly asserting a neutral stance on the Iran/Iraq war, the Reagan and George H.W. Bush administrations sold armaments to Iraq, including chemicals and biological agents intended for military use.[63] In view of his involvement in the process, it's hard to see how Rumsfeld could avoid accepting some responsibility for the alleged possession, by Iraq, of chemical and biological weapons before and during Operation Iraqi Freedom. Of course, no such weapons were found. However, their alleged existence constituted most of the rationale for attacking Iraq.[64]

> *"As you know, you go to war with the army you have, not the army you might want or wish to have at a later time."*
>
> —*Donald Rumsfeld, Kuwait, December 8, 2004*

The above somewhat patronizing statement[65] was in response to the question of a soldier, who wanted to know why he and his fellow soldiers had to improvise in order to install armor plating on their unarmored Humvees. The statement might very well be true in the case of a defensive war for which a country might very well be inadequately prepared. It could hardly be justified for a war of choice. Prewar administration rhetoric (including Rumsfeld's) notwithstanding, the invasion of Iraq was a matter of choice, not of necessity.

---

[63] *Rumsfeld Visited Baghdad in 1984 to Reassure Iraqis, Documents Show, Dana Priest, Washington Post, December 19, 2003, http://washington-post.com/ac2/wp-dyn?pagename=article&contentId=A13558-2003Dec18.*

[64] Of course, we must now take into account the egregious historical revisionism of the Bush administration (and their apologists), for whom the rationale for war has been transformed into one of "bringing democracy to Iraq."

[65] Many of Rumsfeld's statements are patronizing—at least when they're coherent enough to follow. (As an example of incoherence, see the quotation at the beginning of this entry.)

Going into Iraq, Rumsfeld (plus Bush, **Cheney**, **Wolfowitz** and others) ignored the advice of military experts, including then Army Chief of Staff, Eric Shinseki, regarding the number of troops it would take to invade and properly secure Iraq (*see* **lies**).

Rumsfeld used the "shock and awe" approach, recommended by Harlan Ullman,[66] in the initial bombing of Baghdad, using a large number of cruise missiles with very potent warheads. Unfortunately, it was mostly the civilian population, or at least those who weren't killed in the bombing, who were left in a state of shock. And, of course, it's difficult to be awed when your first priority is to find safe refuge where you won't be blown up, crushed by a collapsing building, or maimed by shrapnel. As the population was subjected to being in a state of terror, it isn't too much of a stretch to say that the bombing was an act of terrorism. It was certainly a violation of international law. Whether Rumsfeld, or indeed anyone in the Bush administration, felt any pangs of remorse or was troubled by second thoughts is not known.

After the bombing was over and the troops moved in, the Iraqi Oil Ministry building was secured. In the meantime, looters ransacked unprotected museums and hospitals, taking something like 170,000 irreplaceable and priceless artifacts in two days and depriving the hospitals of essential medical equipment.

> *"It's untidy, and freedom's untidy. Free people are free to make mistakes and commit crimes and do bad things. They're also free to live their lives and do wonderful things."*
>
> —*Donald Rumsfeld, Pentagon daily briefing, April 11, 2003*[67]

---

[66] *Shock & Awe; Is Baghdad the Next Hiroshima?*, Ira Chernus, Common-Dreams.org, January 27, 2003, http://www.commondreams.org/views03/0127-08.htm.

[67] *Free to do bad things*, Guardian Unlimited, April 12, 2003, http://www.guardian.co.uk/Iraq/dailybriefing/story/0,12965,935381,00.html.

The foregoing statements were Rumsfeld's responses to reporters' questions about the looting. His flippancy and insensitivity defy comment.

Rumsfeld's biggest problem seems to have been the *Abu Ghraib* prison abuse and torture scandal. It's one he shares with Attorney General *Alberto Gonzales* and several others. First, the *Taguba Report,* citing abuse of prisoners by the 800th Military Police Brigade, appeared. The administration, Congress and the press did little or nothing until photographs showing prisoners being abused started to appear. The ensuing scandal led to several at the bottom of the command structure being charged, tried and convicted, with the Defense Department hiding behind a "few bad apples" characterization. The latest conviction occurred on March 22, 2006. Sgt. Michael J. Smith was sentenced on five charges, including maltreatment of prisoners, conspiring with another dog handler in a contest to try to frighten detainees at the Iraqi prison into soiling themselves, and directing his dog to lick peanut butter off other soldiers' bodies. [68]

It became very apparent that the problem was systemic and that the climate for the abuses had been established at the top, at which point Rumsfeld said he would accept responsibility. He even offered to resign. It was no surprise when George Bush asked him not to do so.

The trial of a second dog handler, Sgt. Santos A. Cardona, was set to begin on March 22. According to the *New York Times,* Cardona's lawyers will try to direct blame at higher levels, using information not revealed in Sergeant Smith's trial. They will try to have Donald Rumsfeld, Gen. John P. Abizaid, the commander of American forces in the Mideast, and General Ricardo Sanchez, top commander in Iraq when the Abu Ghraib scandal was revealed, testify at the trial.[69] Until now, it has been impossible, through the discovery

---

[68] *Army Dog Handler Gets Six Months in Prison, David Dishneau, Associated Press, March 22, 2006, http://news.yahoo.com/s/ap/ abu_ghraib_dog_handler.*

[69] *Iraq Abuse Trial Is Again Limited to Lower Ranks, Eric Schmitt, New York Times, March 23, 2006, http://nytimes.com/2006/03/23/politics/23abuse.htm.*

process, to follow the trail of responsibility up the line of command.

With the Iraq War over three years old, over 2,400 U.S. and British (and other) troops dead, many thousands of troops with terrible injuries,[70] thousands more emotionally scarred,[71] many tens of thousands of Iraqi civilians dead and injured, an impotent parliament, daily violence, and evidence of an incipient civil war, Rumsfeld has come under more and more pressure to resign.

> *"If this is not civil war, then God knows what civil war is."*
>
> —*Iyad Allawi, former Iraqi Prime Minister, on BBC 2's Sunday AM program, March 19, 2006*

The scenario is about as far from the predictions of his former deputy, **Paul Wolfowitz**, as it possibly could be. Nobody was welcomed with flowers and the whole sorry mess was not, despite Wolfowitz's confidence, financed from Iraq's own oil revenues. Instead, present and future American taxpayers are paying the tab, while essential services are scaled back on the domestic front.

A recent call for Rumsfeld's resignation came from retired Major General Paul Eaton, who said in the March 19, 2006 *New York Times* that Rumsfeld was not competent strategically, operationally, and tactically and is, more than anyone else, responsible for the chaos in Iraq.[72] He claimed that experienced military commanders and civilians are reluctant to stand up to the egotistical Rumsfeld, because of the way he retaliates by undercutting them.

---

[70] Total injuries for US and other non-Iraqi troops are about 18,000. Many of the injuries are really appalling and involve disfigurement or maiming.

[71] For obvious reasons, Pentagon spokespeople don't like to talk about the psychological effects of battle on the servicemen and women in Iraq (and Afghanistan)—things like post-traumatic stress disorder, for example.

[72] *Rumsfeld Singled Out as Crisis Deepens in Iraq*, Julian Borger and Jonathan Steele, *The Guardian UK*, March 20, 2006, http://www.truthout.org/docs_2006/032006M.shtml.

Again, Rumsfeld offered to resign and, once more, George Bush asked him to stay on. This seems to be a well-rehearsed act, but it may not last much longer, as there were more calls for his resignation between March 20 and April 13, 2006— from no fewer than five other generals. In alphabetical order, they were Major General John Batiste, who commanded the 1st Infantry Division in Iraq, Marine Corps Lieutenant General Gregory Newbold, Major General John Riggs, Major General Charles Swannack, who led the Army's 82nd Airborne Division in Iraq, and the most senior of all, Marine Corps General Anthony Zinni.[73]

George Bush came out in support of Rumsfeld, saying something about being the "decider"[74] in the matter. The Defense Department conveniently provided a memorandum, containing talking points, to several retired generals who said they also supported Rumsfeld.[75]

> *"Reports that say that something hasn't happened are always interesting to me, because as we know, there are known knowns; there are things we know we know. We also know there are known unknowns; that is to say we know there are some things we do not know. But there are also unknown unknowns—the ones we don't know we don't know."*
>
> *—Donald Rumsfeld, at a 2003 press briefing*
>
> *(Winner of the Plain English Campaign's*
> *2003 Foot in Mouth Award[76])*

---

[73] *Generals demand Rumsfeld's resignation, Steve Holland, ABC News, April 13, 2006, http://abcnews.go.com/US/wireStory?id=1841350.*

[74] So now he regards himself as a uniter and a decider.

[75] *Pentagon Memo Aims To Counter Rumsfeld Critics, Mark Mazzetti and Jim Rutenberg, New York Times, April 16, 2006, http://nytimes.com/ 2006/04/16/washington/16rumsfeld.html.*

[76] *http://www.plainenglish.co.uk/footinmouth.html.* The last U.S. politician to be recognized (in 1991) by the Plain English Campaign was Dan Quayle, George H.W. Bush's Vice President. There was no Foot in Mouth award in 1991, but Quayle got special mention for, *"We offer the party as a big tent. How we do that (recognize the big tent philosophy) with the platform, the preamble to the platform or whatnot, that remains to be seen. But that message will have to be articulated with great clarity."*

Ryan, George: Former Republican Governor of Illinois, and the focus of a major corruption scandal. After a five-month trial, Ryan was found guilty on April 17, 2006, of all counts brought against him by federal prosecutors. Those counts included racketeering and fraud. Also convicted was a Ryan associate, Larry Warner, who is a businessman.

Ryan and Warner both face a possible twenty years in prison. However, the defense is appealing the verdict, with some help from the revelation that some of the jurors failed to mention relevant facts (including, for three of them, convictions) or lied outright on their juror questionnaires.

S

> S is for Success, as in *"I hope the ambitious realize that they are more likely to succeed with success as opposed to failure."*
>
> —George Bush, AP interview, January 18, 2001
>
> (Nothing fails like failure.)

Saddam Hussein: Former dictator of Iraq, now imprisoned in Iraq and on trial (on and off) for a number of major crimes including crimes against humanity. Because of overwhelming evidence, his conviction seems to be assured.

Contrary to the impression conveyed repeatedly by *Dick Cheney, George Bush* and others, Saddam Hussein and *Osama bin Laden* were about as far from being allies as they possibly could be, with bin Laden, along with many Wahhabi and similar extremists, regarding the former as a secular apostate. Saddam was very tightly in control of Iraq (with the exception of the Kurdish area in the north) and, if he had really continued to possess chemical and biological weapons[1] or had developed nuclear weapons, it is inconceivable that he would have transferred control of any of them to bin Laden.

As for whether, on balance, Iraq is better off without Saddam Hussein, the relatives of the 100,000 or so Iraqi civilians who have died since March 2003[2] are possibly the best judges of that.[3]

---

[1] According to weapons inspectors, Iraq's chemical and biological weapons were destroyed in the years immediately following the 1991 Gulf War. Any that might have remained had a limited shelf life and would have become useless long ago.

[2] Estimate provided as a result of a rigorous survey performed by the Johns Hopkins Bloomberg School of Public Health, the Columbia University School of Nursing and Al-Mustansiriya University in Baghdad, also reported in The Lancet (October 29, 2004 edition), Britain's leading medical journal. Source: *Iraqi Civilian Deaths Increase Dramatically After Invasion, October 28, 2004, http://www.jhsph.edu/PublicHealthNews/ Press_Releases/PR_2004/Burnham_Iraq.html.*

If we look just at Saddam Hussein, though, there is no doubt that his removal, by some means other than all-out war, would have been extremely beneficial.

Safavian, David H.: Former administrator for Federal Procurement Policy in the Office of Management and Budget, which is part of the Executive Office of the President. Safavian was nominated by George Bush to the position on January 22, 2004, and confirmed by the Senate on November 21, 2004. His nomination took a long time, held up by Senator Robert Byrd (D-WV), because he had concerns about how Safavian would administer the administration's competitive sourcing agenda. After Byrd removed his hold, the 2004 Election further delayed confirmation. Prior to his nomination, Safavian was chief of staff in the General Services Administration (GSA).

On September 19, 2005, Safavian was arrested on a three-count criminal complaint, filed in federal court by the Justice Department. The complaint alleges that, while he was at the GSA, he helped a lobbyist (who has not yet been named, at least not officially) acquire GSA-owned property in the Washington, DC, area. *The Hill*[4] quotes sources that say the lobbyist is *Jack Abramoff*, who worked with Safavian at Preston, Gates, a lobbying firm.

Prior to working for the government, Safavian worked for Janus-Merritt Strategies, a lobbying firm founded by hardcore right winger Grover Norquist, who is notorious for saying he wanted to reduce government to a size where it could be drowned in the bathtub.[5]

Safavian apparently resigned on September 16, three days before his arrest.

---

[3] Had Saddam Hussein been removed from power, along with most members of the Baath Party, by means other than all-out war, it would be hard to find anyone (other than Saddam loyalists) who disagreed that it was a good thing.

[4] *The Hill, News official, Abramoff associate arrested, Jonathan E. Kaplan, September 20, 2005, http://www.hillnews.com/thehill/export/TheHill/News/Frontpage/092005/brief1.html.*

[5] It should be noted that Norquist has denied saying that.

Santorum, Rick: Junior Senator from Pennsylvania and darling of the Religious Right.

> *"President ... is once again releasing American military might on a foreign country with an ill-defined objective and no exit strategy. He has yet to tell the Congress how much this operation will cost. And he has not informed our nation's armed forces about how long they will be away from home. These strikes do not make for a sound foreign policy."*
>
> *—Rick Santorum, March 1999,*
> *criticizing President Clinton's Bosnia policy*

The above quotation is often used, humorously, to give the momentary impression (quickly dispelled once the target of his criticism is revealed) that Rick Santorum is capable of being tough on George Bush with respect to his Iraq policy, when he is, in effect, Bush's lapdog.

Santorum is one of several right-wing politicians to have the dubious honor of being the subject of a website dedicated to tracking their legislative and other activities and, more particularly, their stated views. In Santorum's case,[6] what is depicted is far from flattering. For example, although he's a staunch critic of funding for programs that help families, he has not been above taking taxpayer funds to help his own family. Although he and his family live in Virginia, he has benefited from $100,000 in funds (paid for by other people's property taxes) from a Pennsylvania school district to pay for his children's cyber-school tuition. Based on his ownership of a house in the Pennsylvania school district, he registered to vote in that state, where he also obtained his driver's license and car registration. Not only does he not live in the Pennsylvania house (which is occupied by his niece and her husband), but he also usually stays with relatives when he visits the area. When his scheme was revealed, he refused to refund the school dis-

---

[6] *Santorum Exposed, http://santorumexposed.com.*

trict's money, with the result that they had to go to court to recover it.[7]

Santorum's actions would be bad enough, but there's also the hypocrisy aspect. In 1990, when running for Congress, he used a TV advertisement to attack his incumbent Democratic opponent, Doug Walgren, for living in McLean, VA, rather than in his own district in Pennsylvania.[8]

In another example of hypocrisy, Santorum is against stem cell research, while at the same time his re-election committee has accepted well over $50,000 from companies engaged in such research.[9]

The hypocrisy doesn't end there. He voted for a tort reform bill that would limit claims for pain and suffering caused by medical malpractice, notwithstanding his own wife's "pain and suffering" suit for $500,000 in damages against a Virginia chiropractor. He claimed that was a "private family matter." Apparently he doesn't care about other people's "private family matters."[10]

Among Santorum positions too numerous to discuss in detail are his desire to have schools teach "intelligent design" (a belief) as an equal alternative to evolution (which is established science),[11] his leading of the charge to implement George's Bush's Social Security privatization plans (as well as raising the retirement age to 70),[12] and his vote against funding for Amtrak, in spite of the fact that Amtrak's demise would cost about 3000 jobs in his home state and, just

---

[7] *Santorum Exposed: Why is Rick Santorum spending your tax dollars on **his** family? http://santorumexposed.com/pages/issues/issues-tax.php.*

[8] *Ibid.*

[9] *Santorum Exposed: Where exactly does Rick Santorum stand on expansion of stem cell research? http://santorumexposed.com/pages/issues/stemcells.php.*

[10] *Santorum Exposed: Why doesn't Rick Santorum want to protect other people's right to compensation if they're victims of medical malpractice? http://santorumexposed.com/pages/issues/issues-malpractice.php.*

[11] *Santorum Exposed: Why does Rick Santorum want to leave teaching a world-class science curriculum behind? http://santorumexposed.com/pages/issues/issues-science.php.*

[12] *Santorum Exposed: What does Rick Santorum have against Social Security, anyway? http://santorumexposed.com/pages/issues/issues-socsec.php.*

as bad, in spite of having spoken in support of Amtrak funding less than two weeks earlier. Twelve days after the vote, in an opinion piece, he reversed his position again.[13]

> *"In addition, it is critical to Pennsylvania's workers, businesses, visitors, and most specifically to the more than 3,000 Amtrak employees that we do not decrease funding for Amtrak."*
>
> —*Rick Santorum, Philadelphia Inquirer, March 25, 2005*

He must have been counting on the *Inquirer's* readers not following his voting activity in the Senate.

Santorum is up for reelection in 2006 and his poll numbers have been trailing those of his prospective challenger, Pennsylvania State Treasurer Bob Casey, Jr. He may yet be able to return to living in Pennsylvania to legitimize his children's Pennsylvania taxpayer-funded education.

Scaife, Richard Mellon: Reclusive billionaire and financier of right wing (especially extremely right wing) causes. He owns seven newspapers, including the *Pittsburgh Tribune Review* and is part owner of the Internet-based *NewsMax*.

According to a February 7, 2006, article on the Huffington Post website, *"Scaife has given hundreds of millions of dollars to a who's who of right-leaning groups including the Heritage Foundation, the American Enterprise Institute, Judicial Watch, the Federalist Society, Paul Weyrich's Free Congress Foundation, David Horowitz's Center for the Study of Popular Culture, Brent Bozell's Media Research Center, and many others."*[14]

Given such involvement, one would expect Scaife to be an unwavering backer of George Bush and all his policies. However, his *Pittsburgh Tribune-Review* did an about face in February 2006 and endorsed the plan put forward, some weeks previously, by Rep. John Murtha (D-PA) for with-

---

[13] *Santorum Exposed: Why isn't Rick Santorum voting to keep jobs in Pennsylvania? http://santorumexposed.com/pages/issues/issues-jobs.php.*

[14] *The Murtha Effect: Why Republican Are Worried, The Huffington Post, February 7, 2006, http://www.huffingtonpost.com/arianna-huffington/ the-murtha-effect-why-re_b_15262.html.*

drawal from Iraq.[15] Obviously, even hard-line right-wingers have trouble going along with the Bush agenda.

Scaifettes: *Ann Coulter*, Laura Ingraham[16] and the late *Barbara Olson*. All three women were involved in the Independent Women's Forum, under whose banner they appeared frequently on talk shows. Once it became known that the innocent-sounding Independent Women's Forum was funded by the reclusive benefactor of hard-right causes, *Richard Mellon Scaife*, they stopped mentioning their affiliation with it.

school vouchers: A means of financing attendance at private schools, using public money. By moving funds away from public schools, this lowers the quality of public school education. Worse still, because most private schools are religious in nature (e.g., Christian schools), it almost always violates the principle of separation of church and state mandated by the *Establishment Clause* in the First Amendment (see *Bill of Rights*). Most school voucher initiatives have failed, in some cases thanks to the actions of watchdog organizations such as Americans United for the Separation of Church and State and the American Civil Liberties Union (ACLU). In other cases, voters have simply rejected pro-voucher referendums. Wisconsin and Ohio have passed school voucher laws, and Florida Governor Jeb Bush, George Bush's brother, is pushing school vouchers in Florida.

secrecy: Standard operating procedure in the Bush administration, starting on January 20, 2001. This early date is significant, as the administration has repeatedly cited the events of September 11, 2001 as their reason for classifying almost everything as secret.

At the same time, Bush's chief of staff *Andrew Card* told federal agencies to freeze over 300 pending regulations from Bill Clinton's administration. This was ostensibly to *"ensure that the president's appointees have the opportunity to*

---

[15] Ibid.

[16] Right-wing commentator and radio talk-show host.

review any new or pending regulations." That much is normal in the transition to a new administration. What was not normal is the fact that input (comments) on those regulations from average citizens was expressly precluded, as being *"contrary to the public interest."*[17]

> *Democracies die behind closed doors ... When government begins closing doors, it selectively controls information rightfully belonging to the people. Selective information is misinformation.*
>
> —*Damon J. Keith, U.S. Appeals Court Judge, 6th Circuit*[18]

According to an editorial in the Sacramento Bee,[19] the federal agency overseeing the classifying of government documents estimates that 15.6 million were classified in 2004, which is almost double the total for 2001. Declassification of documents in 2004 was at only one seventh the rate for 2001 (28 million pages, against 204 million).

In the Clinton era, the late Senator Daniel Patrick Moynihan brought a breath of fresh air to the issue of open government, when he chaired a bipartisan panel that unanimously called for the declassification of millions of documents, along with a reduction in the period of secrecy from 30 years to 10 years.[20] George Bush and **Dick Cheney**, both very secretive, have reversed that trend with a vengeance.

At the beginning of his first term, George Bush even went so far as to restrict access to the presidential papers of his own father and of Bill Clinton. There is no report of him

---

[17] *Keeping Secrets, Christopher H. Schmitt and Edward T. Pound, U.S. News and World Report, December 12, 2003, http://truthout.org/docs_03/121403A.shtml.*

[18] From a 2002 ruling by Judge Keith, declaring that then Attorney General John Ashcroft acted unlawfully in holding deportation hearings in secret. Judge Keith has been on the Appeals Court since 1977. A more extensive set of quotations from the decision can be found at *http://cantstopwontstop.com/blog/2002/08/democracies-die-behind-closed-doors.html.*

[19] *125 secrets a minute: Time to put some limits on that 'classified' stamp, July 10, 2005, http://sacbee.com/content/opinion/story/13202714p-14045675c.html.*

[20] Ibid.

asking if they agreed with his action. He also moved his own papers, from when he was Governor of Texas, to his father's presidential library, hoping apparently to make access to them more difficult than it would otherwise be. However, in May 2002, then Texas Attorney General John Cornyn (now a U.S. Senator) ruled that although the transfer of the papers was legal, Bush did not have the authority to alter the manner in which they were preserved or made public.[21] On May 4, 2002, the *New York Times* reported the decision under the amusing title, *"Father's Library Can Hold Bush Papers, if Door Is Ajar."*

sex education: It used to be said, jokingly, that the only birth control pill acceptable to the Roman Catholic Church was an aspirin—held firmly between the knees. The Bush attitude towards sex education is not too far from this hypothetical position.

Since the beginning of his first term, George Bush has promoted abstinence-only-until-marriage sex education programs to the exclusion of all other kinds of sex education. No evidence has ever been produced to show that the abstinence-only approach reduces teen pregnancies or the occurrence of sexually transmitted diseases. In fact, studies have shown that the opposite is true and that the only tangible outcome is a delay, in some cases, in teenagers' first sexual experience. Even that is not really a benefit, as sex education programs that simply express a very strong preference for abstinence achieve a similar outcome.

The non-profit Allan Guttmacher Institute[22] has pointed out that abstinence is simply one more type of contraception. Like all others, it has a failure rate, simply because abstinence is an intention and some who intend to be abstinent simply slip. Unfortunately, there are no peer-reviewed studies showing what the failure rate is or, conversely, what the effectiveness (success rate) is. This is not the case with

---

[21] *George W. Bush's Gubernatorial Records Subject to Texas Freedom of Information Law, The Memory Hole, http://thememoryhole.org/wbush-records.htm.*

[22] *http://guttmacher.org.*

the best-known means of contraception, for which there is a known effectiveness for perfect use (i.e., following instructions to the letter) and a lesser effectiveness for typical use.[23]

The only contraceptive normally recommended for both pregnancy prevention and protection against sexually transmitted diseases is the condom. Used as directed, it prevents pregnancy in 97% of cases, on average, over a year of use.[24] That drops to an average of 75.5% for "typical use." Through effective education, the latter figure could almost certainly be improved significantly.[25]

Like so many of Bush's programs, the abstinence-only sex education programs are almost exclusively faith based.[26] In May, 2005, the American Civil Liberties Union (ACLU) filed a lawsuit against a program called *Silver Ring Thing*, alleging that it was "permeated with religion" and that it had, notwithstanding that, received over a million dollars in federal funds.[27] Evidence of its religious nature includes the fact that the teenage graduates of the program sign a covenant, "before God Almighty," to remain virgins, for which the reward is a silver ring with a biblical inscription reminding them that they must "keep clear of sexual sin." The ACLU also alleged that its abstinence-only-until-marriage sex education is a means to bring "unchurched" students to Jesus Christ.

The Silver Ring Thing's legal counsel, who is from the *Alliance Defense Fund*, claimed that Silver Ring Thing offers both a reli-

---

[23] *Understanding 'Abstinence': Implications for Individuals, Programs and Policies, Cynthia Dailard, The Guttmacher Report On Public Policy, December 2003, http://guttmacher.org/pubs/tgr/06/5/gr060504.html.*

[24] This works out to about 99.98% effectiveness for each use, assuming the average frequency of intercourse is 3 times per week.

[25] Ibid.

[26] To be fair, abstinence-only sex educations got their start during Clinton's second term, but Bush has requested vastly increased funding (of which less than one third has actually been approved by the House of Representatives). He also seems to have a limited grasp of the constitutional issues involved in faith-base programs.

[27] *Reproductive Freedom, ACLU Applauds Federal Government's Dscision to Suspend Public Funding of Religion by Nationwide Abstinence-Only-Until-Marriage Program, August 22, 2005, http://aclu.org/ReproductiveRights/ ReproductiveRights.cfm?ID=18941&c=30.*

gious program and a secular one and that "kids can choose which one they want to go to." This is in spite of the statement, on the Silver Ring Thing's own website, that said, "A secular program is also in development"—a promise, not a reality. On August 22, 2005, the Bush administration, specifically the Department of Health and Human Services, suspended a federal grant to the Silver Ring Thing's abstinence program and ordered them to submit a "corrective action plan" if they want to receive a $75,000 grant in the current year.[28] This may be only a minor victory for reason and constitutionality, but it's a start.

Sinclair Broadcast Group: A company that owns, operates, programs or provides services to 61 television stations, reaching 24% of U.S. households. The stations include affiliates of ABC, CBS, Fox, NBC, UPN and WB.

Four of Sinclair's top executives gave the maximum ($2000) to the Bush-Cheney re-election campaign in 2004. As of April 2004, no donations were made to John Kerry, who was at the time the presumptive Democratic nominee. This has some significance because, in April 2004, Sinclair refused to allow any of its ABC stations to air an edition of Nightline in which Ted Koppel was to read the names, without comment, of the over 500 servicemen and women killed in Iraq up to that time.[29] As he read the names, their photographs were to be shown. As planned, and as eventually broadcast on all the other ABC affiliates (and one Fox affiliate), the show, which carried the title of "The Fallen," took no position on the rightness or wrongness of the war in Iraq.

Nevertheless, in response to a wave of criticism and condemnation of Sinclair, including a very strongly worded statement from Senator John McCain (R-AZ), Sinclair's CEO David Smith said, *"Our decision was to stop the misuse of their sacrifice to support an anti-war position with which most, if*

---

[28] *Federal Funds For Abstinence Group Withheld, Ceci Connolly, Washington Post, August 23, 2005, http://www.washingtonpost.com/wp-dyn/content/article/2005/08/22/AR2005082201230_pf.html.*

[29] *McCain rebukes Sinclair's 'Nightline' decision, Owner has ordered affiliates not to broadcast program, CNN Entertainment, April 30, 2004, http://www.cnn.com/2004/SHOWBIZ/TV/04/30/abc.nightline.*

not all, of these soldiers would not have agreed." Earlier, Sinclair had accused ABC of politicizing the war.[30]

Whether or not the soldiers would or would not have agreed with Nightline's recognition of their sacrifice is, of course, unknowable, which leads one to the obvious conclusion that David Smith's comments were simply self-serving speculation.[31]

Smirking Chimp: One of the less attractive socially-acceptable nicknames used by George W. Bush's detractors. The caricatures of Bush, drawn by at least one political cartoonist, depict a very chimp-like appearance. There is also a website called *SmirkingChimp.com,* bearing the motto, "Ask not at whom the chimp smirks – he smirks at you." It is, in fact, a serious site, containing recent news stories about Bush and a blog (web log) for comments and visitor dialogue.

See, also, **Village Idiot.**

Snow, Tony: White House Press Secretary, replacing *Scott McClellan.* Bush announced his appointment on April 26, 2000.

Until his appointment, Snow was an anchor on *Fox News* and a syndicated columnist. Although conservative, he has often been critical of Bush and of Republicans in general.[32] In his announcement, Bush alluded to the criticism and said he had asked Snow about it, to which Snow apparently said, "You should see what I said about the other guy."

> *"Begin with the wimp factor. No president has looked this impotent this long when it comes to defending presidential powers and prerogatives. Nearly 57 months into his administration, President Bush has yet to veto a single bill of any type."[33]*
>
> — *Tony Snow, September 30, 2005*

---

[30] Whatever that is supposed to mean.

[31] Or, of course, Bush-administration-serving speculation.

[32] As have many conservatives since they have grown to realize that Bush isn't really one of them.

[33] *The jury is still out on Bush term,* Tony Snow, September 30, 2005, townhall.com, http://townhall.com/opinion/columns/tonysnow/2005/09/30/158842.html.

This is only one of a large number of Snow's criticisms of Bush.[34] It's a strange one, as Snow will possibly realize now that he's in the White House. Bush has avoided vetoes (which can be overridden by a 2/3 majority) by sneaking "executive signing orders" into bills, permitting him, as long as he can get away with it, to ignore any aspect of a bill that he "considers unconstitutional."[35] Bush is, of course, no constitutional scholar; otherwise he would know that, according to the Constitution, only Congress has the power to pass laws, including all details of those laws.[36] It will be interesting to see if any members of the White House press corps raise this issue with Snow.

> *"Elected Republicans and their legislative leaders nation-wide have fallen prey to the natural temptation to view power as their birthright, rather than a reward for hard and righteous work. This explains why they behave like reckless heirs to someone else's fortune."*[37]
>
> —*Tony Snow, November 11, 2005*

Bush is the ultimate example of a reckless heir to someone else's fortune.

Snow was also a speechwriter in the *George H.W. Bush* administration and he worked for the *Washington Times*.

social contract: The understanding between the government and the governed whereby organized society is brought into being and invested with the right to secure mutual protection and welfare or to regulate the relations among its members. Nations and, within nations, political parties may differ considerably in their view of the social contract. *See, also, **tax and spend liberal**.*

---

[34] *Tony Snow On President Bush: 'An Embarrassment,' 'Impotent,' 'Doesn't Seem To Mean What He Says',* Think Progress, April 25, 2006, http://thinkprogress.org/2006/04/25/snow-on-bush.

[35] Or, more likely, displeasing to his corporate supporters and other wealthy friends.

[36] *Bush annuls a law,* The Hightower Lowdown (page 2), May 2006.

[37] *Lessons from Virginia,* Tony Snow, townhall.com, November 11, 2005, http://townhall.com/opinion/column/tonysnow/2005/11/11/175174.html.

Special Plans, Office of: *See Feith, Douglas J.*

speech, freedom of: *See Bill of Rights.*

stovepiping: A process by which policymakers bypass the usual checks and balances to obtain uncorroborated intelligence that fits and/or justifies whatever case they are trying to make. *Donald Rumsfeld, Douglas Feith* and others have been accused of stovepiping in creating the case for attacking Iraq, which is now known to have been based on false claims (weapons of mass destruction, imminent risk of attack on the United States, involvement with al Qaeda, etc.).

supporting the troops: A perfectly reasonable position that has been corrupted in support of the Bush administration's jingoism. Those who don't blindly support Bush's invasion and occupation of Iraq are accused by some[38] of "not supporting the troops." This is nonsense, of course, and is similar to the reaction of the Bush supporters and campaign operatives in the 2000 election, who accused Democrats who wanted poll workers to properly verify the validity of all overseas ballots (most of which were from military personnel) of not supporting "our boys and girls in uniform."

Swift Boat Veterans for Truth: A Republican-funded[39] group of alleged non-partisan Vietnam naval veterans who endorsed and/or appeared in a TV campaign advertisement slandering Democratic presidential candidate John Kerry and claiming that his Vietnam-era medals (three Purple Hearts, a Bronze Star and a Silver Star) were unearned.

One of the key members of the group was John O'Neill, who served on a Swift Boat in Vietnam after Kerry had returned from his tour of duty. Apparently, the first time he met John Kerry was in a debate on the Dick Cavett show,[40]

---

[38] A dwindling number, as the death toll in Iraq mounts.

[39] Bob R. Perry, who, along with his wife, Doylene, is a big Republican donor, contributed $100,000 of the $158,750 the Swift Boat Group had received by the end of June, 2004 (*http://factcheck.org/article.aspx?docID=231*).

[40] *ABC, June 30, 1971.* A transcript of the debate is available at *http://ice.he.net/~freepnet/kerry/index.php?topic=KerryONeill.*

in which Kerry very easily defended[41] the testimony he had given, in opposition to the Vietnam War, before Congress. O'Neill, whose contribution to the debate was little more than a series of unsupported assertions, had been hand picked by Chuck Colson,[42] at the request of Richard Nixon, to do all he could to discredit Kerry.

In an appearance on CNN's Crossfire, O'Neill denied having any ties to the Republican Party. In fact, since 1990, he had contributed a total of $14,650 to Republican federal candidates or national political organizations.[43]

None of the members of the group served on Kerry's boat. Most of the people who did serve on Kerry's boat, including Jim Rassmann, whose life Kerry saved, appeared in a massive show of support for Kerry at the Democratic National Convention, in Boston, in July 2004. Senator John McCain (R-AZ), also a war hero who was similarly smeared by George Bush's campaign during the 2000 presidential primaries, condemned the advertisement and requested that George Bush repudiate it. Even though Bush refused to do so, McCain continued, inexplicably, to support him on the campaign trail in his bid for his second four years.

On August 10, 2004, the Wall Street Journal carried an opinion piece by Jim Rassmann (who is a Republican), describing his rescue in some detail and condemning the Swift Boat Veterans for Truth group as liars, saying they should "hang their heads in shame."[44]

---

[41] Republican views of the debate will, no doubt, differ from this one.

[42] Chuck Colson served time in jail for obstruction of justice in the wake of the Watergate break-in. The year before he went to jail, he became a born-again Christian and now runs Prison Fellowship Ministries (*http://pfm.org*). By his own admission, he was a White House "hatchet man," responsible for political dirty tricks (*see http://pfm.org/Template.cfm?Section=About_Chuck_Colson*).

[43] *Un-political O'Neill has made nearly $15,000 in contributions to federal races—all Republican, Media Matters for America, http://mediamatters.org/items/200408120012.*

[44] *Man Kerry Rescued Calls Swift Boat Ad False: Gives Vivid Account of Rescue Under Enemy Fire, http://factcheck.org/miscreports.aspx?docid=235.*

T

> T is for Terrorize, as in *"The war on terror involves Saddam Hussein because of the nature of Saddam Hussein, the history of Saddam Hussein, and his willingness to terrorize himself."*
> —*George Bush, Grand Rapids, MI, January 29, 2003*
> (Quick. Hide all the mirrors.)

Taguba Report: A report, ordered by Lieutenant General Ricardo Sanchez and prepared by Major General Antonio M. Taguba, on alleged abuse of prisoners by members of the 800th Military Police Brigade at the *Abu Ghraib* prison in Baghdad. At the time, Sanchez was the senior U.S. military officer in Iraq. He ordered the report in response to persistent allegations of human rights abuses at Abu Ghraib.

In spite of the report, the matter received very little attention from the administration, the U.S. Congress, or the press until photographs started to circulate, depicting many of the abuses. The initial reaction from the Defense Department was that the abuses, and even torture, were the work of "a few bad apples." Eventually, *Donald Rumsfeld* said he would accept responsibility. However, even though there have been some convictions, it remains to be seen how many in the chain of command will be held accountable.

talking point: A fact or feature that aids or supports one side, as in an argument, competition, or the like.[1]

Ideally, talking points are used to reinforce a legitimate message. More often, especially in politics, they are used to misinform, mislead, divert attention from an agenda, or simply to avoid giving a straight answer to a question, especially an embarrassing one. Although members of both major parties are guilty of such tactics, the Republicans

---

[1] *Webster's New Universal Unabridged Dictionary.*

have, in recent years, adopted them as a primary mode of operation.

At White House press briefings, *Scott McClellan* relied almost exclusively on talking points to respond or react to (but not usually to answer) reporters' questions. Republican guests on CNN's now-discontinued Crossfire always seemed to be armed with the latest talking points (old ones too—including many that irrelevantly changed the subject from George Bush to Bill Clinton), which they used in order to avoid directly answering questions from the host on the left (either Paul Begala or James Carville). Their approach on other shows has been similar. In the run-up to the 2004 election, the talking points mimicked those used in Bush campaign commercials, complete with distortions and over-simplification.

Tauzin, Billy: Former 12-term Republican Congressman from Louisiana. He switched from Democrat to Republican in 1995 (at the time the Republicans gained control of the House of Representatives) and went on to become one of the most powerful Republicans in the House. He was Chairman of the House Energy and Commerce Committee, which oversaw the pharmaceutical industry (among others). On January 3, 2005, he started work as the head of the Pharmaceutical Research and Manufacturers of America (PhRMA), which lobbies on behalf of 48 drug companies. For more information regarding Billy Tauzin and this issue, see *revolving door syndrome*.

tax and spend liberal: Frequent Republican characterization of Democrats, used to give the impression that Republicans don't tax and spend.

However, taxing and spending are exactly what governments (all governments!) do. With very rare exceptions,[2] they have no choice. Governments at one level or another

---

[2] One example is Saudi Arabia, which levies no income tax on Saudis or the nationals of other GCC (Gulf Cooperation Council) countries (Bahrain, Kuwait, Oman, Qatar and United Arab Emirates). They do, however, tax corporations and partnerships. *(Ref. http://www.infoprod.co.il/country/saudia2e.htm.)*

are required to spend money on defense, education, infrastructure, security, public safety, law enforcement, and on and on. The money must be raised through taxation. This arrangement is part of what is sometimes referred to as the *social contract*.

The tax strategy (if it can be called that) of the Bush administration and the Republican-dominated Congress seems to be to reduce the marginal tax rate for the very wealthy, make some nominal concessions to the middle class (based on a Democrat-sponsored tax bill amendment), cut programs that affect the needy and near-needy, defund state mandates, and expand corporate welfare and other programs that benefit large corporations, especially energy companies, oil industry service companies (e.g., Halliburton), insurance companies, HMOs and defense contractors. The defunding of state mandates (programs legislated in Washington but implemented by the states) forces cutbacks at the state level and, ultimately, increases state-level taxpayer costs. The net result is that low and middle-income taxpayers are worse off, higher-income taxpayers see little appreciable benefit, and the really wealthy and the corporations make out like bandits.[3]

In the end, the question is one of who is taxed and who gets the most benefit from tax revenues. For the Bush administration and their wealthy friends, the answer is obvious. However, George Bush, like previous presidents from his own party, touts tax cuts as a way to boost the economy.

tax giveaway: This term is often used but rarely defined. Usually, it describes an unnecessary or inequitable tax reduc-

---

[3] A Congressional Budget Office report, issued on August 13, 2004, shows the top 1%, with incomes averaging $1.2 million, getting an average 2004 tax cut of $78,460. The middle 20%, with incomes averaging $57,000 get an average cut of $1,090. Those with incomes in the $51,000 to $75,000 range are, on average, subject to a tax increase. People in the lowest 10% get a measly $250 on average. The figures are for federal income tax only and do not take into account the adverse effect of higher local taxes, fuel costs, usage fees, etc., or of the reduction in services at both the federal and state levels.

tion. Except in a period of government budget surpluses, any tax reduction has a cost, either in increased taxes to those not qualifying for the reduction, or in reduced services, or through budget deficits (or increases in existing deficits) that must be paid for (with interest) in the future—even by future generations. The worst inequities occur when the super-rich (corporations or individual people) are given a tax reduction.

George Bush's tax reductions have affected all three areas. Even though they included some middle class cuts (mainly because of Democratic amendments), reductions in payments to the states have increased local taxes and fees and reduced local services. Also, the rationale for some of the cuts was clearly fraudulent. Cynically renaming the *estate tax* the "death tax," Republicans claimed it was needed, among other reasons, to prevent the loss of family farms. Try as they might, progressive journalists and others could find no case of a family farm being lost because of the estate tax—or even, apparently, any that were subject to the estate tax in the first place. Those that go out of business because they are unable to compete with large (and subsidized) agribusinesses are another matter.

taxation, progressive: *See progressive taxation.*

TeenPact: *See Alliance Defense Fund.*

terrorism: In view of the events of September 11, 2001, and subsequently, Webster's three definitions of terrorism are quite interesting.

The first is "the use of terrorizing methods." Osama bin Laden and his al Qaeda network could certainly be said to use terrorizing methods. One might doubt the sanity of someone who disagreed with that.

The second, which arises from the first, is "the state of fear and submission so produced."

The third is "a terroristic method of governing or of resisting a government."

In looking at these definitions, it would seem to be necessary to distinguish between international terrorism and
other forms. Al Qaeda's terrorism is clearly international.
The terrorism practiced by the Chechen rebels is, for the
most part (but possibly not exclusively), not international.
The terroristic rule of Saddam Hussein was not international, nor is the rule of most other dictators.

Even international terrorism is not the biggest threat faced
by the United States. Hans Blix,[4] among others, has pointed
out that air pollution, which has become worse as a result
of Bush administration environmental policies, will cause
the deaths of more people in the U.S. each year (about
30,000) than were killed in the terrorist attacks of September 11, 2001 (about 3000). Other preventable deaths include
those from firearms (about 28,000 per year) and traffic acci-
dents (over 40,000 per year). Other statistics are similarly
staggering, but those three causes alone add up to nearly
100,000 per year, with something like 50,000 additional ac-
cidental deaths not related to guns or traffic and approxi-
mately 18,000 people whose deaths are attributed to lack of
health care. Tragic as terrorism-related deaths are, the
probability of dying from some other preventable cause is
many times as great. In spite of this, the Bush administration's fear campaign, which contains no compensating reas-
surances based on actual probability, appears to be terrorizing a considerable number of Americans, although a size-
able number have become quite blasé about the repeated
warnings.

terrorist: A person who uses or favors terrorizing methods.[5]

theocon: Contraction of theological conservative. Sidney Blumenthal[6] used the term (but did not invent it) in a March 4,
2004, article in *The Guardian*.[7] A major part of George Bush's

---

[4] Former U.N. Chief Weapons Inspector.

[5] *Webster's dictionary* (first of three definitions).

[6] Former senior adviser to President Clinton and author of *The Clinton
Wars, ISBN 0-3741250-2-3.*

[7] *http://www.guardian.co.uk/comment/story/0,3604,1161399,00.html.*

constituency consists of *neocons,* theocons and, according to Carolyn Kay of *Make them Accountable,*[8] corporocons (corporate conservatives).

Word Spy[9] defines theocon as *a conservative who believes that religion should play a major role in forming and implementing public policy,* and cites December 12, 1996, as the date of its first use.[10]

Thurmond, Strom: Late Republican Senator from South Carolina, who celebrated his hundredth birthday in the Senate on December 5, 2002, just over one year before he died at the age of 101. He retired in January 2003, after eight terms.

Thurmond, who had degrees in horticulture and law, started his political career as an ardent segregationist and, after holding several political offices (including state senator and governor) and a judgeship, ran for President on a segregationist ticket, carrying four states but losing, along with Thomas Dewey, to Harry Truman.[11] His original election to the U.S. Senate was as a write-in candidate. He claimed to have left his segregationist past behind him, but his critics were very skeptical of that.

His supporters admired his longevity in the Senate. His detractors couldn't wait for him to resign. In his last few years, he was dependent on others (and a wheelchair) to get from his office to the Senate floor and back. Towards the end, his main value to the Republican Party was his party-line vote. In 2002, Congressman Lindsey Graham ran successfully for Thurmond's Senate seat, with a ten-point lead over his Democratic opponent, disappointing those who had hoped Thurmond's departure might change the balance of power.

---

[8] *http://makethemaccountable.com.*

[9] *http://wordspy.com/words/theocon.asp.*

[10] *Neocon v. theocon, Jacob Heilbrun, The New Republic, December 12 1996.*

[11] *A short biography can be found on the website of The Strom Thurmond Institute of Government and Public Affairs (part of Clemson University) at http://www.strom.clemson.edu/strom/bio.html.*

Following his death, one of the skeletons came out of Thurmond's closet, when his daughter, Essie Mae Washington Williams, then in her 70s, came forward. She is the product of his fairly long relationship, in the 1920s, with a black servant. Thurmond was well known as a groping womanizer, but this was new to most people, even though a 1998 biography[12] had speculated about it.

TIA: Total Information Awareness, later renamed Terrorism Information Awareness. This was the brainchild of *John Poindexter* and his colleagues, and was set up in the Department of Defense's "Information Awareness Office", whose apparent mission was to gather as much information as possible on as many people as possible with a view to determining who might or might not be a terrorist. It's hard to believe that such a project would not have so many false positive results as to be totally useless, while at the same time invading the privacy of practically everyone. In any event, Congress voted to shut TIA down in 2003. And that was the end of that—apparently. However, it was revealed in a Senate hearing in February 2006 that the project had continued under the codename Topsail.[13] It would appear that today's Congress has little power to rein in the excesses of the executive branch.

Tobin, James: George Bush's former New England campaign manager. Tobin was indicted on December 1, 2004, on four charges related to the Republican jamming of Democrat get-out-the-vote phone lines on election day, 2002 (midterm elections). If convicted, Tobin could serve up to five years in jail. Although it cannot be proved, some Democrats suspected the Justice Department may have deliberately delayed the indictment until after the 2004 presidential election. Two of Tobin's associates have already been convicted.

---

[12] *Ol' Strom, by Jack Bass and Marilyn W. Thomson, University of South Carolina Press, January 2003, ISBN 1-57-003514-8.*

[13] *Wanted: Competent Big Brothers, Michael Hirsh, Newsweek, February 8, 2006, http://msnbc.msn.com/id/11238800/site/newsweek.*

Tobin's trial date was set for February 1, 2005, but was post-poned until December. He was convicted[14] on December 15, 2005, of conspiracy to commit telephone harassment and of aiding and abetting telephone harassment. Sentencing was set for March 16, 2006. Following his conviction, Tobin said he would appeal.

tort reform: This is one of the most misleading issues pursued by the Republicans. Tort is the legal term for a wrongful act that leads to injury or death to a person, or his or her property or reputation, for which he or she or a survivor is entitled to compensation.

The primary focus of the tort reformers has been in the health care field, where, rather than address the real reasons for soaring medical costs, the Republicans blame the tort system. In other words, they blame medical liability lawsuits.

What the tort reformers would rather you didn't know is that, according to both government and academic data, lawsuits have very little to do with the cost of health care. The Congressional Budget Office places that cost at around 2% of total health care spending, and points out that George Bush's proposed malpractice reforms would reduce doctors' malpractice insurance premiums by something under 0.5%, in spite of which Bush claims that lawsuits are *"driving docs (sic) out of the practice of medicine."*

Only about 13% of malpractice victims actually file a claim, with only 2% going so far as to file a lawsuit. Where lawsuits are filed, an arbitrary cap on non-economic damages (which is what the tort reform proponents propose—and is already the practice in a number of states) would penalize those who are injured the most.[15]

---

[14] *Former RNC New England Regional Director Convicted In New Hampshire Phone Jamming Case, Department of Justice, December 15, 2005, http://www.usdoj.gov/opa/pr/2005/December/05_crm_672.html.*

[15] *President Bush's Rhetoric on Medical Malpractice Doesn't Match Reality (Democratic Policy Committee, Senator Byron Dorgan, Chairman), http://democrats.senate.gov/~dpc/pubs/108-2-026.html.*

Because most lawsuits are handled on a contingency basis, where the lawyers get a percentage of the proceeds if an award is made, but nothing if they lose the case, a cap on damages is likely to make a litigation practice a losing proposition. The result is a reduction in the likelihood that someone seeking compensation, through the courts, for physical or financial injuries will be able to find a lawyer willing or even able to take the case. All of this is fine with most Republican politicians, as political contributions by trial lawyers are overwhelmingly to Democratic candidates and campaigns.

See, also, **Article VII,** *under* **Bill of Rights.**

torture: *See* **Abu Ghraib** *and* **Camp Delta.**

Towey, Jim: Former head of the White House *Office of Faith-Based and Community Initiatives.* Towey (pronounced tooey) was appointed in February 2002, five months after the departure of John DiIulio from the position. He announced his resignation on April 18, 2006, with effect from June 2.

Whereas DiIulio's background was academic, Towey's was political and legal. Although, like DiIulio, a Democrat, he endorsed Jeb Bush in his run as Lawton Chiles' successor for Governor of Florida.

Unlike DiIulio, Towey did not report directly to George Bush, indicating that what was initially a signature issue for Bush was somewhat diminished in importance[16] — a result, no doubt, of criticism, not only from the left and center, but also from the right.

One of Towey's stated goals in his White House role was to "heal the nation's soul." Given that the Establishment Clause of the First Amendment would seem to exclude any governmental involvement in defining what a nation's soul (or a person's soul) might be, measuring his achievement in that area would seem to be somewhat problematic.

---

[16] Or at least in visibility.

In November 2003, Towey committed a major gaffe in the course of a scheduled on-line chat session about Bush's faith-based projects. In response to a question as to whether pagan faith-based groups should be given the same consideration as other groups seeking aid, he answered, according to a White House transcript[17] of the session:

> *"I haven't run into a pagan faith-based group yet, much less a pagan group that cares for the poor! Once you make it clear to any applicant that public money must go to public purposes and can't be used to promote ideology, the fringe groups lose interest. Helping the poor is tough work and only those with loving hearts seem drawn to it."*

Given that most or possibly all pagan groups (which would include Wiccans, for example) are involved in charitable work, helping the poor and disadvantaged, there was an understandably negative reaction once the media published his statement. Americans United for Separation of Church and State conducted a survey[18] of pagan activists, soliciting information about social service work done by members of their organizations. The response was enormous, and included the following four:

- Portal of Light Pantry, southwestern Missouri: Pagan-run distribution center delivering food to elderly and ill people. Stays open late to allow low-income people to stock up on food after work.

- Diamond Charities, Glendora, CA: Distributes food, blankets and clothing to the homeless.

- The Spiral Grove (a Pagan worship group), Stephens City, VA: Sponsors a food bank, spearheads clothing collections, and provides emergency funds to distressed households.

- Southern Illinois Pagan Alliance: Collects books for hospitalized children, participates in

---

[17] The transcript may be found at *http://whitehouse.gov/ask/20031126.html*.
[18] *Church and State, January 2004, page 15.*

local food and clothing drives, and collects new toys for poor children every Christmas.

Notwithstanding such activity, Towey's backers, including representatives of *Concerned Women for America* and *The Heritage Foundation*, averred that Towey was only *"stating a fact."* Such a position would appear to come from closed minds not wishing to be confused with facts.

Later in the same chat session, asked about Muslims participating in the faith-based programs, Towey answered:

> *"Muslims are welcomed* (sic) *to participate in this initiative. The issue isn't whether a group believes in God or not but whether their program works. So the faith-based initiative isn't faith-specific. I think America needs to do all it can to avoid religious rivalry and competition—that is the beauty of our heritage of pluralism."*

Apparently, consistency wasn't Towey's forte. To paraphrase George Orwell, it seems that some religions are more equal than others.

Finally, Towey said that he believed that God "speaks to us through the poor." Given the rate at which the Bush administration has been increasing their numbers, the future promises to be very noisy.

traitor: Webster's provides two definitions: *1. One who betrays a person, a cause, or any trust. 2. One who betrays his country by violating his allegiance; one guilty of treason.*

Ann Coulter provides one definition: *Anyone who is a **liberal**.* Unfortunately, many on the right appear to agree with Ann Coulter.

Trashing the White House: The subject of a minor work of fiction, created by some members of the incoming Bush administration in January 2001. A subsequent (and expensive) GAO investigation revealed that outgoing members of the Clinton Administration left their offices and office equipment in much the same condition as did outgoing members of previous administrations (i.e., with a great deal of trash, but no evidence of deliberate "trashing").

Treene, Eric W.: Special Counsel for Religious Discrimination in the U.S. Justice Department. Treene was appointed to the newly created position, reporting to R. Alexander Acosta, Assistant Attorney General for the Civil Rights Division, in June 2002. His appointment was celebrated by *Faith and Action*, a conservative Christian group that likes to remind legislators of *"the prominent role that the word of God played in the creation of our nation and its laws."* That the framers of the Constitution were predominantly deists,[19] who scrupulously avoided references to any God, seems to have escaped their attention.

In early 2003, Treene's department lent its support to a lawsuit, by the very conservative **Alliance Defense Fund** (which counts James Dobson, of **Focus on the Family**, and D. James Kennedy, of Coral Ridge Ministries, among its founders), in the case of the L.I.F.E. Bible Club at Westfield High School (in Westfield, MA), whose members were suspended for engaging in religious proselytization, in defiance of the principal's withholding of permission, by handing out scripture verses and candy canes bearing religious messages to fellow students on school property.

More recently, Treene's department intervened on the side of the Salvation Army in a lawsuit challenging the latter's practice of imposing a religious litmus test on employees in (or applicants for) positions related to projects financed by taxpayer dollars.[20]

trifecta: A bet in which the first three finishers in a horse race are selected in what is hoped to be the correct order. Be-

---

[19] A deist believes in the existence of a God on the evidence of reason and nature only, with rejection of supernatural revelation. More concisely, a deist believes in a God who created the World (or the Universe), but has since remained indifferent to that creation.

[20] For employees working on core Salvation Army projects, financed by its own fundraising efforts, a religious test for employment is not illegal and follows historically accepted practices.

cause of the long odds against the success of such a bet, the payoff is typically very large.

After September 11, 2001, George Bush used the word in at least three speeches on fiscal policy or fiscal responsibility. Examples can even be found on the White House website. On April 16, 2002, Bush addressed a meeting of the Leaders of the Fiscal Responsibility Coalition in Room 450 of the Dwight D. Eisenhower Executive Office Building. Right from the White House Press Office's own transcript, we have the following:

> *"The recession — no question, I remember when I was campaigning, I said, would you ever deficit spend? And I said, yes, only if there were a time of war, or recession, or a national emergency. Never thought we'd get — (laughter and applause). And so we have a temporary[21] deficit in our budget, because we are at war, we're recovering, our economy is recovering,[22] and we've had a national emergency. Never did I dream we'd have the trifecta. (Laughter.)"*

In addition to the obvious bad taste involved in including the aftermath of 9/11 in his attempt at humor, the reference to his alleged campaign statement is a bald-faced lie. In none of his 2000 campaign statements or speeches has anyone been able to find a statement linking those three conditions. The transcript does not tell us, of course, whether the laughter was genuine or merely a nervous reaction by his audience. The appalling thing about this particular lie is that a similar statement was made, in 1998, by Al Gore, who was still Vice President at the time. Not content with stealing the election from Gore (*see felon purge, Felonious Five and Harris, Katherine*), Bush stole his words, too.

TRMPAC: Texans for a Republican Majority Political Action Committee, established and controlled by former House Majority Leader *Tom DeLay*.

---

[21] One problem with the word "temporary" is that it's not very instructive with respect to duration.

[22] Wishful thinking. There was no evidence of economic recovery at the time Bush made the speech.

U

> U is for Unrest, as in *"I understand that the unrest in the Middle East creates unrest throughout the region."*
> —George Bush, Washington, DC, March 13, 2002
> (He's misunderstood.)

unfunded mandate: A requirement imposed by Congress on state or local governments with no funding to pay for it.[1]

unions, civil: *See gay marriage and civil unions.*

USA PATRIOT Act: This is the legislation that was passed in the dead of night, not long after the attacks of September 11, 2001. There were very few dissenting votes in either the House or the Senate and no members of either house had been given time to actually read it.

Its full name is *The Uniting and Strengthening America by Providing Appropriate Tools Required to Intercept and Obstruct Terrorism Act.* As a pronounceable initialism, it qualifies as an acronym. However, it seems apparent that the term USA PATRIOT Act came first and words to fit the initials were contrived. Possibly many in Congress felt too intimidated to vote against a bill with "patriot" in its name. No doubt its flag-waving connotations caused others to support it uncritically. Obviously, in the aftermath of 9/11, the "we must do something" syndrome was at work.

Since its implementation, its threats to privacy and due process have moved more than 380 cities and communities, representing 60 million people, to pass resolutions calling for its reform. In California alone, there have been no fewer than 64 resolutions opposing the Act.[2]

---

[1] *C-SPAN Congressional Glosssary, http://c-span.org/guide/congress/glossary/unfunded.htm.*

[2] *ACLU News (American Civil Liberties Union of Northern California), Summer 2005 Edition.*

The Act contains a sunset provision, in which some parts of it were slated to lapse, if not renewed, at the end of 2005. Although the House of Representatives voted for renewal, as of December 17, 2005 it was stalled in the Senate, with a bipartisan group of senators saying that a compromise of House and Senate bills doesn't do enough *"to protect innocent people from unnecessary and intrusive government surveillance."* They have vowed to ensure that renewal doesn't occur unless changes are made. [3] As of the end of February 2006, the Act was expected to become permanent and have very few changes.

> *"In the House, bipartisan majorities supported bills to limit the reach of the Patriot Act by placing better checks and balances into the law—moves that were ultimately overridden by the Republican House leadership at the behest of the Bush administration's knee-jerk opposition to common-sense reforms."*
>
> *—The Patriot Act: Where It Stands, ACLU, March 2006*[4]

At the beginning of March 2006, both the House and the Senate passed the USA Patriot Act reauthorization bill. The good news was that some sunset provisions remain, but with the date moved to the end of 2009. The bad news was that fourteen of the original sixteen sunset provisions were made permanent. The other two authorize roving wiretaps and permit secret warrants for books, records and other items from businesses, hospitals and organizations such as libraries.[5]

There are only three real (but small) improvements in the revised Act: the right of recipients of National Security Letters to challenge them in court, the right of recipients of

---

[3] *Electronic Privacy Information Center, USA Patriot Act Sunset, http://epic.org/privacy/terrorism/usapatriot/sunset.html.* (This web page is updated as the situation changes.)

[4] *Reform the Patriot Act, Talking Points, ACLU, http://action.aclu.org/ reformthepatriotact/whereitstands.html.*

[5] *Congress Renews Patriot Act, With Some Changes, Charles Babington, The Washington Post, March 8, 2006, http://truthout.org/docs_2006/ 030806K.shtml.*

court-approved subpoenas for information in terrorist investigations to challenge a requirement that they refrain from telling anyone, and a clarification stating that most libraries are not subject to demands in National Security Letters for information about suspected terrorists.

The Senate vote was 89 to 10 and the House vote was 257 to 171, nothing like the near unanimity of the original 2001 vote. House Republicans approved it by 214 to 14, with the Democrats, plus Bernie Sanders (I-VT), disapproving by 157 to 43. If the 43 Democrats who voted for it had voted against it, there would have been a 214 to 214 tie, which could have been broken, one way or the other, if any of the six House members who didn't vote at all had voted. George Bush signed it into law on March 9, one day before the original Act was due to expire. In the meantime, various members of Congress have been working on legislation, including the SAFE Act,[6] to correct excesses in the Patriot Act.[7]

U.S. Constitution: A document with which George W. Bush and members of his administration seem to have only a passing acquaintance, especially with the ten articles of the *Bill of Rights* and the Fourteenth Amendment.

---

[6] *Security And Freedom Ensured Act (S. 1709), Senator Larry Craig (R-ID) and Senator Dick Durbin (D-IL), http://www.eff.org/patriot/safe_act_analysis.php.*

[7] *Reform the Patriot Act, What You Should Know, ACLU, http://action.aclu.org/reformthepatriotact.*

V

> V is for Vision, as in *"I have a different vision of lead-ership. A leadership is someone who brings people to-gether."*
>
> —*George Bush, Bartlett, TN, August 18, 2000*
>
> (Not your father's vision thing.)

Veneman, Ann M: Secretary of Agriculture in George Bush's first term. She resigned in November, 2004 and was re-placed, in January 2005, by *Mike Johanns,* former governor of Nebraska.

Village Idiot: Subject of bumper sticker, on which the full mes-sage is, *"Somewhere in Texas… A village is missing its idiot."* There are, of course, no prizes for guessing the alleged idiot's identity.

violence, recent surge in: *See recent surge in violence.*

Vitter, David: The first Republican to win a U.S. Senate seat in Louisiana since Reconstruction. Although he agrees with George Bush on most issues, including opposition to same-sex marriage and support of tax cuts for the wealthy, he disagrees with the Bush policy that opposes importation of lower cost prescription drugs. He replaced the retiring De-mocratic Senator, John Breaux.

voodoo economics: *George H.W. Bush's* description of Ronald Reagan's proposed supply-side, or trickle-down, economics during the 1980 Republican Primaries. After Bush lost the primary to Reagan and was offered the role of Vice Presi-dential running mate, he managed to forget his criticism. George W. Bush's economic policy is similar enough to that of Reagan to have inspired Robert S. McIntyre, in a column in *The American Prospect* (May 1, 2003, edition), to coin the term, "Déjà Voodoo Economics." (*See also **dubyanomics** and **tax giveaway**.*)

vote, right to: Contrary to popular belief, the U.S. Constitution contains no explicit statement about the right to vote. It states a requirement that one be a citizen and, in the 15th, 19th and 26th Amendments, provides for nondiscrimination in voting, with respect to race, sex and age. In the *Bush v. Gore* Supreme Court case, in 2000, Justice Antonin Scalia made life difficult for the Gore Campaign lawyer, Lawrence Tribe, by bombarding him with questions predicated on the assumption that there was no universal right of suffrage in a presidential election. Had Gore won in the Supreme Court and had he won a subsequent complete recount, the Republicans in the Florida Senate could have sent Florida's Republican Electoral College members to Washington, in addition to their Democrat counterparts. In fact, they had already indicated their intent to do so. That would, as it happens, have nullified the Florida vote and put Gore in the White House anyway, as he already had more electoral votes than Bush. Congressman Jesse Jackson, Jr. has proposed to add a voting rights amendment to the U.S. Constitution.[1]

voter rights: *See vote, right to.*

vouchers: *See school vouchers.*

Vulcans: A loosely constituted group of extremely hawkish foreign policy advisors, consisting of, among others, Richard Armitage, ***Dick Cheney, Stephen Hadley, Colin Powell, Richard Perle, Condoleezza Rice, Donald Rumsfeld*** and ***Paul Wolfowitz***. They advised George Bush during his 2000 election campaign. The Vulcans are all proponents of the National Missile Defense (NMD) system (also known as Star Wars). Colin Powell even said, *"Star Wars is an essential part of our strategic system."* The view of the scientific community and of many military strategists, in the U.S. and elsewhere, including among U.S. allies, is that NMD is useless, ruinous and destabilizing—not exactly a ringing endorsement.

---

[1] *Do Americans Have The Right To Vote? Congressman Jesse L. Jackson, Jr. (D-IL), September 1, 2004, prepared for Tavis Smiley's PBS "Election 2004 Special Features,"* http://house.gov/jackson/DoAmericansHaveRightTAVIS.doc.

W

W is for We, as in *"Our enemies are innovative and re-sourceful, and so are we. They never stop thinking about new ways to harm our country and our people, and neither do we."*

—*George Bush, August 5, 2004*

(Honesty can be so refreshing.)

Walters, John: Director, Office of National Drug Control Policy. Not surprisingly (for a Bush appointee), Walters has a history of arguing for jail time over voluntary treatment for drug offenders, although he had argued for leniency for users for a first offense. Around the time of his nomination, a teenager in Alabama was sentenced to 26 years for selling 120 grams of marijuana to an undercover agent. It would have been interesting to find out how he felt about such a draconian punishment.

" … but listen to [John Walters] and he stands out as a bellicose drug warrior."

Ethan Nadelmann, Executive Director,
Lindesmith Center—Drug Policy Foundation

War on Drugs: This is a concept that has similar semantic problems to *War on Terrorism*. A war on wholesale drug pushers might make some sense, coupled with a campaign to discourage drug use (through education) and programs to treat and rehabilitate addicts—and there is something of a trend, in some states, in this direction. George Bush is probably only somewhat worse than his predecessors on this issue,[1] although his former Attorney General, *John Ashcroft*, exhibited extraordinary zeal in opposing the in-

---

[1] Even Bill Clinton had a Drug Czar, General Barry McCaffrey, during whose tenure drug use by children in junior high school increased 300% (in spite of a billion dollar anti-drug propaganda program) and the U.S. involved itself in a civil war in Colombia.

nocuous practice of smoking marijuana to alleviate such things as the nausea suffered by people undergoing chemotherapy.[2,3] In the meantime, opium production in Afghanistan is at a record high, making that country, supposedly still subject to strong U.S. influence, the world's leading heroin exporter. *See, also,* **Walters, John**.

War on Terrorism, War on Terror: The terms used by George W. Bush, his Republican allies and, unfortunately, his Democrat opponents, to describe what should, in fact, be called a war on terrorists (if, indeed, it should be called a war at all). The trouble with a war on terrorism or terror is that it's impossible to know when victory has been achieved.[4] Given his propensity for calling himself a **War President**, that may very well be exactly what Bush wants, providing him with a perpetual excuse to curtail civil liberties, issue executive orders, provide his buddies in defense and defense-related industries with lucrative contracts, and scare more than half the U.S. population into voting for him and his congressional allies in November 2004.[5]

Interestingly though, in August 2005, Bush and those around him substituted, for a few days, a new term for war on terror. Apparently, he decided he was engaged in a *"global struggle against violent extremism."* This is odd, if not in fact hypocritical, in that both George Bush and **Dick Cheney** attacked John Kerry, in the 2004 campaign, for his reluctance to use the word *war* in the context of terrorism. Kerry's view, which he stated in the October 2003 Democratic primary debate, was that the so-called war on terror

---

[2] George Bush, himself, also opposes the medical use of marijuana.

[3] Ultimately, Ashcroft was successful, in that the U.S. Supreme Court ruled that federal law trumped state law and that it was up to Congress to change the federal law if they chose.

[4] As "isms" will always be with us, there can be no victory over them, leading to a phony "perpetual war," as envisaged by George Orwell in his famous 1948 novel, *1984*. The forecast implicit in *1984* was off by less than 20 years.

[5] A tactic which, in conjunction with other tactics, was evidently successful.

was *"far less of a military operation and far more of an intelligence and law-enforcement operation."*[6]

War President: One of George Bush's favorite self-descriptive terms. The apparent relish with which he uses the term might lead one to believe that he sees himself as a latter-day Franklin Roosevelt or Winston Churchill. That perception is reinforced by the uncritical comparisons made by members of a compliant press, especially regarding FDR. An examination of FDR's record shows how foolish this is. FDR's famous *"We have nothing to fear but fear itself"* is the antithesis of Bush's fear mongering approach. FDR called for sacrifice; Bush encourages spending on consumer goods and rewards his extremely wealthy supporters with tax breaks and corporate subsidies they don't need. Comparing Bush's speeches with those of FDR is one of the biggest exercises in self-deception, with Bush apparently more dependent on his professional speechwriters than any previous president.[7]

Some wishful thinking may be involved, in that Roosevelt was elected to a second and third term. Identifying himself as a wartime president certainly seemed to be part of Bush's strategy for winning a second term—and that quest was certainly successful.[8] Theoretically, Bush could serve a third term, as the 22nd Amendment only says that no person may be **elected** President more than twice.[9]

warming, global: *See global warming.*

---

[6] *No major newspapers noted that Bush had bashed Kerry with now-defunct "war on terror" term, Media Matters, posted August 3, 2005, http://mediamatters.org/items/200508030001.*

[7] All presidents have speechwriters, of course. However, many of them were also excellent extemporaneous speakers, a talent not to be found in George Bush.

[8] Notwithstanding allegations of fraud, in some cases massive fraud, in most states.

[9] This is said with tongue firmly in cheek, of course, as the U.S. Supreme Court decision ending the Florida recount is probably regarded, for 22nd Amendment purposes, as affirming Bush's election (certainly by the five justices who voted in the affirmative), notwithstanding numerous well-informed opinions that the Supreme Court was party to a coup d'état.

warmonger: A person who advocates, wants, or tries to precipitate war.[10] Those in the Bush administration who could justifiably be called warmongers include (but are not limited to) George Bush himself (*see, also,* **War President**), *Dick Cheney, Donald Rumsfeld, John Bolton, Douglas Feith, I. Lewis "Scooter" Libby* and *Paul Wolfowitz.*[11] Others having a certain amount of influence on (and who are certainly supportive of) the Bush administration would include *Kenneth Adelman,* Frank Gaffney and *Richard Perle.*

weapons of mass destruction (WMD): This category of weapons is usually understood to include strategic nuclear devices, poisonous chemical agents and lethal biological agents. There is universal agreement with respect to strategic nuclear devices, but some disagreement regarding the other two, for two reasons. First, they don't destroy property; second, they are hard to deploy in such a way as to kill more than a few hundred or a few thousand people. That is not to say that killing so many people is a trivial matter. However, "mass destruction" is a term traditionally confined to situations where entire populations (e.g., of cities) are wiped out (or nearly wiped out), usually with massive destruction of property. The World War II bombing of Coventry, by the Luftwaffe, and of Dresden, by the Royal Air Force, could certainly be characterized as mass destruction, although the weapons were conventional. Obviously, used in sufficient numbers, all military weapons could be considered to be weapons of mass destruction.

As for the WMD Saddam Hussein was alleged to possess prior to Operation Iraqi Freedom, the most recent information indicates that his fledgling nuclear program was destroyed after the Gulf War[12] and that his chemical and bio-

---

[10] *Webster's New Universal Unabridged Dictionary.*

[11] Libby (indicted) and Wolfowitz (head of World Bank) are no longer members of the Bush administration.

[12] As Mohamed El Baradei, head of the International Atomic Energy Agency (IAEA) said on several occasions. More recently, Jafar Dhia Jafar, the former head of Saddam Hussein's nuclear weapons program, said that Saddam ordered the destruction of all banned weapons in 1991. He said, moreover, that

logical agents were effectively gone by the mid 1990s.[13] Even if any of his chemical and biological stockpiles escaped destruction, their shelf life is apparently quite limited.

America's stockpile of chemical weapons dwarfs anything ever attributed to Saddam Hussein. As part of an international treaty, 30,000 tons of deadly chemicals at several U.S. sites are scheduled for destruction, by incineration, by 2007. All but two sites are behind schedule and the best-case estimate is now 2008, with possible delays making 2013 more realistic.[14] The U.S. stockpile of nuclear weapons is, of course, enough to destroy the world several times over. Although neither the chemical (and biological) nor the nuclear stockpiles can be blamed on George W. Bush, his attitude towards international treaties does nothing to improve the situation—and, indeed, cannot help but exacerbate it.

Weyrich, Paul M.: *See Free Congress Foundation.*

White House Iraq Group (WHIG): *See Card, Andrew H., Jr.*

willing, coalition of: *See coalition of the willing.*

WMD: *See weapons of mass destruction (WMD).*

Wolfowitz, Paul: Former Deputy Secretary of Defense, and now head of the World Bank.

Although Wolfowitz is a *neocon* and one of the signatories to **Project for the New American Century**, he is, unlike the other well-known neoconservatives, a registered Democrat. However, his position on Iraq, in the run-up to *Operation Iraqi Freedom,* was similar to that of his boss, **Donald Rumsfeld,** and the other hawks.[15] In fact, he was pushing both

---

the Special Republican Guard carried out the destruction. Source: *Saddam had WMDs destroyed in 91, claim scientists, http://thescotsman.scotsman.com/international.cfm?id=273532004.*

[13] As many, including, most prominently, Scott Ritter, were saying in the months leading up to the invasion of Iraq.

[14] *Depot faces longer timeline, Mary Hopkin, Tri-City Herald, October 3, 2001, http://www.tri-cityherald.com/news/2001/1003/story3.html.*

[15] Yes, there is such a thing as a Democrat hawk. One of them, former Senator Zell Miller (D-GA), springs somewhat readily to mind.

Rumsfeld and Bush to attack Iraq immediately after the attacks of September 11, 2001. Most embarrassing in retrospect, though, are his prewar statements on the cost of that war, which turned out to be very different from the eventual reality.

> *"There's a lot of money to pay for this that doesn't have to be U.S. taxpayer money, and it starts with the assets of the Iraqi people ... and on a rough recollection, the oil revenues of that country could bring between 50 and 100 billion dollars over the course of the next two or three years ... We're dealing with a country that can really finance its own reconstruction, and relatively soon."*[16]
>
> —*Paul Wolfowitz, March 27, 2003, in testimony before the House Committee on Appropriations*

In spite of a great deal of controversy, based mostly on his war hawk reputation, the directors of the World Bank elected him unanimously as its president. Possibly his excellent record as an academic (Yale and Johns Hopkins) and as a diplomat (including being U.S. Ambassador to Indonesia) carried more weight than his uncharacteristically dismal performance in his most recent position.

---

[16] *Iraqi Oil Will Pay For This: PAST COMMENTS ABOUT HOW MUCH IRAQ WOULD COST, http://www.house.gov/schakowsky/iraqquotes_web.htm.*

xenophobia: An unreasonable fear or hatred of foreigners or strangers.

Xenophobia was at its peak in early 2003, among Republicans, after France and Germany (among others) refused to support a U.S.-proposed U.N. resolution to attack and invade Iraq. It led to the renaming of French fries to "freedom fries" (failing to recognize that French fries are, in fact, of Belgian origin) and the ceremonial pouring of French wine into the gutter. The latter act highlighted the irrationality of xenophobes, in that those dumping the wine had already paid for it. Thus, the punishment they presumably thought they were inflicting on the French was only in their heads and to their own pocketbooks.

Y

Yoo, John: Professor of Law at the University of California at Berkeley and former Deputy Assistant Attorney General under *John Ashcroft*. John Yoo is interesting in that he was the co-author, in January 2002, of a legal brief that argued that fighters captured by U.S. troops in Afghanistan were not protected by the *Geneva Conventions*. This led to George Bush's policy in which the prisoners at Guantánamo's *Camp Delta* were declared to be *"enemy combatants,"* with no right to counsel or even to a hearing. With neither counsel nor a hearing, it was impossible, of course, to know whether any prisoner's "enemy combatant" status was simply a convenient assertion or based on actual evidence. This was complicated by the fact that it was virtually impossible for any outsider to know who, indeed, was being held at Camp Delta. The denial of Geneva Convention protections led to abuses, both at Camp Delta and, later, at the *Abu Ghraib* prison in Baghdad. Yoo has denied, for obvious reasons, that his arguments were intended to apply to conditions in Iraq (the invasion of which didn't occur until the following year). However, the practices at Camp Delta eventually served as a model for the Abu Ghraib abuses.

George Bush's second Attorney General and former White House Counsel, *Alberto Gonzalez*, bears significant responsibility for Bush's policy, in that he advised Bush that Yoo's analysis was a legitimate one.

Ultimately, of course, the responsibility lies with George Bush himself. It is highly improper (but, unfortunately, not entirely rare) and quite possibly an impeachable offense for a president to seek ways to circumvent international law. The U.S. Constitution (Article VI, Clause 2) quite clearly states that international laws ("Treaties"), to which the U.S. is a signatory ("made … under the Authority of the United States"), are the law of the United States ("supreme Law of the Land"), and binding upon judges in every state.

Because of his actions at the Justice Department, Yoo's appointment at U.C. Berkeley Law School was met by protests by a significant number of the students.

See, also, **Bybee, Jay S.**

Z

Zarqawi: *See al-Zarqawi.*

Zoellick, Robert B.: Deputy Secretary of State since February 22, 2005. Secretary of State, *Condoleezza Rice,* to whom he reports, recommended his nomination.

Zoellick was formerly the United States Trade Representative, a cabinet-level position with the rank of Ambassador. His Senate confirmation was unanimous.

Another retread from Bush's father's administration, Zoellick was Bush Senior's Economics Undersecretary, working for Secretary of State James A. Baker III.

As Trade Representative, he was responsible for negotiating free trade agreements, although his approach seemed to be that of a bully, expecting cooperation—or **better** (emphasis added)—from nations wishing to participate. Zoellick came to that position directly from being a paid consultant for, among others, Enron Corporation, by whom he was paid $50,000 in fees, and where he served on the company's Advisory Council. His critics claimed that the deals he negotiated would favor rich multinationals like Enron (almost certainly at the expense of workers and consumers). One potential deal (under CAFTA—Central American Free Trade Agreement) was with Costa Rica, which stood firm against a demand that it privatize its telecommunications, electricity and insurance industries if it wanted to join CAFTA. Based on a claim that it would increase efficiency and lower costs, another Central American republic, El Salvador, had allowed itself to be pressured into privatizing its telecommunications industry (among others). Instead of lower costs, residents of El Salvador saw their telephone rates, formerly lower than those in Costa Rica, increase 274%.[1]

---

[1] Source for most of this entry: *CorpWatch, Robert Zoellick's Free Trade Evangelism,* November 17, 2003, http://www.corpwatch.org/issues/PID.jsp?articleid=9108.

On the positive side, Zoellick's academic credentials are impeccable. He graduated Phi Beta Kappa from Swarthmore in 1975 and went on to get a Doctor of Jurisprudence degree (JD) at Harvard and a Master of Public Policy Degree from Harvard's Kennedy School of Government.

As of May 25, 2006, there were rumors that Zoellick was planning to resign, possibly taking a senior job on Wall Street. He was apparently disappointed that he was not going to be succeeding John Snow as Treasury Secretary.

9

9/11: As if any of us need to be reminded,[1] this was the day, in 2001, of the notorious attack on the World Trade Center and the Pentagon (with possible intent to attack the White House, using the plane that ended up in a field in Pennsylvania). From George Bush's point of view, it was a great opportunity to dramatically improve his sagging position in the polls (and, quite possibly, to celebrate the demise of the "That's my George" TV comedy series, which lampooned him mercilessly).

For suspicious minds (i.e., those that can see beyond the headlines), Bush's behavior on that day was (and still is) cause for concern. Why, after he was told what had happened, did he continue to listen, for seven or more minutes, to the children at the Emma T. Booker Elementary School as they read the **Goat Story** (*My Pet Goat*)? Why did he later claim (on more than one occasion) to have seen, live on TV, the first plane crash into the World Trade Center? Why did he not immediately fly back to Washington, DC? Why did he not immediately refute the claim, made by White House staff, that a threat had been made against Air Force One? Why did he subsequently tell (on several occasions) the **trifecta** story (dishonestly taking credit for a statement actually made by Al Gore when he was Vice President)?

Unfortunately, the National Commission on Terror Attacks ("9/11 Commission") obtained answers to none of these questions. George Bush and **Dick Cheney** were not called to testify, under oath, before the Commission. Rather, they were allowed to answer questions, together, in the White House, with the questioners taking no notes.

See, also, **Rice, Condoleezza.**

---

[1] Something George Bush appears to do in a significant number of his speeches (several times per speech), usually as an implied justification for the Iraq War.

Acknowledgements

I would like to particularly acknowledge the help of Edd Doerr, President of Americans for Religious Liberty, for his encouragement and support as I put this book together. He also proofread the entire book and provided input for the Thirteenth and Fourteenth Amendment parts of the Bill of Rights entry, and for the last-minute addition of the reproductive rights and school vouchers entries.

I'd like to offer special thanks, too, to my wife Elaine, who has put up with the long hours I've spent in my office, researching and writing.

As this book is launched, there will be others I need to thank. I'll take care of that in subsequent printings.

Bill Potts, June 2006